THE SOUNDS
OF SPEECH
COMMUNICATION

A Volume in the Perspectives in Audiology Series

THE SOUNDS OF SPEECH COMMUNICATION

A Primer of Acoustic Phonetics and Speech Perception

by

J. M. Pickett, Ph.D.
Professor of Speech Communication Research
Sensory Communication Research Laboratory
Gallaudet College

ALLYN AND BACON
Boston London Toronto Sydney Tokyo Singapore

Copyright © 1980 by Allyn and Bacon
A Division of Simon & Schuster, Inc.
160 Gould Street
Needham Heights, MA 02194

Printed in the United States of America

10 9 8 7 6 5 4 3 2   96 95 94 93 92

ISBN 0-205-13542-0

Library of Congress Cataloging in Publication Data

Pickett, J. M.
The sounds of speech communication.
(Perspectives in audiology series)
Includes bibliographies and indexes.

1. Speech perception. 2. Phonetics.
3. Bioacoustics. 4. Auditory perception.
I. Title.   II. Series
BF463.S64P52   612'.78   79-21729
ISBN 0-89079-119-8
(previously 0-8391-1533-4)

To the Memory of R. H. Stetson

CONTENTS

PREFACE TO PERSPECTIVES IN AUDIOLOGY

Audiology is a young, vibrant, dynamic field. Its lineage can be traced to the fields of education, medicine, physics, and psychology in the nineteenth century and the emergence of speech pathology in the first half of this century. The term *audiology,* meaning the science of hearing, was coined by Raymond Carhart in 1947. Since then, its definition has expanded to include its professional nature. Audiology is the profession that provides knowledge and service in the areas of human hearing and, more broadly, human communication and its disorders. As evidence of the growth of audiology as a major profession, in the 1940s there were no programs designed to prepare "audiologists," while now there are over 112 graduate training programs accredited by the Education and Training Board of the American Board of Examiners in Speech Pathology and Audiology for providing academic and clinical training designed to prepare clinically competent audiologists. Audiology is also a major area of study in the professional preparation of speech pathologists, speech and hearing scientists, and otologists.

Perspectives in Audiology is the first series of books designed to cover the major areas of study in audiology. The interdisciplinary nature of the field is reflected by the scope of the volumes in this series. The volumes currently in preparation (see p. ii) include both clinically oriented and basic science texts. The series consists of topic-specific textbooks designed to meet the needs of today's advanced level student. Each volume will also serve as a focal reference source for practicing audiologists and specialists in many related fields.

The **Perspectives in Audiology** series offers several advantages not usually found in other texts, but purposely featured in this series to increase the practical value of the books for practitioners and researchers, as well as for students and teachers:

1. Every volume includes thorough discussion of all relevant clinical and/or research papers on each topic.
2. Every volume is organized in an educational format to serve as the main text or as one of the main texts for graduate and advanced undergraduate students in courses on audiology and/or other studies concerned with human communication and its disorders.
3. Unlike ordinary texts, **Perspectives in Audiology** volumes will retain their professional reference value as focal reference sources for practitioners and researchers in career work long after completion of their studies.
4. Each volume serves as a rich source of authoritative, up-to-date information and valuable reviews for specialists in many fields, including administration, audiology, early childhood studies, linguistics, otology, psychology, pediatrics, public health, special education, speech pathology, and speech and hearing science.

A thorough knowledge of acoustic phonetics and speech perception is critical to audiologic assessment, habilitation, and education of the hearing impaired and to the broader area of communication and its disorders. Thus, with its general introduction and thorough overview of acoustic phonetics, *The Sounds of Speech Communication: A Primer of Acoustic Phonetics and Speech Perception* covers major basic science areas that are essential to the professional preparation of audiologists, speech pathologists, speech and hearing scientists, linguists, psycholinguists, educators of the hearing impaired, and others concerned with human communication and its disorders. As with most books in the *Perspectives in Audiology* series, this volume is designed both as a textbook and as a handy reference for the active professional. J. M. Pickett's years of research with the hearing impaired and experience in teaching acoustic phonetics to students have enabled him to write an easy-to-read volume that focuses attention on critical knowledge necessary in the professional preparation of clinicians and teachers.

PREFACE

My aim in this book is to teach a technical subject, the acoustics of speech and its perception, to the nontechnical student. The book goes fairly deeply into its field because there is no way to understand speech acoustics without technical concepts, but I have tried to make the immersion gradual and logical. Thus the early part explains basic concepts, the middle applies them to the description of speech sounds, and the last part presents acoustic research on the perception of speech sounds and their meanings. The line of study develops a technical background for practical, clinical work on speech communication. It should also prepare the student for advanced reading on speech research.

My personal stimulus for writing such a book goes back to an example set by my early mentor, R. H. Stetson, and his student, C. V. Hudgins. Stetson was a phonetic scientist deeply interested in clinical problems. He believed in a thorough technical preparation for all practitioners dealing with problems of impaired speech and hearing. Hudgins became the first speech scientist to work full-time in an institution for the deaf, in 1936 at Clarke School for the Deaf. He and Stetson drafted a technical text on phonetics for teachers of the deaf. It was trial taught but never published. Much later, when I came to Gallaudet, I taught acoustic phonetics to student teachers and to audiology students. My book grew out of this teaching, my students' contributions, and the encouragement of colleagues, especially my wife, Betty H. Pickett, with her dazzling blue pencil.

Many people in the field helped me. The foremost, whose comments led to substantial revisions and additions, were Arthur House, Gunnar Fant, Dennis Fry, Arthur Boothroyd, Ilse Lehiste, Ludmilla Chistovich, Lawrence Feth, William Strong, Ingo Titze, Earl Schubert, Noriko Umeda, John Ohala, and Martin Rothenberg. Among other colleagues who made important suggestions are Arthur Abramson, Robert Bilger, J. R. Boston, Cecil Coker, Ellen Danaher, Roy Gengel, A.-M. Hammock, Ira Hirsh, Peter Ladefoged, Alvin Liberman, Philip Lieberman, Daniel Ling, Lyle Lloyd, Sally Revoile, Sadanand Singh, Henry Tobin, and Michael Weiss. I am deeply indebted to all of these people and I hope I have used their contributions correctly.

Helping me to clarify many points, and patient students of drafts, were my research assistants: Kathy Foust Blane, Sue Colten, Harriet Kaplan, Mary Joe Osberger, Regan Quinn, Phyllis Segal, David Talkin, and Mary Pat Wilson.

Colleagues who frequently cheered me on over a too-lengthy writing process were Donald Baker, Dan Bode, Frank Cooper, Edith Corliss, Dave Coulter, James Curtis, Peter Denes, Earleen Elkins, Lois Elliott, Norm Erber, Jim Flanagan, Adrian Fourcin, Moise Goldstein, Sandy Hamlet, Kathy Harris, Dennis Klatt, Harry Levitt, Christy Ludlow, Anna and Igor Nábělek, Peter MacNeilage, Jim D. Miller, Al Montgomery, Susan Smith, Betty Stark, Ken Stevens, Brian Walden, and Charles Wood.

Finally, the manuscript and figures could never have been properly put together without the careful work of my administrative secretary, Zeda Daniel.

J. M. Pickett

THE SOUNDS
OF SPEECH
COMMUNICATION

CHAPTER 1

SPEECH PRODUCTION
AND ACOUSTIC PHONETICS

CONTENTS

> ...speech is a series of movements made audible...
>
> R. H. Stetson, 1928

Speech is our prime way to communicate. Speech is communicative because it is coded to form words and sentences in a language. The code of speech resides in its sounds. Thus a deep understanding of speech communication depends on knowing the sound patterns of the speech code.

The scientific study of speech sounds is acoustic phonetics, which focuses especially on the sound patterns that function in language. Thus acoustic phonetics is the branch of linguistic science that deals with the sound code of speech.

Acoustic phonetics is a part of the general field of speech science, or experimental phonetics, which also includes physiological phonetics. Physiological phonetics describes how the nervous system, muscles, and other organs operate in speech. Acoustic phonetics describes the speech sounds themselves and how they are formed acoustically. Acoustic and physiological phonetics are closely related, as we will often see in this book.

Speech science is basic to the scientific study of a very broad range of interesting problems, including speech perception and hearing, child language acquisition, teaching of language and speech, pathologic speech and language, speech communication technology and speech processing, synthetic speech, automatic recognition of spoken messages, speech communication aids for handicapped people, personal voice characteristics and voice identification, signing, dialects, phonetic comparison of languages, linguistics, and general communication theory when speech is a prime example. Acoustic phonetics contributes to each of these. This book contains discussions of some of these topics, but only very brief ones; there is a classified bibliography at the end. The main aim is to present the facts and theories of acoustic phonetics, and thus to provide a background for further study in the many fields related to speech science and linguistics.

The quotation at the start of this chapter epitomizes the approach taken in this book to acoustic phonetics: proceeding from articulatory shapes and movements to the sound patterns produced. This is because articulations can be seen and felt, but sound patterns have to be described with special acoustic concepts. Once you have learned the acoustic concepts, and have used them to describe the relations between articulations and sound patterns, you will find that many of the sound patterns are as easy to understand as articulations. Finally, toward the end of this study, you will see that the perception of the speech code also seems to be based on articulation.

To begin this acoustic study of speech, the communication units of spoken language are defined and the production of speech sounds is described generally.

SPEECH UNITS

Linguists have found that the code of a spoken language consists of units that are arranged in a hierarchy from small units to large units. The smallest units are the individual sounds, i.e., the vowels and consonants. The sounds form syllables, which contain one or more sounds. The syllables form words of one or more syllables. Words form sentences of one or more words, to express a thought.

The speech sounds that differentiate words are called *phonemes*. Consider for example the spoken words *man, ban,* and *pan,* each of which consists of a sequence of three sounds. These words differ only in the first sound. Other sets of words are differentiated in the same way, such as *main, bane,* and *pain; moot* and *boot.* In *mam* and *map,* the difference is in the third sound; in *bean, ban* the difference is in the second sound. These are all examples for defining the phonemes /m, b, p, i/ and /æ/ of spoken English. By convention the phonemes are written within slashes, using symbols of the International Phonetic Alphabet. The phonemes of General American English are listed in Table 1; for each phoneme key words are given containing the phoneme in different positions.

The phonemes of a language are determined by linguists, who make many comparisons between many utterances in the language, construct lists of examples, and revise the phoneme lists to reach a consensus. The

Table 1.   The phonemes of General American English[a]

Consonants		Vowels and diphthongs	
/m/	me, aim, smile, ramp	/i/	heed
/w/	wet, swoop	/ɪ/	hid
/ʍ/	whet	/ɛ/	head
/b/	be, mob	/æ/	had
/v/	van, give	/ɑ/	odd
/p/	pan, map, spill, apt	/ɔ/	all
/f/	fan, wife, soft	/ʊ/	hood
/ð/	that, bathe	/u/	who
/θ/	thing, bath	/ʌ/	ton
/n/	no, pan, snap, bend	/ə/	a ton
/l/	lawn, pole, slap, belt	/ɝ/	earth
/d/	dawn, good	/aɪ/	hide
/z/	zip, ways	/oɪ/	coin
/t/	tan, bat, still, cats	/au/	pout
/s/	sip, face, fast, cats	/eɪ/	pain
/tʃ/	chop, each	/ou/	code
/dʒ/	joke, age	/iu/	few
/j/	you		
/r/	ran, press, hard		Regional vowels
/ʒ/	azure, garage		
/ʃ/	show, fresh	/a/	Bostonian "hard"
/ŋ/	sing, think	/ə/	Northeastern "better"
/g/	give, bag	/ɸ/	Northeastern "earth"
/k/	key, sick, skip, picked		
/h/	had		

[a]Each phoneme is given by its symbol in the International Phonetic Alphabet followed by examples of words containing the phoneme.

linguist's ear and knowledge of the language are the main tools for this type of study. A linguist who is not a native speaker of the language under study uses native speakers to pronounce sentences and words for comparison.

It is important to understand that phonemes are determined by their function in differentiating the words of a language. Thus a phoneme is defined within a language system and not acoustically. Phonemes *do* have some consistent acoustic features, which are covered in this book, but the acoustic features of a phoneme vary a great deal depending on the context of adjacent speech events. Thus the acoustic features of a phoneme are subunits that are not determined solely by their function in the language, as are the phonemes.

The different variants of a phoneme are called *allophones.* Consider some variants of the phoneme /s/; in the words *sill, still,* and *spill,* each example of /s/ is slightly different acoustically from the others, and the same differences occur between the /s/'s in the words *seed, steed,* and *speed.* All such systematic variants of /s/ comprise its allophones. Each phoneme thus actually designates a large class of sounds. For example, the phoneme /s/ consists of more than 100 allophones.

In most acoustic discussions of a speech sound we are describing only its most general or common features and are not concerned with all of its allophones. Then it is called a *speech sound* or *phone,* not a phoneme. To label such a sound, the same symbols as in Table 1 are used with brackets instead of slashes; thus [s], for example, refers to a sound pattern produced like other [s] sounds that may be classed within, or serve as an example of, the phoneme /s/.

The phonemes are, in one sense, the basic sequential segments of speech and thus the features of phonemes are sometimes called *segmental features.* However, in the acoustic stream of speech the phonemic segments are often not clearly demarcated. This is because speech production is a rapid, flowing activity, involving overlap of the acoustic features of one phoneme on others. The basic unitary aspect of the phoneme resides not in acoustic demarcation, but in linguistic evidence that the phoneme is the smallest interchangeable element in a language. In addition, perceptual and behavioral evidence prove the phoneme to be a basic unit. For example, in "slips of the tongue" phonemes often interchange as units (Fromkin, 1972).

The syllable is the next larger unit of speech after the phoneme. A syllable typically consists of a vowel and one or more consonants. The vowel functions as the "carrier" of the syllable, with the consonants riding on the beginning or end. For this reason the vowel has sometimes been called the *syllable nucleus.* Some syllables consist of a single vowel, or of a single voiced consonant, such as /n/, or /l/, forming the second syllable of words like *garden* /gaɚdn/ and *ladle* /leɪdl/.

The rhythms and melodies of speech for stress, emphasis, and expression are organized by groups of syllables. This aspect of speech is called *prosody* and certain acoustic features of syllables and groups of syllables are called *prosodic features.*

Syllables, like phonemes, are linguistic units, not acoustic units. Some linguists view the syllable as the basic building block of spoken language, citing evidence from the organization of speech production, certain aspects of speech perception, and the study of slips of the tongue (Fry, 1964a; Kozhevnikov and Chistovich, 1965).

For the study of acoustic phonetics in this book we concentrate first on acoustic patterns that serve to differentiate the vowel phonemes. Then the prosodic features are described. Further chapters describe the features of consonant phonemes. Finally, some of the acoustic effects seen in phoneme interaction are studied.

GENERAL CONDITIONS OF SPEECH PRODUCTION

Before we begin a detailed study of speech sounds, we need a general knowledge of how speech is produced. Only an overall picture of the breathing movements, the speech articulatory movements, and the basic mechanisms of speech sound production is given here. Later each of these topics is studied in more detail.

Speaking is a motor skill and, like other skills, it consists of coordinated movements acting upon an object. In speaking, the object acted upon is the air contained in the respiratory and oral tracts, i.e., the air in the lungs, trachea, larynx, pharynx, nose, and mouth. When we speak, we perform movements that act on this air space. The movements occur in consistent gestural patterns to produce the speech sounds.

The gestures of speech are performed by the organs of respiration and the organs of the upper alimentary tract. When referring to speech the term *vocal tract* is used for the passages of the larynx, mouth, and nose. The organs and passages involved are diagrammed in Figure 1.

Respiration for Speech

In the production of speech the air in the lungs is pressed upon by the chest and lung tissues, resulting in a flow of air from the lungs toward the outside; we call this flow the *breath stream*. If the vocal tract is open, the breath stream is unimpeded and the air flows out the nose or mouth, as in ordinary breathing. During speech, however, some part of the vocal tract is constricted to a degree that impedes the outward airflow so that the pressure of the tracheal air rises. This tracheal air pressure is the fundamental basis of speech sounds; in fact the sounds originate in variations in the flow of air from the trachea powered by the tracheal air pressure.

Let us examine the control of the breath stream in more detail, referring to Figure 1. Breathing is controlled by two opposed sets of forces on the lungs: forces of inspiration and forces of expiration. The *inspiratory forces* expand the lung volume by raising the rib cage and lowering the floor of the lung cavity. The major inspiratory muscles are the diaphragm and external layer of the intercostal muscles between the ribs. The diaphragm forms the floor of the chest cavity. Contraction of these muscles expands the chest, air flows in, and the lungs expand.

The *expiratory forces* contract the lung volume by lowering the rib cage and pushing the floor of the chest cavity upward. Major expiratory muscles are the abdominal muscles, which pull the abdominal wall inward, thereby pressing on the viscera and pushing the floor of the chest upward, and other abdominal muscles that pull downward on the rib cage. The intercostal muscles also exert a contracting force on the rib

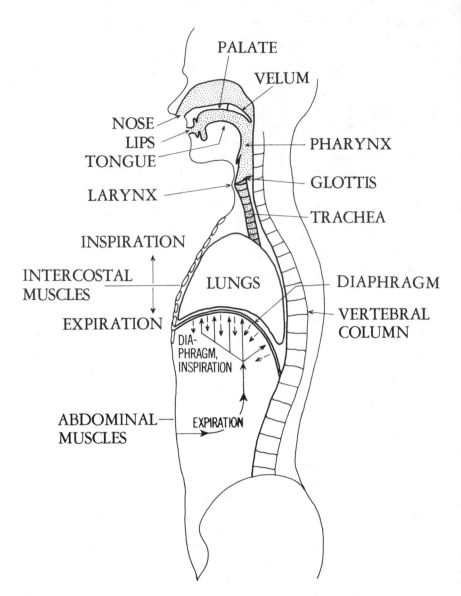

Figure 1.   Diagram of the organs used in speech production. In breathing and in speaking the expiratory muscles act to move air from the lungs through the trachea and onward toward the outside. The expiratory muscles are the internal intercostals, which lower the rib cage, thus compressing the lungs, and the abdominal muscles, which push the viscera and diaphragm upward. The airstream moving outward (breath stream) is modified by movements of the glottis and the other downstream organs to produce speech sounds.

cage. Another expiratory force is provided by the elastic recoil of the lung tissues and other chest tissues that are stretched by the increased volume of the chest after an inspiration of air. The expiratory forces push air out of the lungs causing air to flow outward through the respiratory passages.

How are these breathing muscles used in speech? A brief summary based on research studies by Draper, Ladefoged, and Whitteridge (1959) and Ladefoged (1963, 1967) illustrates this.

The chest movements for conversational speech are light, easy movements that are not noticeably effortful. The lungs are only slightly distended; thus the elastic recoil force is low, and the internal intercostal muscles between the bony parts of the ribs probably provide the main expiratory force. This force, on the average, is quite moderate, producing a pressure in the trachea, under vocal tract constriction for speech, that is only slightly above atmospheric pressure. Atmospheric pressure is 1055 cm of water and the tracheal pressure in speech is about 10 cm above atmospheric pressure, with small variations up and down because of the speech rhythm or stress pattern. Thus the tracheal air pressure, constituting the energy source of speech, averages only about 1% above the ambient atmospheric pressure.

The average outward flow of air during speech is also rather low; it is on the order of 100 to 300 cc of air per second, which is less than ½ pint per second. During certain speech sounds the flow is much lower or is even completely blocked momentarily, as in stop consonants like [p, t, k]. For other sounds the airflow can be much higher than average. For example, during fricatives like [s] and [ʃ], and in the release of stop consonants like [t] in the word *tea,* the airflow briefly reaches rates equivalent to about 1000 to 2000 cc of air per second.

The chest movements of shouting and of very low vocal effort can be radically different from those of normal conversations. In shouting, the pressures and flow rates may be higher; with very low effort they are lower. However, adequate volume of voice is primarily a matter of the voice action of the glottis in the larynx, not of strong pressure by the chest.

Long streams of speech, uninterrupted by air intakes, require a very large air reservoir at the beginning, and thus the elastic recoil force may be too high for the voice level desired; in this case the inspiratory muscles contract in order to oppose the recoil and hold the tracheal pressure to the desired low level. Then, as air is expended in speaking and the lung tissues become less distended, the recoil force decreases and the opposing inspiratory contractions disappear. When the air reservoir reaches normal and lower levels, the expiratory muscles come into play to maintain the tracheal pressure.

The expiratory muscles are also contracted to produce increases in tracheal air pressure at places in the stream of speech where stress or emphasis is required. These pressure pulses for stress may also be produced by sudden relaxations of the inspiratory opposition to the elastic recoil. The vocal mechanisms for stress are described in Chapter 5 in more detail.

Articulation of Speech

The action of the glottis, pharynx, velum, jaw, tongue, and lips to produce speech sounds is called articulation. The coordinated action of the respiratory movements and the articulatory movements produces the phonemes, syllables, and sentences. These coordinations involve rapid movements resulting from very complex muscular contractions, and yet they seem very easy and natural to make. Perhaps speaking is basically a simple act despite the diversity and complexity of the muscles involved. In general speaking is like other rhythmic body movements where a postural adjustment serves as a base on which smaller, rapid movements are superimposed. In tapping a rhythm by hand, for example, the shoulders and arms provide a postural base for the rapid tapping movements of the hand. In speech the postural base is the adjustment of the breathing muscles to provide the outward airflow of the breath stream, and the articulatory movements of the tongue, lips, and jaw are small, rapid movements rhythmically superimposed on the breath stream. Thus speaking is basically like making any simple rhythm. Another indication of the simplicity of speaking is the fact that it is so easily learned so early in life; this suggests that speech coordinations may be largely innate (Lenneberg, 1967).

General Time Features of Speech

The sequence of breathing and articulation for an utterance is as follows. The tracheal air pressure rises at the start of an utterance. The articulatory movements perform a sequential pattern to produce the sequence of phonemes and syllables of the utterance. Then the tracheal air pressure falls back to atmospheric at the end of the utterance.

Let us examine the time sequence of a very simple sequence of articulations. Consonant articulations constrict the vocal tract more than vowel articulations. Typically, there are no gaps between syllables. Thus, for a fluent sequence of syllables we can think of the utterance simply as an alternation over time between a constricted articulation and an open articulation. This is schematized in Figure 2; we assume that each syllable has only one consonant. The open states produce the vowel sounds; the constricted states produce the consonant sounds. Thus the time sequence of syllables appears in the sound flow of speech as consonant sound representing the constricted phase of the syllable, alternating with vowel sound, the open phase of the syllable.

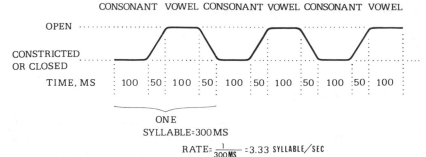

Figure 2.   Schematic representation of the consonant and vowel articulatory movements for a series of syllables. The durations of the movement phases are idealized, average durations, typical of those found in speech at a moderate rate of utterance.

The time pattern of syllables determines many of the time features of speech sounds. Therefore it is important to know the typical character of syllable timing; later this timing pattern is used in describing the time patterns of vowel sounds and consonant sounds.

The syllables of speech occur at an average rate of two to five syllables per second, depending on the style of speaking. The slow rate of two syllables per second is typical of careful, exaggerated enunciation; the fast rate of five syllables per second would be for very rapid, fluent conversation that is still clearly articulated.

For a medium rate of speaking we can assign typical time durations, based on average measurements, of the constricting and opening movements. For simplicity let us assume that the constricting and opening cycles succeed each other at exactly equal intervals of time; this is not actually true, because some syllables are stressed or emphasized more than others and these differences are highly important in language, as shown later in Chapter 5, but at this stage of our study we need some simple, easily remembered durations that can be used for a description of the timing of speech events. Events for a succession of equal syllables are sketched in Figure 2; these events are very rapid, so it is customary to use a time unit of 1/1000 second, or milliseconds, ms. The constricted period (consonant) is about 100 ms, the opening transition between constricted and open is about 50 ms, the open period (vowel) is about 100 ms, and the closing transition from open to constricted is about 50 ms. The total time for one consonant-vowel syllable, from constricted to open and back to the beginning of the consonant constriction in the next syllable, would be the sum of these periods; the sum is 300 ms, which corresponds to a rate of 3.33 syllables per second. This rate is a typical average rate for careful speech falling somewhere between slow, exaggerated enunciation and rapid but clear conversation. This is only an average syllable rate. In actual speech at this rate syllables of about 300 ms are common, but the shortest syllables may be as little as 50 ms in duration and the longest syllables as long as 500 ms.

SPEECH SOUND SOURCES

The gestures of speech produce sounds by modulating the airflow from the trachea (breath stream). The sounds are based on three types of sound source, which are now considered in a general way and described briefly for orientation. Later these sound types are described in much more detail.

Voiced Sound Source

One type of modulation of the breath stream produces periodic sounds, which are called *voiced* sounds. Voiced sounds are based on a periodic modulation of the breath stream by the action of the glottis. The action is a repeated opening and closing of the glottal slit between the vocal folds in the larynx. Voicing action occurs more or less automatically when the vocal folds are adjusted for "voicing" and supplied with appropriate tracheal air pressure. The action produces periodic pulses of airflow by repeatedly passing and shutting off the breath stream. The airflow pulses succeed each other at a very rapid rate, about 125 pulses per second for adult male talkers and about 200 per second or higher for women and children. This pulsing sound has a buzz-like quality. It propagates up through the vocal tract to the air outside the speaker. Examples of speech sounds produced with this voiced sound source are the vowels and the nasal consonants [m, n, ŋ].

The airflow of the breath stream for voicing is low in both average volume and average velocity. However, the voice pulses produce sound waves that are loud and propagate at the velocity of sound.

Turbulent Sound Source

The second type of modulation of the breath stream is produced when it passes through a narrow constriction and the flow of air through the constriction becomes turbulent. The turbulence produces a sound that has a hissing quality; the turbulent breath stream does not pulse periodically as for the voiced sounds, but has random variations in airflow. This type of sound is called *aperiodic*. Aperiodic sound is the basic type of sound source, which is further modified to produce speech sounds like the fricatives, [s], [ʃ], and [f].

Transient Sound Source

Sudden, step-like increases in the airflow occur whenever there is a sudden release of the air pressure behind a constriction in the vocal tract. This occurs upon the release of the complete constriction of consonants like [p], [t], and [k]. Later we see how these transients generate sound.

The three types of sound source described here are the ones employed in English and many other languages of the world. There are several other interesting sound sources used in certain languages. Some African languages employ "clicks" that are formed by oral sucking actions released by the lips or tongue, and some languages employ vocalization with an inspiratory breath stream as well as with expiration. Speakers of English use clicks and inspiratory sounds as expressive interjections, but they have no phonemic function, as they may in other languages (Appendix B, Ladefoged, 1975).

SUMMARY

Thus far we have seen that speech consists of linguistic units of sound sequences, the phonemes and syllables, that form words and sentences in a language. Speech production is based on movements of the breathing mechanism, which produce a flow of air through the vocal tract. This airflow is modified by articulatory movements to produce sequences of syllables consisting of a rapid alternation between constricted articulation for consonant phonemes and open articulation for vowel phonemes. Three basic types of airflow modulation provide the sound sources of speech: 1) a periodic or voiced sound source, 2) a turbulent, hissing sound source, and 3) a transient, step-like sound source.

CHAPTER 2

SOUNDS, RESONANCE, AND SPECTRUM ANALYSIS

CONTENTS

Speech sounds are complex in form but they can be represented in simple terms that give us a concise description of any speech sound. We do this by analyzing the sound and breaking it into its components. This chapter introduces the basic principles of sound analysis that we will apply later in our study of all the sounds of speech. How sound waves are produced and propagated is first considered. Then the sine wave, a wave resulting from simple harmonic motion, is described. Sine waves are the simple waves that are used as components to describe complex sounds. The sine wave components represent the spectrum of a sound, and the spectrum is the concise description that we need. Resonance, how it occurs in the vocal tract and how resonant sound waves are analyzed into sine waves to represent the spectrum of a resonant sound, is discussed. Finally, the sound spectrograph, which is the instrument used to analyze and record the sound spectrum, is described.

SOUND PRODUCTION AND PROPAGATION

Sound originates as a disturbance of the positions of molecules within a substance. The initial disturbance also moves all the neighboring molecules, these in turn move their neighbors, and in this way the sound is propagated outward through all parts of the substance. The disturbance propagates as a change in position, to and fro, of each molecule. Air is the substance that usually propagates sound to us from its place of origin. Air-borne sounds generated at one place reach us at another place because the disturbances of the air molecules at the original location are faithfully relayed or propagated through the intervening air.

In speech the vocal organs produce sound by causing a local disturbance in the air molecule positions at some point in the vocal tract. The
disturbance causes successive motions of the molecules, to and fro, at
each adjacent point in the vocal tract, thus propagating the vocal sound
outward to the outside air and through the air to distant points. For example, during a vowel sound the air molecule disturbances that initiate the
sound are pulses of air emitted by the glottis. Each pulse is propagated upward from the glottis to the lips, and to the outside air. In the production
of a fricative consonant the breath stream is forced through a constriction
in the vocal tract, causing a turbulent disturbance of the air molecules that
is propagated away from the constriction to the lips and the outside air.

The propagation speed of sound, both inside and outside the vocal
tract, is about 1129 feet per second. This is a very high speed compared
with the rate of flow of the breath stream, which averages only about 1
foot per second. Thus, although disturbances in the breath stream are the
initiating sources of speech sounds, the sounds themselves are propagated
through the vocal tract air at a much higher speed than the breath. The
speech sounds, traveling at the speed of sound, or about 770 miles per
hour, can be thought of as riding on the very slow wind of the breath
stream, which is traveling at less than 1 mile per hour.

SIMPLE HARMONIC MOTION

The air molecule motions of speech sounds are complex in form. However, complex motions can be described concisely by considering them to
be made up of simple oscillations. This is done by dividing the complex
motions into a set of simple vibrations called *simple harmonic motions.*
Simple harmonic motion is the basis for describing all forms of motion no
matter how complex. A familiar example of simple harmonic motion is
the swing of a pendulum. An ideal pendulum, one that has no friction,
moves back and forth in simple harmonic motion. The pendulum motion
is very regular in time, but still it involves many different speeds and positions. Fortunately this motion can be represented very simply by relating
it to uniform motion on a circle. Let us see how this happens.

Imagine the situation illustrated in Figure 3. In the figure we view
together, and from the side, the motions of a pendulum and of a peg fixed
on a turntable. When we adjust the turntable speed so that the oscillation
cycles of the peg and pendulum are the same, then their motions are found
to be in perfect synchrony at every moment. In other words, the simple
harmonic motion of an ideal pendulum is the same as a constant circular
motion viewed from the side looking along the plane of rotation or, in

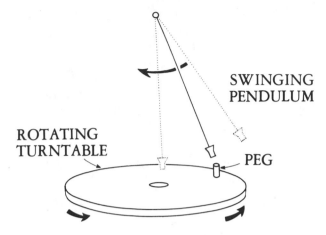

Figure 3. Demonstration showing that the back-and-forth motion of a pendulum can be represented by uniform motion in a circle viewed from the side. When the turntable speed is adjusted to one revolution for each swing of the pendulum, the peg and pendulum will be seen always to be at the same horizontal position, exactly opposite each other, even though the peg moves in a circle and the pendulum moves along a line. (Adapted from Benade, 1960).

terms of geometry, the same as circular motion projected on a line in the plane of rotation. This affords a very simple description of the pendulum motion because the circular motion can be described just by specifying two values, one giving the rate of motion and another giving the size of the motion. If we find other types of motion produced by the same type of force mechanism as in the pendulum, we can describe them too in terms of projected circular motion.

   The motion of a pendulum is produced by a restoring force that is proportional to the distance of the pendulum bob from its resting position. There are many other types of motion produced by forces proportional to the distance from a resting position; all such motions have a form related to simple harmonic motion. Examples of such motions that produce sound are the vibrations of the prongs of a tuning fork, the main vibration of a plucked guitar string, and the vibration of the sides of a wine glass when tapped. Because all these motions are like simple harmonic motion, each can be described using the two aspects that describe a uniform circular motion: 1) the time, or period, for one complete revolution, and 2) the size of the motion, which is determined by the distance from the center of rotation to the moving point. In sound vibrations, these two aspects are: 1) the period for one complete cycle, to and fro, of

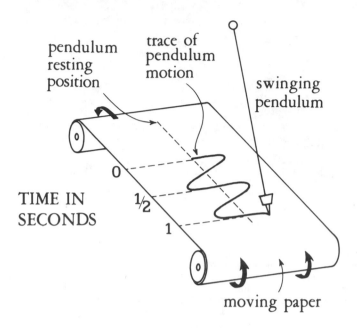

Figure 4.   The motion of the pendulum traces a path in time that is a sine wave. The period, that is, the time for one complete cycle of oscillation is ½ second and the frequency of oscillation is 2 Hz. (Adapted from Benade, 1960.)

air molecule vibration, and 2) the extent or amplitude of the air molecule motion.

   A plot in time of the motion of the ideal pendulum gives a wave like the one shown in Figure 4. This wave is called a sine wave; its sinuous form is the form in time for all simple harmonic motions. The form of this wave is called sinusoidal.

   The period of a sine wave is the time for one complete cycle; this aspect, related to the rate of oscillation, is often given as the *frequency of repetition* of the cycle in a unit of time. The *frequency* is simply the reciprocal of the period. The *frequency* is given in cycles per second or Hertz (Hz). For example, in Figure 4, the period of the pendulum motion is ½ second and the frequency is 2 cycles per second or 2 Hz.

   The distance or amount of sine wave motion is called the *amplitude*. It corresponds to the extent of the oscillation from the original resting position. This is illustrated in Figure 5 where a sine wave of 1 Hz is traced

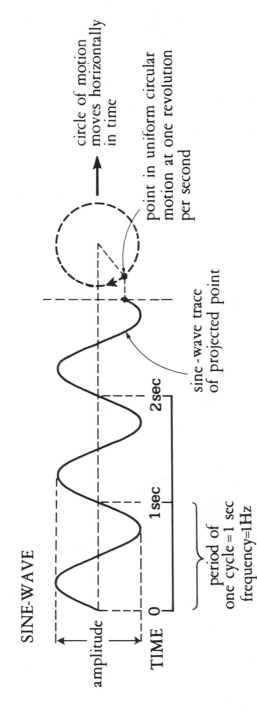

Figure 5. The amplitude, period, and frequency of a sine wave generated by a point projected on a line from uniform circular motion at one revolution per second moving horizontally. As a concrete example, the sine wave would be the path traced by the projected vertical position of a peg on a rotating turntable that is facing us on its side and moving horizontally at a constant speed.

17

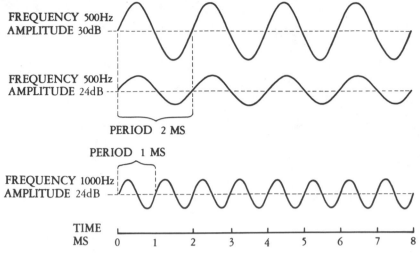

Figure 6.   Some sine waves having frequencies and intensities found in components of speech.

by a point projected from a uniform circular motion that is translated horizontally in time.

The frequencies of sound vibrations are usually much higher than 1 or 2 Hz; e.g., notes of the guitar go up to about 2000 Hz. The range of the frequencies found in speech is from about 50 Hz to over 10,000 Hz, covering almost the entire range of hearing. Figure 6 shows some sine waves having frequencies and amplitudes like those in speech. Here there is a time scale in 1/1000ths of a second (milliseconds or ms) instead of the seconds involved in our slow-swinging pendulum.

In sound vibrations the air molecules move back and forth. If the original disturbance is a simple harmonic motion, the resulting air molecule motions will also be simple harmonic in form, and the frequency and amplitude of their movement will follow perfectly the sine wave form of the original disturbance. For any sound wave the extent or amplitude of the motion and its form describe the sound completely, in physical terms. When a sound is received by ear, the extent of air molecule motion determines the loudness of the sound heard; the form of the motion determines the timbre or quality of the sound heard. The heard quality and loudness of sound are very important to us and these are very neatly represented by means of the frequency and amplitude of simple harmonic motions.

Consider the form of the sound from tapping a wine glass. After the tap, which displaces the glass molecules from their resting position, the sides of the glass continue to vibrate in a form similar to simple harmonic motion. The moving sides of the vibrating glass move the adjacent air molecules; that motion is propagated through the air to our ears, and we hear the beautiful ringing tone of the wine glass. The "pure" tonal quality of this sound is caused by a sinusoidal motion of air molecules at our ears. Sinusoidal sounds are called *pure tones*. The sensation of a pure tone is hard to describe but the sound wave producing it can be described exactly just by noting that it is sinusoidal in form and that it has a given frequency and amplitude of motion. If the amplitude were to remain constant and not die out, the vibration would be pure simple harmonic motion and the wave of motion in time would be a sine wave, like that traced in time by the ideal frictionless pendulum.

Vibrations of actual objects are always affected by "damping" forces that affect the amplitude of motion. These cause a regular decrease in amplitude of oscillation, as in the gradual dying away of the tone from a ringing wine glass. The same thing happens to the vibration of a guitar string and to the swing of a real pendulum: the vibrations die out gradually in time. The forces of *damping* are air friction and the internal resistance to bending of the wine glass and the guitar string. The resulting waves are called *damped oscillations*. A damped oscillation will be sinusoidal in form if it is produced by restoring forces proportional to the displacement from resting position, but a sinusoidal damped oscillation is not a sine wave because it is not constant in amplitude.

RESONANCE

An oscillating object, like the swinging pendulum or the ringing wine glass, vibrates at just one frequency, called its natural or resonant frequency. Another example is air resonance in a bottle. The air in a bottle has a natural, resonant frequency of vibration; if we displace the air molecules at the mouth of a bottle, by pulling out a cork or by blowing across the open mouth, the bottle produces a resonant, tonal sound. This type of resonance plays a very important role in speech.

Let us now see exactly what makes a bottle give a resonant "pop" when the cork is pulled and then we will apply it to speech. In essence, pulling the cork produces a pulse of airflow that results in a damped sinusoidal oscillation of the air molecules at the mouth of the bottle. First let us see why the oscillation is sinusoidal in form.

The form of the air oscillation is related to the way forces operate to move the air molecules. In simple harmonic motion the force is proportional to the displacement (or distance) from resting position. This type of force relation also operates for the cork and bottle; the force here is a pressure difference at the mouth of the bottle. The sequence of forces and oscillation are illustrated in Figure 7. At the moment when the cork leaves

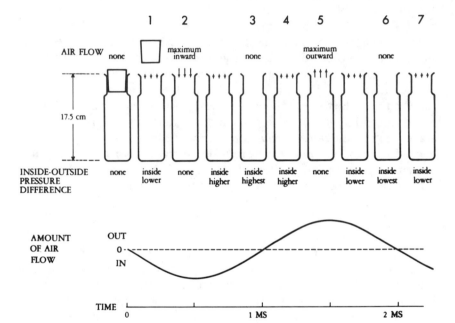

Figure 7.   Illustrating how a resonant oscillation is produced in the air in a tube-like bottle. The diagrams show the airflow and pressure changes in the bottle after a cork is suddenly pulled from the mouth. The bottle and successive airflow conditions are shown in time along the top row of the figure; the bottom row shows how the amount of airflow varies sinusoidally in time corresponding with the conditions of pressure in the top row. The airflow is propelled by the pressure difference between the air inside and outside the bottle, which is described below the bottle at each ¼-ms interval. The amount and direction of airflow in the mouth is schematized by arrows, which are exaggerated greatly in length. The actual extent of air-molecule motion is extremely small.

The resonant oscillation is established as follows. After the cork is pulled, at time 1, the pressure inside is lower because the cork has been removed; this causes air to flow in, as shown by the arrows in the bottle mouth. At time 2, which is ½ ms after the cork was pulled, the airflow has increased to its maximum and the pressure inside is now equal to the pressure outside. However, the momentum of the airflow continues to force air into the bottle and this causes the pressure inside to rise above the outside pressure until, at time 3, the inward airflow has stopped completely. Now the inside pressure is at its maximum amount, higher than the outside pressure. This causes air to begin to flow out, with a moderate flow at time 4 and a maximum at 5, at which time the inside-outside pressure difference is zero. The momentum of the high outward flow then reduces the pressure inside the bottle to become lower than the outside until, at time 6, the inside pressure is at its lowest and the flow is zero; now, however, the situation is similar to the beginning, with a lower pressure inside, as it was after the cork was pulled, and so the cycle begins again and, as can be seen, the airflow oscillation must continue and repeat itself more or less indefinitely. Actually, the loss of some of the original energy, in moving the air molecules outside the bottle, adjacent to the molecules moving in the mouth, causes each successive flow cycle to be a little weaker, and so the oscillations die out in a second or two.

The form of the oscillation is sinusoidal; its frequency is the reciprocal of the period of 2 ms, or 500 Hz; the reasons for the form and frequency are explained in the text.

This type of resonant oscillation of air is the same as the type that occurs in the vocal tract to produce resonance in speech sounds, as further explained in the text.

the mouth of the bottle, at 1 in the figure, the air pressure in the bottle is lower than the outside pressure at the mouth because of the space vacated by the cork. Air flows inward in response to this difference in pressure, but the difference decreases as the air flows in and causes the pressure in the bottle to increase. In other words, as more and more air molecules move into the bottle the pressure difference becomes less and less, and finally becomes zero at 2. Thus we have a situation analogous to the pendulum; a form of simple harmonic oscillation of the air occurs because the air molecules move in response to a force (the pressure difference) that is proportional to their displacement from resting position. At the moment when the pressure difference becomes zero, the air molecules are still moving inward and their momentum carries them farther into the bottle (just as a pendulum swings past its resting position). This cause a rise in the pressure inside the bottle. This rise continues until the pressure in the bottle is high enough to stop the air molecule motion at 3 and reverse it at 4; then the molecules move outward and the excess pressure decreases to zero at 5, but now the molecules have an outward momentum and continue outward, reducing the pressure in the mouth sufficiently to stop the outward movement at 6 and produce inward movement again at 7. As air molecules again move inward the situation is like the initial movement after pulling the cork, and we can see that the oscillation process will continue more or less indefinitely. Actually it gradually dies out because of the damping effects of air friction and the energy dissipated in moving the outside air molecules at the mouth of the bottle. The form of this oscillation is a damped sinusoid; the first cycle of the oscillation is traced as a graph of the airflow in time along the bottom of Figure 7. (In the graph, the form of the sinusoidal airflow oscillation is stretched out on a long scale in order to be synchronous with the bottle sequence.)

Now let us account for the frequency of oscillation. The frequency depends on the size of the bottle. A small bottle makes a high pitched pop and a large bottle makes a low pitched, boom-like sound. This is because the resonant sound is the result of the propagation and repeated reflection, back and forth within the bottle, of the initial air molecule disturbance (the pulse of airflow) from pulling the cork; there are longer intervals between the reflections in a large bottle than in a small bottle, and, of course, longer intervals between repeated reflections should result in a lower frequency of oscillation.

As a concrete example we can calculate the frequency of the oscillation in the bottle, using the speed of sound propagation and the distance from the bottle mouth to the bottom where the main reflection occurs. We simply calculate the time between the appearances of reflections at the mouth. In Figure 7 we have chosen a distance giving a round-trip travel time, from mouth to bottom to mouth, of 1 ms. The corresponding distance is for a bottle like a uniform tube that is 17.5 cm long. The time sequence of the reflections of the initial pulse is as follows. The in-flow pulse at 1 in Figure 7 is propagated down to the bottom, reflected by the bottom, and propagated back outward to appear at the mouth 1 ms later at 3. The airflow direction at the mouth is now outward instead of inward. Thus this first reflected pulse acts now as an out-flow pulse disturbance of the air at the mouth; it is propagated back down the bottle and reflected from the bottom to appear again 1 ms later at the mouth, at 7 in the figure. This second pulse returned to the mouth is an outward-directed out-flow pulse, equivalent to an in-flow pulse having the same airflow direction as the initial pulse at 1. It is propagated back toward the bottom, to be reflected again, and so on; thus there is repeated reflection of the pulse disturbance. The reflected pulses are 1 ms apart and every other pulse is opposite in direction to the initial pulse.

We see in Figure 7 that the time for the fluctuation of the airflow at the mouth to go through a complete cycle and just begin to repeat itself in the original direction requires two round-trip reflection cycles of 1 ms each, giving a total time of 2 ms, or 1/500 second. This value is the period of each cycle of resonant oscillation. The cycle repeats at a rate of 500 times per second (500 Hz), and this is the *resonant frequency*. The air column in the bottle is a resonant system having a natural frequency of 500 Hz. The damped sinusoidal wave of the air column oscillation is illustrated in Figure 8 together with the corresponding air pressure fluctuation that is propagated away from the bottle by the surrounding air.

The resonances seen in speech sounds are caused by the same process of oscillation just described. For example, when a vowel is spoken, the vocal tract has a tube-like shape and production of a vowel is perfectly analogous to what took place in the corked bottle example. In vowel production, pulses of airflow are emitted by the glottis into the pharynx; each glottal pulse is propagated upward to the open mouth; at the mouth the pulse acts as an outward airflow disturbance and so it is propagated back toward the vocal fold surfaces. The vocal folds act like the bottom of a bottle and reflect the pulse; it then is propagated upward again, and so on, so that the glottal pulse is repeatedly reflected back and forth between the vocal folds and the mouth. The round-trip propagation is so rapid that quite a few reflections can take place, after each glottal pulse, before the vocal folds open to emit another glottal pulse. Typically, 10 round-trip reflections producing five cycles of oscillation can occur between the glottal pulses of an adult male speaker.

The analogy between the corked bottle reflections and glottal pulse reflections is exact, allowing for the differences in origin and direction of

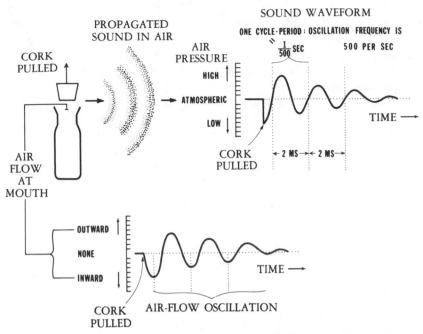

Figure 8.   Diagram of the airflow oscillation at the mouth of a tubular bottle and corresponding sound wave produced by pulling a cork from the bottle. The main resonance of the bottle is at a frequency of 500 Hz. The horizontal scale of the wave has been compressed for the diagram (as opposed to Figure 7, where only the first cycle could be shown on the time scale). The sound wave of air pressure and the airflow oscillation are both damped sinusoids; the pressure is at a maximum or minimum whenever the flow is at 0 and the flow is maximum or minimum when the pressure is at atmospheric.

pulse flow. Both have the same reflection mechanism, namely, that of a tube that is closed at one end, at the bottom of the bottle or at the vocal folds, and open at the other end, the mouth. The bottom-to-mouth distance of the bottle in Figure 7 was chosen to be the same as the average distance, from the vocal folds to the lips, in adult male speakers. Thus the basic resonant frequency of 500 Hz for the bottle is the same as that for the average adult male speaker. In speech *the resonances of the vocal tract are called formants;* the basic formant frequency of the average size adult male is 500 Hz.

The vocal tract, like any tube, has other resonances at frequencies higher than the basic one; these also affect the form of speech sounds. The resonant frequencies also depend on the shape of the vocal tract. In fact many of the sounds of speech are distinguished by specific patterns of resonant frequencies. In later chapters this is explained in detail.

SPECTRUM ANALYSIS

Consider again the form of the sound wave produced by a resonant air column like that in a bottle, a tube, or the vocal tract. How can this wave be analyzed, i.e., how can it be represented in the simple sine wave terms of frequency and amplitude as was the pendulum motion? We can do this by using a set of sine waves instead of a single wave.

The form of any wave can be constructed by adding together a number of sine waves of the proper amplitudes and frequencies. Sine waves that can be added to form a more complex wave are called the *components* of the complex wave. The fact that any wave, no matter how complex, can be represented by a certain set of component sine waves gives us the basis for the analysis of complex waves by their patterns of frequency and amplitude. To analyze a complex wave we find the set of component sine waves that would, when added together, produce a wave identical to the complex wave. That is how we analyze speech waves.

Speech waves often consist of resonant damped oscillations, so let us see how to represent a resonant wave by means of sine wave components.

Figure 9 shows a damped sinusoidal wave from a resonator whose resonant frequency is 500 Hz, together with a sinusoid of the same frequency. The resonant wave is similar to the sinusoid; however, the damped resonant wave decreases in amplitude as it dies out whereas the sinusoid is constant in amplitude. Obviously one component of the analysis could be a sinusoid having a frequency of the resonant frequency and the total duration of the damped oscillation. By adding to it other sinusoids, having frequencies higher and lower than the resonant frequency,

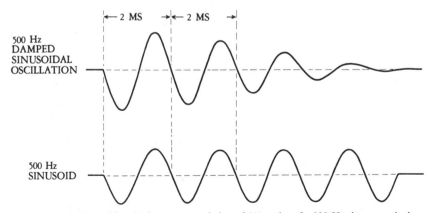

Figure 9.   The sinusoid at the bottom, consisting of 4½ cycles of a 500-Hz sine wave, is similar to the damped sinusoidal oscillation of 500 Hz, except for the damping of the amplitude.

we can produce a wave that is sinusoidal in form and damps out in amplitude in a regular fashion. This can be partially accomplished with three sinusoids, as shown in Figure 10, where we approximate the 500-Hz damped sinusoid by combining sinusoids of 450, 500, and 550 Hz. The sinusoids of 450 and 550 Hz, above and below the resonant frequency, have amplitudes less than the sinusoid at the resonant frequency.

In order to represent completely the damped resonant wave it is necessary to add to the resonant frequency component a very large number of other sinusoids having frequencies both above and below the resonant frequency, and all the other sinusoids must have lower amplitudes according to their distance from the resonant frequency.

The pattern of the amplitudes of all the component frequencies of a sound is called the *amplitude-frequency spectrum.* For brevity it is called simply the *spectrum,* or the *frequency spectrum.* The spectrum is the result of analyzing the sound and thus deriving its sine wave components.

The spectrum is plotted as a graph of the amplitudes at each of the frequencies, as in Figure 11, where we have plotted 55 components of the damped resonant oscillation of 500 Hz. Actually an infinite number of sine waves, infinitely close together in frequency, are necessary to represent a single occurrence of a resonant oscillation. The components would have amplitudes on the curved line drawn through the amplitudes of the 55 components in Figure 11.

The line connecting all the amplitudes is called the *spectrum envelope.* The spectrum envelope of Figure 11 describes the shape of the spectrum of the 500-Hz damped resonant wave in Figures 8 and 9. The frequency spectrum represents the analysis of that wave.

In much work on speech analysis the amplitude-frequency spectrum of sound is measured and the time relations (phases) of the components are ignored. This is because the phases of the spectral components do not have large effects on the identity of the different sounds of speech. However, the phases of the components do affect voice timbre or voice quality. The term *spectrum* is used herein to mean only the amplitude-frequency spectrum.

The concept of the amplitude-frequency spectrum is used to analyze and describe sounds of all types, not just speech. Sounds whose spectra have been studied extensively range from noises, such as the roar of jet aircraft, the clatter of machinery, and vehicle exhaust noise, to musical sounds like those of bells, trumpets, violins, and opera singers.

The resonance characteristics of the vocal tract are studied by finding and plotting the shape of the spectrum envelope of the sounds emitted from the mouth. There are definite relations between the shape of the vocal tract and the sound spectrum shape, as is seen in the next chapter.

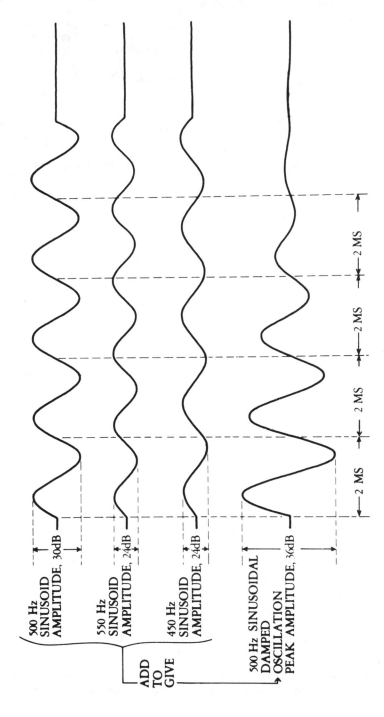

Figure 10. The three sinusoids having frequencies of 450, 500, and 550 Hz add together to produce a damped sinusoidal oscillation of 500 Hz, as seen in the lower wave.

27

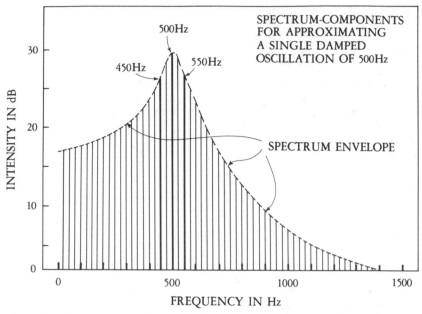

Figure 11.   The top end of each spectrum line gives the amplitude (intensity) of a sine wave spectrum component of a 500-Hz damped sinusoidal oscillation. There are 55 components, one every 25 Hz. Adding all 55 of these sine waves together, even though they are of infinite duration, gives only an approximation of a single damped sinusoidal oscillation of 500 Hz like the one at the bottom of Figure 10. The frequencies of the three sine wave segment components used in Figure 10 are indicated by the darker vertical lines. The spectrum envelope describes the amplitude-frequency shape for the infinite number of components necessary to produce the single damped oscillation.

SPECTRA OF RECURRING RESONANT OSCILLATIONS

In speech, the vowel sounds are produced by repeatedly "pulsing" the vocal tract air column with a train of glottal pulses. Let us now see how a vocal tract resonance would be represented by the spectrum of repeated occurrences of damped oscillations. Let us go back to our pulsed-tube model of the vocal tract. Assume that the tube is pulsed repeatedly and that the pulses succeed each other very rapidly, at intervals of 10 ms; this amounts to assuming a glottal pulse rate of 100 pulses per second, a typical rate for a low-pitched male speaker. The wave produced in this way would look like the wave in Figure 12A, which is simply the same wave as that at the bottom of Figure 10 but now it recurs every 10 ms. The rate or frequency of the pulses is 100 pulses per second and it will be noted in the waveform of Figure 12 that the wave has two types of periodic, repeated fluctuation. First there is a periodicity of 100 per second, that is, the wave shows a damped oscillation recurring at a rate of 100 times per

RESONANT 500-Hz OSCILLATION
PULSED 100 TIMES PER SECOND

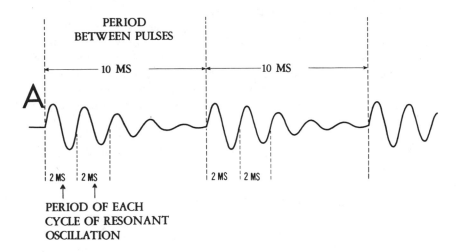

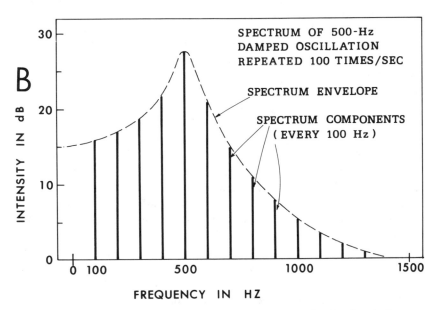

Figure 12.   Waveform and spectrum of a 500-Hz damped oscillation that is pulsed at a rate
of 100 times per second. In the spectrum there is a component at every multiple of 100 Hz,
corresponding to the 100 per second frequency of pulsing; the most intense component, 500
Hz, corresponds to the frequency of the resonant oscillation.

second. Second, there is the periodicity of each damped oscillation at the resonant frequency. This frequency is 500 Hz. It is the frequency of the basic formant for a 17.5-cm vocal tract.

The spectrum of this wave appears in Figure 12B. Compare the spectrum in Figure 12 with the spectrum in Figure 11; you will note that the shape of the spectrum envelope is the same in both. This is because the spectrum envelope depends only on the physical characteristics of the air column that determine its resonant frequency and the damping.

The individual components of the spectrum for the tract pulsed at 100 pulses per second are different from the components of the wave resulting from a single pulsing. Instead of a very large number of components, close together in frequency, there are components at 400 Hz, 300 Hz, 200 Hz, and 100 Hz below the resonant frequency, and components at 600 Hz, 700 Hz, 800 Hz, etc. above the resonant frequency. The frequency component of 100 Hz in this wave is referred to as the *fundamental frequency* of the wave, or simply the *fundamental*. Because of the way the wave was produced, by pulsing at 100 times per second, the other components of the wave are all multiples of this frequency. In listening to the wave a person will hear a fundamental pitch corresponding to the fundamental frequency of 100 Hz and will also hear a timbre corresponding to the resonant frequency of 500 Hz.

It is important that the strongest component in the spectrum is at 500 Hz, the resonant frequency, and that all other components of the sound, including the fundamental component, are weaker in amplitude than the component at the resonant frequency. This is because of the resonance of the air column. It is true for the spectrum of any sound produced by a resonant system: the most intense component of the spectrum is the one closest to the resonant frequency.

Some resonant systems respond to a pulse with more prolonged vibration than an air column because their materials do not damp out the oscillations to such a great degree. A wine glass is a good example of a resonant system with rather little damping. If a wine glass is tapped very rapidly say at 100 taps per second, then the resonant oscillations decay only a little between taps. The spectrum of this sound would show the amplitude of the component at the fundamental frequency to be extremely low compared with the amplitude of the component at the resonant frequency. In listening to such a sound the ear can still discriminate the low periodicity corresponding to the fundamental pulsing rate of the tapping and hear this as the lowest pitch of the sound wave. In addition a very strong tonal pitch is heard corresponding to the resonant frequency of the glass.

Imagine a resonant system that has no damping at all. The oscillation from one pulse would continue forever and we would hear a pure tone at the resonant frequency; the spectrum of this wave would be a single component at the resonant frequency with no other components.

At this point we need some definitions of terms that are used in describing spectra like the one in Figure 12. When the spectrum of a wave consists of components whose frequencies are all multiples of a fundamental frequency, the spectrum is said to be *harmonic*. This term arose because the components of the wave are synchronously (harmoniously) produced by the fundamental pulsing activity at a constant frequency. The components are called *harmonics* and individual harmonics are always at frequencies that are simple integer multiples of the fundamental, for the type of wave we are now considering. The harmonics are numbered in order from low to high frequencies, using numbers that correspond to their multiples; thus the wave component next above the fundamental is the *second harmonic* since its frequency is twice that of the fundamental; the frequency of the next component is three times the fundamental, so it is the *third harmonic,* and so on. The component at the resonant frequency in Figure 12 is 500 Hz, which is five times the fundamental, so it is the fifth harmonic.

The spectrum of a harmonic wave is usually plotted as in Figure 12, using a line for each component. The line has a length representing the amplitude (intensity) of the wave component and a position on the frequency scale representing the frequency of the component. A spectrum plot of such component lines is called a *line spectrum*. If the spectral lines are harmonically related, that is, if they are multiples of a single frequency, the line spectrum is also a *harmonic spectrum;* if not, it is an *inharmonic spectrum*.

In speech, voiced sounds are produced with various pulsing rates of the glottis, so let us now consider what would happen to the line spectrum of the sound that would be produced if the vocal tract were pulsed at different fundamental rates. If the glottal pulses were delivered at a rate of 200 per second, a typical rate for adult female speakers, the spectrum would appear as in Figure 13A. Here we note that the components of the spectrum are now at intervals of 200 Hz: there is a component in the spectrum at every multiple of the fundamental pulsing frequency. The spectrum envelope is still the same as before (in Figure 12) because the resonant characteristics of the tract have not been changed; we have only increased the rate of the pulsing that periodically excites the air column to vibrate, but the form of resonant vibration between pulses remains exactly the same and this determines the shape of the spectrum envelope.

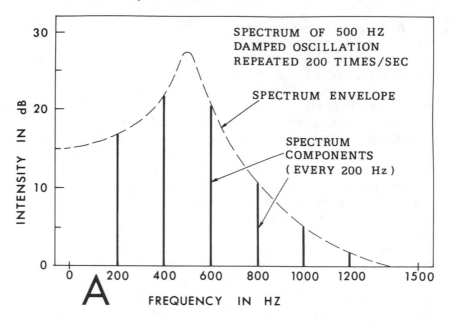

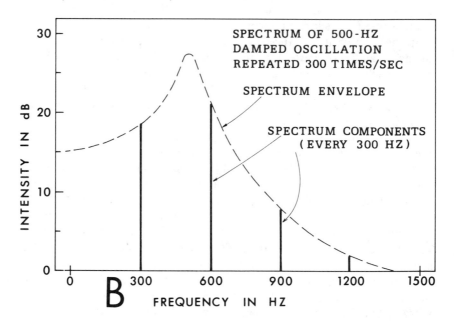

Figure 13.   Spectra of 500-Hz damped oscillation pulsed at 200 times per second (A) and 300 times per second (B).

Similarly, if the tract is pulsed at a rate of 300 pulses per second, the spectrum envelope will again remain the same. We show this in the spectrum in Figure 13B.

APERIODIC SPEECH SOUNDS

Up to this point we have dealt only with the *periodic sounds* of speech, those based on the periodic pulses of air emitted by the glottis. The aperiodic, turbulent sounds of speech are equally important. The *aperiodic sounds* are, as the name indicates, sounds that do not have a periodic form of sound wave. This is because the airflow disturbances that produce aperiodic sound waves are events that occur randomly in time. Aperiodic speech sounds are produced by two types of disturbance: 1) sudden transient releases of the air pressure built up behind consonant closures, and 2) turbulence in the breath stream as it rushes through a constriction. Air turbulence is random in time.

Sources of sound produced by transients and turbulence have spectra showing components at all frequencies. The form of the spectrum depends, as with periodic sounds, on the spectrum of the source and on the resonances of the vocal tract through which the source sound passes. We will examine later the production and spectra of aperiodic speech sounds.

THE SOUND SPECTROGRAPH

The sound spectrograph is an instrument for analyzing the spectrum of complex sounds that are changing over time. The rapid articulation of speech causes rapid changes in the shape of the oral tract and in the source of sound and we would expect the spectral patterns of speech to change rapidly in time. Consider, for example, that the lips and tongue move rapidly between the consonant constrictions and the more open vocal tract shapes for the vowels. This causes the formants of the vowels to move rapidly from one frequency location to another. In addition, when the vocal tract becomes very constricted, forming turbulent, aperiodic sounds, there would be corresponding changes in the sound pattern. In fact it often happens that the sound suddenly shifts from pulsing periodicity to aperiodic turbulence. During different phases in the formation of the vowels and consonants, rapid changes occur in the amplitude of sound depending on the amount and type of constriction in the vocal tract. We shall also see later how the expressive and rhythmical aspects of speech are embodied in changing patterns of the frequencies and amplitudes of speech.

Many of the most important characteristics of speech can thus be seen in the spectrum patterns as they change in time. The sound spectrograph operates on speech waves in order to analyze their spectra and make a picture of the spectral changes showing the patterns in time, frequency, and intensity. We use these pictures (sound spectrograms) in describing the detailed characteristics of speech, and thus they are very useful as an aid to learning acoustic phonetics.

The way in which the spectrograph analyzes the spectrum is to measure the amplitude of sound in a narrow range of frequencies. This is done by means of electrical *filters*. A filter is a resonating system that can be tuned as an analyzer to isolate one or more frequency components of a complex wave. The wave to be analyzed is fed through the filter and the amplitude of the electrical output of the filter represents the amplitude of the component of the wave that is isolated by the filter.

One type of spectrograph provides an instantaneous picture. It employs a large number of filters, each tuned to a different range of frequencies. These are shown in Figure 14. These filters are arranged in order from low to high frequencies and the electrical outputs of the filters stimulate a phosphorescent belt, which is passed under the array of stimulators. The belt retains the image of the different frequency patterns as they change in time and shows the picture of these changes. This is how one of the first sound spectrographs operated. It was built at the Bell Telephone Laboratories in the 1940s. This type of instant display of speech sounds has been proposed for helping deaf persons in their speech communication.

For acoustic analysis, a permanent record is needed so that we can measure and study the speech sound patterns. Also it would be desirable to have a very large number of filters so that we detect all the components of speech. For this purpose a sound spectrograph is provided with a single filter, which is then scanned gradually over the frequency range while a permanent record of the speech patterns is marked on a paper record. To do this the speech to be analyzed must first be recorded so that it can be played back repeatedly, over and over again, while the filter making the analysis is slowly scanned over the range of frequencies (see Figure 15). Each repetition of the recorded speech traces a horizontal line across the paper; the darkness of the line is determined by the amplitude of sound measured by the filter. Thus a picture is built up in which the horizontal extent of the many lines represents the time axis of speech and the vertical position of the line in the picture represents the frequency location of the filter. The darkness of the line represents intensity. The final picture shows the energy (intensity) in the speech frequencies at different points along a vertical scale of frequency. This picture is called a *spectrogram*.

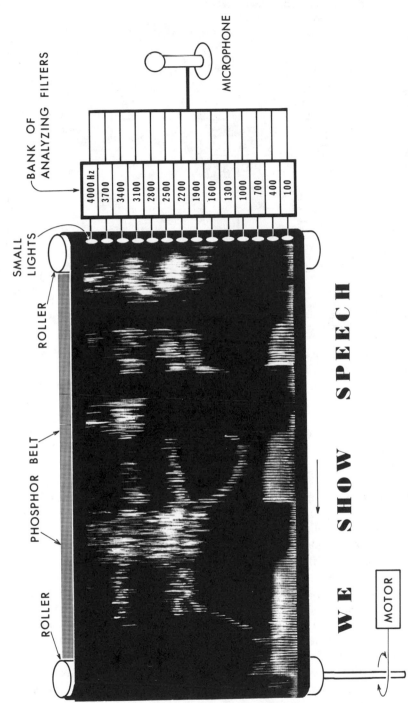

Figure 14. Bell Laboratories' early phosphor belt spectrograph. Time runs from left to right in the phosphorescent pattern and frequency runs from low to high frequencies as shown by the frequency number of each filter on the right.

35

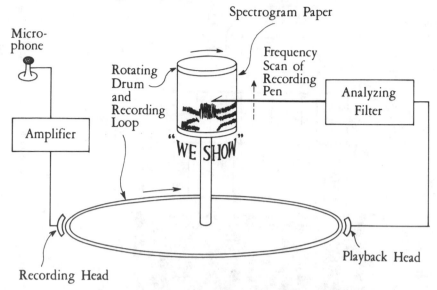

Figure 15.   Schematic diagram of the operation of the sound spectrograph, as available in models by Kay Elemetrics Co. and Voice Identification, Inc.

Examine the spectrogram at the top of Figure 16; the vertical frequency scale is in kilohertz (kHz) or thousands of Hertz and a 100-ms time interval is marked at the bottom of the spectrogram. The dark bars in the vowels, below a frequency of about 3 kHz, are due to the peaks in the spectrum caused by the three lowest formants (resonances of the vocal tract). These formants change in frequency as the speech is articulated. Above these formants we can see another dark bar at about 3.5 kHz; this is due to the fourth formant; its frequency does not change greatly with articulation, as do the frequencies of the three lower formants. The fricative consonants [s] and [tʃ] in the word "speech" show strong high frequency sound above 2 kHz and, unlike all the other sounds, the fricatives have little or no sound below 2 kHz.

The formant locations stand out boldly in the spectrogram because the analysis process in the spectrograph is deliberately designed for this. The filter for this type of display in the spectrogram is intentionally made rather wide in its frequency coverage so that the individual spectrum components of these sounds do not appear individually in the spectrogram. Only when the total sum of the energy of several components within the filter reaches a rather high level is the paper marked to indicate the presence of a high amount of energy. This allows the instrument to skim effectively over the top of the spectrum and pick off the areas of high amplitude, namely, those places where the formant peaks occur in the spectrum. This results in a very effective display of some of the most important spectrum changes, i.e., the formant frequency changes, as they occur in time. Formants are explained in greater detail in later chapters.

In addition to being able to see indications of the positions and course of the formants in time, as in the spectrogram, we also want to be able to examine the individual components of the spectrum at points of interest. For this purpose the sound spectrograph has an arrangement for operating in a different mode to pick out selected time points on the spectrogram and make a plot of the detailed spectrum at each of these points. Each of these plots is called a *spectral section*. In Figure 16 there are several spectral sections taken at the time points shown on the spectrogram. The spectral sections clearly show the individual components of sound and their amplitude relations to each other. Also the spectrum components are pictured on a linear scale of frequency so that their frequency locations can be measured and formant frequencies can be estimated; the fundamental frequency of periodic sounds can be measured by counting the frequency intervals between components. This is done by measuring the span in frequency of several successive components and then dividing by the number of intervals spanned. This gives the frequency spacing between components, which is the same as the fundamental frequency, as noted earlier.

The next two chapters deal with the vowel sounds of speech and how the spectral patterns of all the vowels are produced and analyzed.

SUMMARY

We have seen in this chapter how sound, which originates as a disturbance of the resting positions of air molecules, propagates the form of the disturbance faithfully and rapidly through the air. In speech, sound is produced by the vocal organs and propagated through the vocal tract to the outside air. The air molecule motions of speech sounds are complex in form but they can be represented as combinations of the simple oscillations of simple harmonic motion, a type of motion like that of a pendulum, where the motion is caused by a restoring force that is proportional to the displacement from resting position. Simple harmonic motion produces a sine wave. The amplitude, frequency, and sinusoidal form of a sine wave sound (pure tone) define its physical and auditory character.

A natural vibrating system, such as a pendulum, a ringing wine glass, or an air column in a tube like the vocal tract, responds to a disturbance from the resting state with a sinusoidal damped oscillation. This is called resonant oscillation.

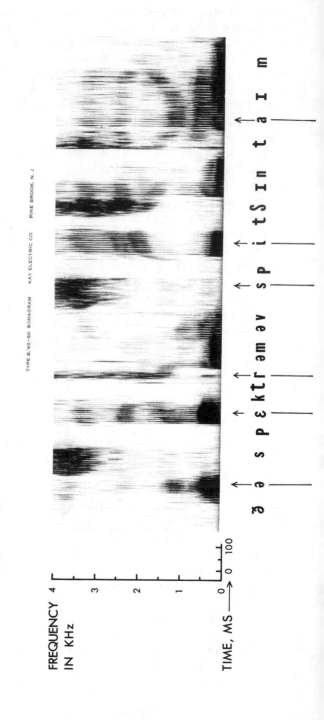

38

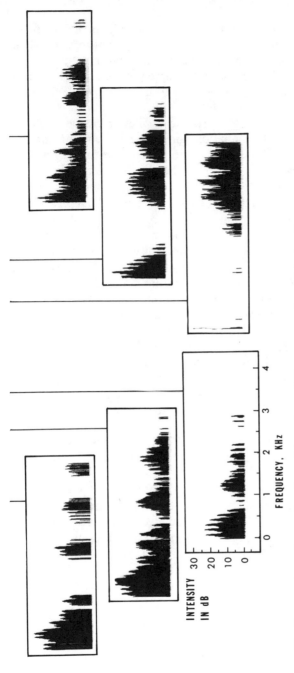

Figure 16. Spectrogram and spectral sections of the utterance ''The spectrum of speech in time.''

The frequency of resonant oscillation of the air column in a tube-like bottle, and in the vocal tract, can be explained in terms of reflections up and down the length of the air column. The form of resonant oscillation of an air column is sinusoidal because the force producing air molecule motion is a pressure difference proportional to the air molecule distance from resting position.

The sound wave produced by a resonant oscillation can be analyzed by sine-wave components; the main component is a sinusoid having the same frequency as the resonant oscillation; other components having frequencies higher and lower than the main component are necessary and these have amplitudes that are less than the main component. The amplitudes of the components, when plotted on a frequency scale, represent the spectrum of the resonant oscillation.

In speech the vowel sounds are produced by a periodic series of pulses emitted by the glottis. Each such pulse causes damped oscillations of the vocal tract air column. The resulting wave of recurring damped oscillations is analyzed by deriving its spectrum components. The frequencies of the spectrum components depend on the pulsing rate, which determines the fundamental frequency and the frequencies of the other spectrum components. The components are harmonics, all of which are simple multiples of the fundamental frequency. The amplitudes of the spectrum components are determined by the resonant frequency of the damped oscillation and by the amount of damping. The harmonic at the resonant frequency always has the highest amplitude and the other components have lower amplitudes according to their distance from the resonant frequency.

Aperiodic sounds also occur in speech. These are caused by random pulsing of the vocal tract by transient or turbulent disturbances in the air molecule distribution.

The articulation of speech causes the speech sound spectrum to change rapidly in time. The sound spectrograph is an instrument for analyzing these changes and displaying them visually. The spectrograph may be operated in one mode to display the changing resonances, or formants, of the vocal tract, and in another mode to display the individual components of the spectrum.

CHAPTER 3

VOWEL SHAPING
AND VOWEL FORMANTS

CONTENTS

The purpose of this chapter is to explain how the vocal shapes of vowels produce the spectrum patterns of the different vowels. We need only a few concepts and rules to go from the vocal tract shape for a vowel to its spectrum envelope. The rules give relations between the formant frequencies of the vocal tract and its shape. To demonstrate these relations we use a simple tube model of the vowel tract. The tube model produces sounds with formant frequencies similar to those of vowels. The formant frequencies are related to the length of the tube and to constrictions in the tube like those formed in the vocal tract by the pharynx, lips, and tongue. A set of rules is given for these relations. The rules are used to develop a set of formant frequencies for model vowels.

MODEL OF THE PHARYNGEAL-ORAL TRACT

All the different vowel sounds begin as a single common sound produced by the glottis; this sound is propagated through the pharynx and mouth to the air outside. The form of the pharyngeal and oral passages determines what the resulting vowel sound will be. This passage is called the pharyngeal-oral tract or simply the oral tract. When the oral tract has a given shape, the vowel sound produced has a certain pattern; when some other shape is formed, a different pattern of vowel sound is formed.

    Acoustic research on vowel shaping has found that a surprisingly simple model of the tract will produce artificial vowel sounds very similar to those of natural speech. The model is a shaped tube. It provides an easy way to remember the different spectrum patterns of vowels and, at the same time, it is a true physical model of how these patterns are produced.

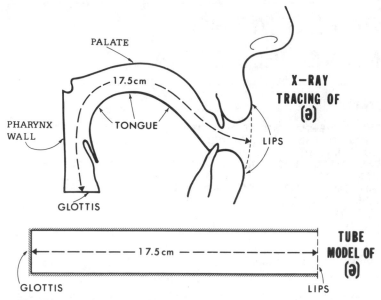

Figure 17.   Diagram of an x-ray tracing of the shape of the pharyngeal-oral tract and a tube model of the tract for the neutral vowel [ə].

The adequacy of the tube model was demonstrated by research comparing the sounds from models with sounds from natural speakers. First, natural vowel sounds were spoken and recorded. At the same time x-rays were made of the vocal tracts of the speakers. The shapes of the pharyngeal oral tract for each vowel were then sketched from the x-rays. Using these shapes and dimensions, tube models were made that had the same shapes seen in the x-rays. Finally, sound was passed through the tube models and the emerging sound patterns were compared with the natural vowel patterns. The agreement was good.[1]

This research model is used herein to explain the main sound patterns of vowels. We start with the vowel that has the most simple shape—the neutral vowel [ə], as in the phrase, *a toy* [ətɔɪ]. For this vowel sound the shape of the oral tract is neutral. That is, the tract has no appreciable constriction at any point; it is like a tube that has the same width at all points.

---

[1]This research began with the work of Chiba and Kajiyama (1941) and was continued in the 1950s by Dunn, Fant, Stevens, and House. Fant related vocal x-ray shapes to the acoustic theory of tube shapes and developed an acoustic theory of speech production that brought both acoustics and phonetics to bear on a unified description of speech. For details the student should read Dunn (1950), Fant (1960, 1968), Jakobson, Fant, and Halle (1967), Lindblom and Sundberg (1971), and Stevens and House (1955, 1961), but not before reading this chapter and the next one on the spectra of vowel sounds.

A simple straight tube is the model for this vowel. Figure 17 illustrates the relation between the tract shape and the model.

In Figure 17, an x-ray sketch of the pharyngeal-oral tract shape for [ə] shows the neutral position of the tongue and lips forming a tract that is nearly constant in width from the glottis through the lips. The length of the tract from glottis through lips is important for the vowel pattern; it is 17.5 cm long. This length is used for the model because it is the average distance through the tract from the glottis to the lips for adult males. The curvature of the tract does not affect sound propagation appreciably. Thus the tube model for this vowel is straight, of equal width throughout, and is 17.5 cm long, as shown in the lower part of Figure 17. The natural tract has minor deviations from equal width at the teeth and just above the glottis, but these have only minor effects on the vowel patterns.

Our object is to compare the sound pattern from the natural tract with that derived from the tube model. We do this by comparing the spectrum of sound from the model tube with the spectrum of a natural vowel sound. Each vowel sound has a characteristic shape of spectrum envelope depending on the formant frequency locations. Some simple rules relate the formant frequencies to the vowel shape, and this makes it easy to describe the sound pattern for a number of the vowel shapes assumed by the pharyngeal-oral tract.

SPECTRUM OF THE NEUTRAL VOWEL [ə]

Now let us see how the spectrum envelope of the neutral vowel [ə] arises from its oral tract shape. In Figure 18 we can see how the spectrum of a model [ə] vowel is formed by the tube model and compare the model spectrum with the natural vowel spectrum. Examine first how the sound is formed in the tube model. The sound that is inserted into the tube at the "glottis" end has a spectrum envelope that slopes downward in intensity as we go from low to high frequencies. This spectrum represents the sound emitted from the natural glottis; it is the spectrum of the glottal sound source, the source of sound for vowels.

Now note that the spectrum of the sound coming out of the tube also slopes downward, but it is scalloped with regular peaks and valleys of sound intensity. The general downward slope of the scalloped spectrum is the same as the slope of the glottal spectrum that was inserted into the tube. However, when we compare the spectrum of the emitted sound with that of the inserted sound we see that passage through the tube has emphasized some frequencies more than others in a very regular pattern. The first peak is at a frequency of 500 Hz; at frequencies above the first peak there are peaks at 1500 Hz, 2500 Hz, 3500 Hz, and 4500 Hz. In other

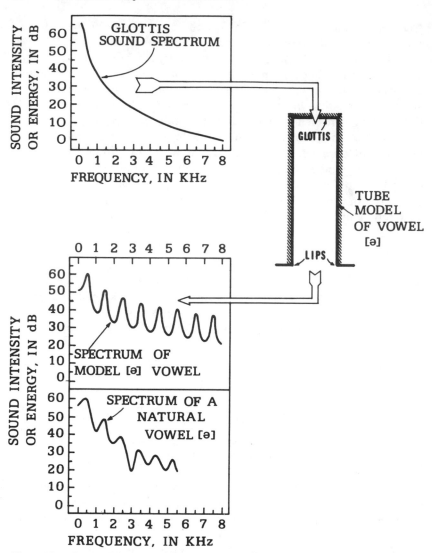

Figure 18.   Illustration of the modification of the glottal sound spectrum by transmission through a tube model of the neutral vowel [ə] and comparison spectrum of a natural [ə].

words *there is a peak every 1000 Hz beginning with the first peak at 500 Hz.* These repeated peaks occur at intervals of 1000 Hz, up to infinitely high frequencies, but we ended our graph at 8000 Hz.

As we saw in the previous chapter, the peak at 500 Hz represents the basic resonance of a 17.5-cm tube. It is the resonance that is lowest in frequency. The other peaks represent resonances at frequencies above the basic resonance. The resonant frequencies of a tube depend on its particular shape and dimensions. For a uniform tube the resonances occur at regular frequency intervals above the lowest resonance.

Going back to Figure 18, examine the spectrum of the natural vowel [ə] and compare it with the spectrum of the sound from the tube model. There is a considerable similarity between the two spectra. In the natural vowel, the peaks of sound intensity occur at 475, 1450, 2375, 3350, 4300, and 5200 Hz; these peaks are regularly spaced at intervals of about 950 Hz. The pattern of resonances of this natural [ə] seems to be shifted downward slightly in frequency compared with the pattern of the model [ə].

It is through acoustic modeling in this way that we know how the frequency locations of the resonant peaks in vowels depend on the length and shape of the vocal tract or, in the model, on the length and shape of a tube with the same dimensions. In the modeling process different sections of the model tube are given different diameters representing sections of the vocal tract where the lips are more or less rounded, protruded, or spread, and where the tongue is humped up in a given location or the pharynx is constricted. Using x-ray pictures of the lip, tongue, and pharynx constrictions, the resonance patterns and spectrum envelopes of many spoken vowels have been compared with those produced by tube models constricted according to the x-ray pictures. Good agreement has been found and we conclude that the resonance patterns of natural vowels are formed by the same physical effects that determine the resonances of tubes.

SPEECH FORMANTS

Before describing how the spectrum patterns, with various resonant peaks, are formed for different vowels, we need some exact definitions of the acoustic terms to be used.

The resonances in sound transmission through the vocal tract are called *formants. A formant is a resonance of the vocal tract.*

The effects of the formants are seen in the spectrum pattern of a speech sound because the spectrum is strongly affected by the resonances of the vocal tract. When the effects of the vocal resonances are apparent in the spectrum of a speech sound, the spectrum peaks may be called the "formants" of the speech sound but, strictly speaking, this is not correct because it is not the sound that has formants or resonances, it is the vocal tract. The formants are not the peaks seen in the spectrum; they are physical properties of the vocal tract, which produced the spectrum.

Sometimes spectrum peaks are called "formants," but this not strictly correct. We should always keep in mind the fact that formants are really properties of the vocal tract; this basic approach is essential when we try to explain the spectrum peaks and their relation to the vocal tract shape.[2]

The formants of a speech sound are numbered from low to high frequencies and are called the first formant (F1), second formant (F2), third formant (F3), fourth formant (F4), and so on, as far as needed.

The frequency locations of the formants, especially F1 and F2, are closely tied to the shape of the vocal tract as the lips, tongue, pharynx, and jaw move to articulate the consonants and vowels. The frequency of the third formant, F3, is related to only a few specific speech sounds, which are discussed later. The fourth and fifth and higher formants, F4, F5, and so on, remain rather constant in frequency location regardless of changes in articulation. First we will concentrate on F1 and F2, especially on their frequency locations for the different vowel sounds.

The formant frequency locations for vowels are affected by three factors: the length of the pharyngeal-oral tract, the location of constrictions in the tract, and the degree of narrowness of the constrictions.

VOWEL FORMANT LOCATIONS
AND LENGTH OF PHARYNGEAL-ORAL TRACT

The age and physical size of a person determine the length of his pharyngeal-oral tract. The length of the tract affects the frequency locations of all of the vowel formants; this fact helps us to predict where the formant peaks in the spectrum will appear for children, women, and men.

A very simple rule relates the frequencies of the formants to the overall length of the tract from glottis through lips. The rule for this relation is:

Length Rule. The average frequencies of the vowel formants are inversely proportional to the length of the pharyngeal-oral tract. In other words, the longer the tract, the lower are its average formant frequencies.

The neutral vowel formants for the average man, with an oral tract 17.5 cm in length, are at 500, 1500, 2500 Hz, etc., with the lowest formant at 500 Hz and frequency spacing of 1000 Hz between all formants.

An easy way to remember the neutral formant frequencies is to think of the odd numbers 1, 3, 5, 7, 9, and so on, because the formant frequen-

---

[2]In practice we often want to infer the formant pattern of the vocal tract that produced a given speech sound by examining the spectrum of the sound; then the frequencies and intensities of the formants are estimated by examining the peaks in the spectrum. However, the way to measure the formants exactly would be to measure the transmission of sound through the actual vocal tract shape.

cies of a uniform tube that is closed at one end, like the pharyngeal-oral tract, are always odd multiples of the frequency of the lowest formant. For example, begin with the basic formant frequency, 500 Hz, as the unit or 1; then the formant frequencies above that are $500 \times 3 = 1500$ Hz, $500 \times 5 = 2500$ Hz, etc. This method, calculating the formants above F1 as multiples of F1, applies only to a neutral tract shape.

The pharyngeal-oral tract length of an infant is approximately half the length for a man. Therefore, following our Length Rule about formant frequency locations, the formants of a neutral-shaped infant tract in relation to a man's would be at frequency locations that are a factor of the reciprocal of ½, or twice those of the man. On this basis the infant formant locations for a neutral vowel would be as follows: F1 is $500 \times 2 = 1000$ Hz, F2 is $1500 \times 2 = 3000$ Hz, F3 is $2500 \times 2 = 5000$ Hz, and so on.

Following the same procedure, a woman's vocal tract, on the average, is about 15% shorter than that of a man. The ratio is approximately ⁵/₆. The reciprocal of ⁵/₆ is ⁶/₅, which is equal to a factor of 1.20, which, when multipled by the man's neutral formant frequencies, gives the women values that are 20% higher: F1 is $500 \times 1.2 = 600$ Hz, F2 is $1500 \times 1.2 = 1800$ Hz, F3 is $2500 \times 1.2 = 3000$ Hz, and so on.

It should also be noted that the frequency spacing between the formants can be calculated by the Length Rule, i.e., simply by applying a factor that is the reciprocal of the length ratio taken relative to the 17.5-cm length.

Figure 19 illustrates these relations between the model tract lengths for women, men, and infants and the corresponding formant frequency positions in the spectra of model neutral vowels.

For another example of applying the Length Rule, return to Figure 18 and ask the following question about the natural [ə] vowel. Why were the formant frequencies indicated by the spectrum of the natural [ə] vowel a little lower and more closely spaced than those of the model [ə] vowel? The natural formants in this case seem to be about 5% lower than those for the 17.5-cm model; 5% lower is a ratio of 0.95, the reciprocal of which is 1.053, so it may be that the pharyngeal-oral tract of the natural speaker was 5.3% longer than 17.5 cm.

The relation of model formant frequency locations and formant spacing to the length of the vocal tract is a useful aid in analyzing speech patterns. The Length Rule tells us approximately where we may find the formants, for the very young as well as for older, larger persons. However, the neutral locations of F1 and F2 for an individual are also affected by the length proportions of his vocal tract between the oral and pharyngeal cavities (Fant, 1973; Chapter 4). In general the location and spacing of formants F3 and above are more closely correlated with length of vocal

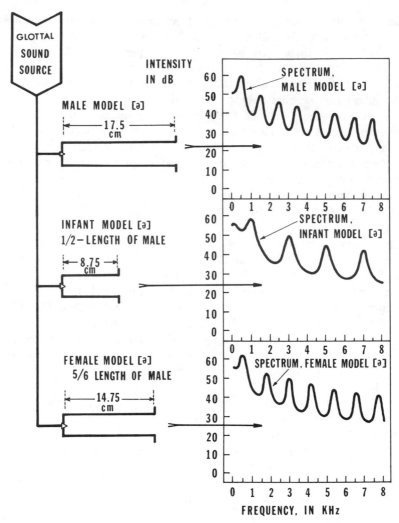

Figure 19.   Production of model [ə]-vowel spectra using tubes having lengths appropriate to the lengths of the pharyngeal-oral tract of an adult male, infant, and adult female. A constant model glottal sound is passed through each tube model, resulting in vowel spectrum envelopes with formant peaks as shown. The formant frequency locations and spacing are inversely related to tube length.

tract than for F1 and F2. The average locations of F1 and F2 for an individual are also affected somewhat by language environment and training.

In view of the Length Rule, some very interesting questions can be asked about how children acquire speech. As children grow, their vocal tracts grow longer and their formants shift downward in frequency. In other words, as children learn to speak, between the ages of 18 and 48 months, the sounds they produce are gradually changing in the frequency location of the formants! How do they learn to make the correct sounds, if the results of their productions are changing in sound pattern? Speculations on this question are most intriguing. It may be that auditory self-monitoring for speech development is unnecessary after the initial stages of learning a sound, or it may be that the child's auditory system somehow readjusts its frequency scale for listening as the vocal tract is growing. Some sort of built-in readjustment or rescaling may take place automatically in the auditory system, because, in addition to adjusting for growth changes in his own speech sounds, the child also uses adult sounds as models; adult sounds cannot correspond to the child's own proper sounds because of the large difference in size between adult and child vocal tracts.

VOCAL TRACT CONSTRICTIONS
AND FORMANT FREQUENCY LOCATIONS

Having located the neutral formant positions, we now need to see how different articulatory shapes of the pharyngeal-oral tract affect the formant locations. The simplest way to do this is to consider, for modeling purposes, just the constriction point of the articulation, ignoring the particular shape assumed by the tongue and lips to form the constriction. First we consider just the amount of constriction, i.e., the narrowness at the narrowest place of constriction. Figure 20 shows diagrams of the tract shape for several vowels. The diagrams are based on an x-ray study by Lindblom and Sundberg (1971). The tongue positions in Figure 20 for the front vowels, [i, e, ɛ, æ], can be seen to form a series with progressively less constriction at the front of the palate. In addition the jaw position is more open for [ɛ, æ] than for [i, e], and the pharynx is more constricted.

The back vowels [u] and [o] differ in amount of constriction by the tongue at a place near the back of the palate, with [u] being more constricted than [o]. Also the lips are narrowly rounded for [u] but are less so for [o]. The back vowels [ɔ] and [ɑ] have progressively less lip constriction but are formed by constricting the pharynx progressively more going from [o] to [ɔ] to [ɑ]. In addition the jaw position is more open for [ɑ].

In describing rules that relate vowel shapes to formant locations we begin with the effect of amount of constriction on the frequency of F1. A constriction also affects F2, but in different ways, which are described separately.

There are two rules relating constriction and F1, one for oral constrictions and another for pharyngeal constrictions.

BASIC VOWEL SHAPES

FRONT VOWEL SHAPES

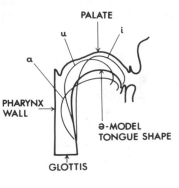
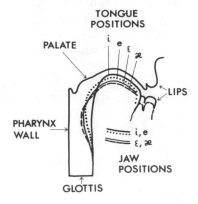

BACK VOWEL SHAPES

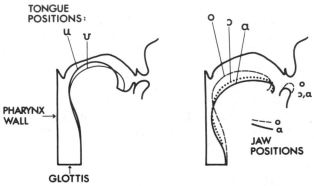

Figure 20.   Diagrams of pharyngeal-oral tract shapes for front and back vowels. (Adapted from Lindblom and Sundberg, 1971.)

Oral Constriction/F1 Rule.   The frequency of F1 is lowered by any constriction in the front half of the oral part of the vocal tract, and the greater the constriction the more F1 is lowered.

Thus, if the tongue is somewhat humped up close to the middle of the palate, or to the front of the palate, instead of being in the position forming a neutral uniform area tube, then F1 tends to be lower in frequency than the neutral 500 Hz. This also applies to a constriction formed at the lips or teeth.

Pharyngeal Constriction/F1 Rule. The frequency of F1 is raised by constriction of the pharynx, and the greater the constriction the more F1 is raised.

As we saw in Figure 20, different degrees of constriction of the pharynx occur in the back vowels, going from the least pharyngeal constriction for [o] to the most pharyngeal constriction for [ɑ]. This causes F1 of these vowels to be progressively higher than 500 Hz.

Next we give rules relating F2 frequency to vocal tract constrictions. The frequency of F2 depends on whether the tongue constriction is near the front of the oral tract, as for front vowels, or near the back, as for the back vowels. First we consider back constrictions.

Back Tongue Constriction/F2 Rule. The frequency of F2 tends to be lowered by a back tongue constriction, and the greater the constriction the more F2 is lowered.

If the tongue is humped up toward the back of the palate to constrict the oral tract and form one of the back vowels, [u] for example, the effect is to lower the frequency of F2. In fact the vowel [u] is formed by humping the tongue rather close to the soft palate, and the frequency location of F2 for this vowel is very low because of the rather narrow constriction. Compared with the frequency location of F2 for the neutral vowel shape, the F2 for [u], for a man, is about 800 Hz instead of a neutral F2 of 1500 Hz. The next vowel in the series of back vowels, [o], is formed with less tongue constriction and less lip-rounding than [u]; therefore, since the amount of lowering of F2 depends on the amount of constriction, F2 is at a higher frequency location for [o] than for [u]. In a typical man's [o], F2 is at about 900 Hz. Later these relations between vowels are summarized by giving a set of model frequency locations for F1 and F2 for all of the vowels.

When the constriction of the tongue is at the front of the palate, F2 is affected by the constriction in a way just opposite to that for back tongue constrictions. The rule relating front tongue constriction and frequency of F2 is:

Front Tongue Constriction/F2 Rule. The frequency of F2 is raised by a front tongue constriction, and the greater the constriction the more F2 is raised.

The front vowels can be arranged in a series where the amount of tongue constriction is least for [æ] and greatest for [i] (cf. Figure 20); the series is [æ], [ɛ], [e], [i]. Following our rules for the frequency location of F1 and F2 over the series of front vowels from least constricted to most constricted, the frequency of F1 decreases in frequency; however the frequency of F2 goes from a frequency of 1700 Hz, just slightly higher than the neutral position for F2, to a high frequency for the most constricted front vowel, [i], where F2 is at a frequency of about 2200 Hz for an average man. The pharyngeal constrictions of [æ] and [ɛ] raise F1 above the neutral F1 of 500 Hz.

Our final rule describes the effects of lip-rounding on the formants as follows:

> **Lip-Rounding Rule.** The frequencies of all formants are lowered by lip-rounding. The more the rounding, the more the constriction, and the more the formants are lowered.

Lip-rounding plays an important part in forming the back vowels and some of the consonants. The series of back vowels involves a series of lip positions beginning with wide-open lips for [ɑ] and progressing to more and more rounded, i.e., more and more lip-constricted, configurations as we proceed to [ɔ], [o], and [u]. In addition, the back tongue constrictions for the back vowels are more and more constricted going from [ɔ] to [o] to [u]. Thus two effects cause the frequency locations of F1 and F2 to be progressively lower over the back vowel series going from the most open, unrounded vowel [ɑ] to the [u] vowel with the most tongue constriction at the back and the most lip-rounding at the lips. The pharyngeal constriction also comes into play going from [ɑ] to [o]. The frequency of F1 begins, with [ɑ], at a high frequency and is lowered by the decrease in pharyngeal constriction for [ɔ] and [o]. The increasing back tongue constriction causes F2 to decrease between [o] and [u] while, at the same time, increasing lip-rounding causes further decrease in F2, as well as decrease in F1.

The rules given above provide a simple framework for predicting formant patterns from vocal tract shape. However, they have some limitations in their effective range of operation. They operate best when a single constriction is the dominant feature of the shape of the vocal tract. Single-constriction shapes occur for the close front vowels, [i, e], and the open back vowels, [ɑ, ɔ], when they are spoken in isolation, or in words at points where the vowel shape is not greatly affected by consonant constrictions. For these shapes different degrees of the constriction cause large shifts of formant frequencies in the directions given by the rules. When there are two constrictions involved in the shape of the tract, a rule may or may not operate over the entire range of constrictions. For example different degrees of lip-rounding have strong effects when superimposed on a front vowel shape, but have more limited effects when added to back vowel shapes. In running speech where the constriction move-

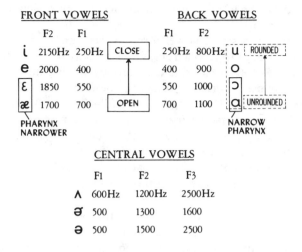

FRONT VOWELS

	F2	F1	
i	2150Hz	250Hz	CLOSE
e	2000	400	
ɛ	1850	550	
æ	1700	700	OPEN

PHARYNX
NARROWER

BACK VOWELS

	F1	F2	
	250Hz	800Hz	u ROUNDED
	400	900	o
	550	1000	ɔ
	700	1100	ɑ UNROUNDED

NARROW
PHARYNX

CENTRAL VOWELS

	F1	F2	F3
ʌ	600Hz	1200Hz	2500Hz
ɚ	500	1300	1600
ə	500	1500	2500

Figure 21.   Scheme of model formant frequencies for vowels.

ments of the lips, tongue, and pharynx frequently overlap each other in time, it is only during phases of single constriction dominance and during certain combined constrictions that our formant/constriction rules apply strongly. Stevens and House (1955) and Fant (1960) have provided quantitative relations between formant frequencies and degrees of constriction.

The purpose of the five rules relating vocal tract constrictions and formant frequencies is to provide a simplified framework that summarizes the acoustic shaping of normal vowels. The rules may not always apply to defective speech because abnormal (compensatory) shaping of the vocal tract, and abnormal vocal fold action, can produce spectral patterns not explained by the rules.

A set of model formant frequencies for vowels is given in Figure 21. The set of frequencies is constructed in a somewhat artificial way to serve as a mnemonic device. The end values of F1 and F2, at the ends of the front series and the back series, are set at frequencies that are fairly close to the average formant frequencies found for American men. However, the end values were also selected to allow equal steps of either 100 or 150 Hz between formants of two adjacent vowels. The 150-Hz steps are used for F1 and for the F2 range of the front vowels from [i] to [æ]. The 100-Hz steps are used for the F2 steps between adjacent back vowels and 150-Hz steps are used for F1.

This results in a set of vowel formant frequencies that are easy to keep in mind, or even to reconstruct, knowing only the extreme F values and step sizes. For example, one can start by writing down just the F values for the close vowels, [i] and [u]; these are front F1 and back F1=250 Hz, front F2=2150 Hz, and back F2=800 Hz. Then, following the constriction rules, from close to open, go down in frequency in 150-Hz steps of F2 over the series of front vowels, next go up in frequency in 150-Hz steps of F1 over the series of front vowels, then go up in frequency in 100-Hz steps of F2 over the back vowels, and up in 150-Hz steps for the F1 values. This constructs a table of model formant frequencies for the front and back vowels.

If you study this table, you will see that for each front vowel there is a corresponding back vowel having a similar degree of constriction and, therefore, a very similar location in the frequency of the first formant. We might predict that when a listener hears vowels in a noisy situation such that the noise interferes with hearing the second formant region, he will interconfuse the pairs of front and back vowels that have similar frequencies of the first formant, namely, he will confuse [i] with [u], [e] with [o], [ɛ] with [ɔ], and [æ] with [a]. Such an effect actually does occur in listening to speech in some noises where the second formant region cannot be heard. The same effect would be expected to occur for deaf listeners who have a type of deafness where hearing is more impaired in the frequency range of F2 than in the range of F1.

CENTRAL VOWELS

Two English vowels are formed with constriction in the central part of the oral tract. These are [ʌ] and [ɚ]. The vowel [ʌ] is similar to the neutral vowel [ə] but the tongue is often retracted slightly backward so that this vowel has a larger portion of the oral tract in front of the constriction than behind it. F1 for [ʌ] is at about 600 Hz, slightly higher than the neutral position of F1. F2 of [ʌ] is at about 1200 Hz; as with other back tongue constrictions, F2 is lower than the 1500-Hz neutral position.

The vowel [ɚ], unlike other vowels, is usually formed with the tongue tip flexed backward forming a midpalatal constriction. The first formant of [ɚ] is in a rather neutral position at about 500 Hz; the second formant is at about 1300 Hz. In these respects [ɚ] is similar to a neutral vowel. However, when there is a midpalatal constriction, the frequency location of the third formant is strongly affected. The third formant is lowered by this constriction. For the vowel [ɚ] the third formant for a man is very low, at about 1600 Hz, compared with the F3 neutral position of 2500 Hz.

SUMMARY

Acoustic research on speech production has developed a physical model of the pharyngeal-oral tract representing the production of natural vowel sounds. The physical model is a tube, the length and shape of which determines the formant frequencies of the tube.

Five simple shape rules can be used to give model positions of the first and second formants for the front vowels and for the back vowels. Referring again to Figure 21, we see that it is a simple matter, with the rules in mind, to reconstruct a set of model formant frequencies for F1 and F2, over the back vowel series and over the front vowel series, knowing only the rules and the starting points of the formants at the extreme ends of each series.

CHAPTER 4

THE SPECTRA OF VOWELS

CONTENTS

> In...vowels sounded on a succession of different larynx notes...what the ear hears...is the...resonant characteristics of the cavities through which that larynx note has passed...due to the relative volume and areas of orifices produced by the different attitudes of the tongue and lips.
>
> R. A. S. Paget, 1924

Thus far vowel sounds have been described according to vocal tract shape and its effects on the formant locations. A complete description of a vowel sound also includes characteristics arising from the action of the glottis. In this chapter the effects of vowel shape and glottal action are combined. First the glottal action and how it affects the spectrum of the glottal source-sound is described. Then the effects of the vocal tract resonances on the glottal spectrum are presented, using the source-filter theory of vowel production. We also study the effects on the vowel spectrum of low- and high-pitched voice, of vocal effort, and of nasalization. Finally, typical spectrograms are given of English vowels and diphthongs.

THE GLOTTAL SOUND SOURCE

The production of voiced speech sounds begins with the repeated opening and closing of the glottis, in response to the tracheal air pressure; this action forms a train of glottal pulses, which is the basic sound source for vowels and all other voiced sounds. The spectrum of this sound source depends on just how the glottis forms the pulses. For each glottal pulse, the exact form of the airflow through the glottis has an effect on the glottal sound spectrum, so we must first examine how the glottal airflow occurs.

The action of the glottis to produce a sound source is called *phonation*. Phonation depends on how the airflow interacts with the muscular and elastic tensions of the vocal folds; these interactions are now described following the widely accepted *aerodynamic-myoelastic theory of phonation*.

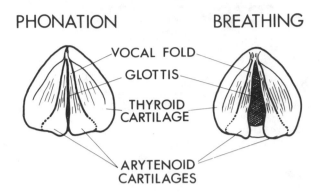

Figure 22.   Diagrams of the larynx as seen from above, illustrating the positions of the arytenoid cartilages and vocal folds for breathing and for phonation.

The vocal folds are held in various positions by the arytenoid cartilages, to which the rear portions of the folds are attached (see Figure 22). During breathing the arytenoid cartilages are held outward, keeping the glottis open in a wide-open position. When phonation is about to begin, the arytenoids move inward and bring the vocal folds together; this closes the glottis and blocks the flow of air from the trachea. The chest and lungs press inward, causing the air pressure below the glottis to rise. When this subglottal pressure is sufficiently higher than the air pressure above the glottis, the closing tension on the folds is overcome and they begin to open in a glottal slit between the folds. The sequence of events that then occurs to produce glottal pulsing is as follows: as the glottal slit opens, air begins to flow out through the glottis. The subglottal pressure continues to force the glottis to open wider, and there is an increasing airflow[1] through the glottis, until the natural elastic tension of the folds, which increases dynamically with increased opening, balances the separating force of the air

---

[1]The term *airflow* is called glottal volume velocity in acoustic research on speech. It is equal to the area of the glottal opening multiplied by the air molecule velocity through the glottis. The air molecule velocity, to a first approximation, is simply proportional to the difference in air pressure above and below the glottis. This transglottal pressure difference is approximately constant throughout a cycle of glottal action, although, of course, it is under the influence of external changes in pressure from the chest action or from a narrow constriction in the vocal tract above the glottis and may be slowly rising or falling due to these influences.

  Recent theory of glottal action is discussed in Ishizaka and Flanagan (1972) and Titze (1973, 1974).

pressure. Then the glottal opening and the rate of airflow through the glottis have reached their maximum value. At this point the kinetic energy that the vocal folds received during the opening movement is stored as elastic recoil energy, resulting in a restoring force large enough to overbalance the separating force of the airflow. This stored energy also causes the folds to begin to move inward. The inward movement gathers momentum and continues. When the glottis becomes sufficiently narrow, the high velocity of movement of the air particles within the narrow glottis creates a suction effect, which tends to further pull the vocal folds toward each other. This suction is an example of a physical flow effect called the Bernoulli force.[2] The elastic restoring force and the Bernoulli force together act to close the glottis. The Bernoulli force especially comes into play just before closure; as the glottal slit becomes very narrow there is a further increase in the velocity of the air particles moving through the glottis, thus increasing the suction of the Bernoulli force, and causing the glottis to close very abruptly, completely stopping the airflow. Elastic restoring forces during this collision of the vocal folds, in conjunction with the subglottal pressure, then start a new cycle of action similar to the cycle just described.

To summarize the forces in the cycle of glottal action, the subglottal pressure forces the vocal folds to open and then move outward; the momentum of the movement forces the folds to an extreme of elastic tension where they reverse and then move inward; the momentum of inward movement and, finally, the increased suction of the Bernoulli effect cause the vocal folds to close abruptly; the subglottal pressure and elastic restoring forces during closure cause the cycle to begin again.

As long as the subglottal pressure remains at a sufficiently high level and the arytenoid cartilages hold the vocal folds together, voicing phonation occurs and the glottis will continue to emit a rapid series of air pulses; there is one air pulse emitted during each open-close cycle of glottal action.

---

[2]The Bernoulli pressure is a difference in pressure that must exist to maintain equal energy in a duct with varying cross section. The total flow energy depends on the pressure and air particle velocity. The particle velocity at a constriction is higher than it is at the adjacent larger areas; therefore, because the total flow energy must remain constant, the pressure in the constricted area is lower than the pressure in the adjacent areas.

A Bernoulli force exists wherever there is a difference in fluid pressure between opposite sides of an object. Two other examples of a Bernoulli force in a constricted area of flow are: 1) blowing between parallel sheets of paper held close together (they pull together instead of flying apart because the air velocity is greater, and the pressure is lower, between the sheets than on the outer sides) and 2) the attraction of a hose nozzle toward the bottom of a pail because of the increased velocity of the water when the nozzle is near the bottom (if the nozzle outlet is too close to the bottom, the Bernoulli suction is strong enough to completely shut off the water flow in spite of the water pressure outward through the nozzle).

THE SPECTRUM OF THE GLOTTAL SOUND SOURCE

The exact form of the pulses of air emitted by the glottis is extremely important because this form is the waveform of the glottal sound source and the spectrum of this waveform is the spectrum of the glottal sound source. For this reason the spectrum of the glottal source has been studied by many scientists. However, only recently have we had powerful experimental techniques that promise to lead to a complete description of all the factors that affect the glottal spectrum. The first modern technique, ultra high speed cinematography of the movement of the vocal folds during phonation, was developed at Bell Laboratories (Farnsworth, 1940). The method was to take several thousand pictures per second through a small mirror looking down on the glottis. A series of such pictures is shown in Figure 23. These pictures showed the change in degree of opening between the vocal folds, which can then be converted to an open-area measurement for each picture. This method was used by W. W. Fletcher in 1950 at Northwestern University to determine glottal area waveforms in time, and to study how these waveforms were related to voice intensity. Flanagan (1958) used Fletcher's waveforms, and certain physical flow assumptions about how the area waves would be related to the wave shapes of airflow pulses, to derive the first detailed plots of the spectrum of glottal pulses. Flanagan and his colleagues at Bell Laboratories then proceeded to develop a computer model of the action of the vocal folds (Flanagan and Landgraf, 1968). Computer models produce directly their own wave forms of glottal pulses, and assumptions about the area-flow relationship are not necessary. This is because a computer model can simulate many of the anatomic and physical conditions, the forces on the air in the glottis, and the resulting actions of the vocal folds. In the computer simulation, an input of constant subglottal pressure produces movements of simulated vocal folds and corresponding pulses of air escaping through the simulated glottis between the folds.

The veracity of the glottal pulses produced by computer models has been checked by other methods. One of the best methods is to analyze actual speech waves by filtering to remove the effects of the resonances of the pharyngeal-oral tract, and leave as an output from the filters the original glottal pulses. This method is called inverse filtering; it consists of first determining the resonant frequencies and bandwidths of the main formants of a steady portion of a vowel sound, then setting inverse filters at the same frequencies and bandwidths, and finally passing the vowel sound through this inverse filter set. The output wave has the same wave shape as the pulses of glottal airflow. For examples of the resulting waves of glottal airflow see Rothenberg (1973).

Next consider the spectrum of the glottal sound source, the *glottal source spectrum*. This spectrum is the basis of the spectrum characteristics of all voiced sounds. The spectrum depends on the shape of the glottal wave form.

Figures 24 and 25 illustrate the origin of the source spectrum; Figure 24 shows a wave form of the glottal area for two cycles of vocal fold vibration and the resulting waves of glottal airflow, and Figure 25 shows the spectrum of the glottal airflow waveform. The waves of Figure 24 were generated by an advanced computer model of the vocal folds; the model incorporated typical conditions of the subglottal pressure, of the physical characteristics of the folds, and of the muscle tensions on the folds. This biomechanical model of phonation was developed by Titze and Talkin (1979), who kindly furnished the curves of Figure 24. The pressure and tension conditions were chosen to produce an idealized glottal source spectrum having a slope with the same general pattern as found at Bell Laboratories, and by other investigators in previous studies of the actual glottal spectrum.

There are two characteristics of the glottal spectrum that are especially important: 1) the frequency spacing of the spectral components, i.e., the fundamental and the harmonics, and 2) the amplitude pattern of the components over frequency. The frequency spacing depends on the repetition rate of the pulses in the glottal wave. The amplitude pattern of the spectral components depends on the exact shape of the pulses.

The spacing of the components of the glottal wave of Figure 25 is 100 Hz between components; this spacing corresponds to the repetition rate of the glottal pulses and to the fundamental frequency of the glottal wave. In other words, the glottal pulses repeat at a rate of 100 pulses per second, the corresponding fundamental frequency of the wave of glottal pulses is 100 Hz, and the harmonics in the spectrum of this wave are spaced 100 Hz apart. The fundamental frequency of the spectrum shown in Figure 25 is typical for a low-pitched adult male voice, that is, a fundamental frequency of 100 Hz.

The amplitudes of the components in the glottal spectrum have a pattern that generally decreases from low frequency harmonics to higher ones; that is, the spectrum slopes generally downward. The intensity slopes downward at an average of 12 dB per octave change (doubling) in frequency. The spectrum of the glottal flow wave in Figure 25 therefore has a slope of $-12dB/octave$.

For actual glottal waves there are variations in the component amplitudes of the glottal spectrum that are related to the degree of rounding of the corners, the duration of the closure, and other fine details of the glottal waveform. These relate physiologically to the style and force of speak-

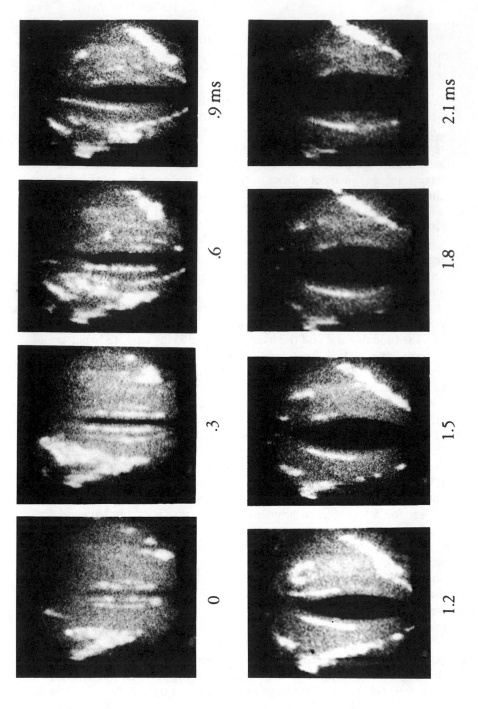

.9 ms

.6

.3

0

2.1 ms

1.8

1.5

1.2

62

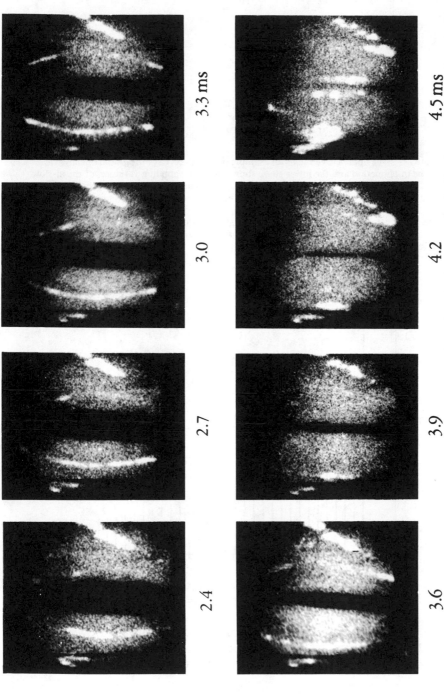

3.3 ms

3.0

2.7

2.4

4.5 ms

4.2

3.9

3.6

Figure 23.   A series of high speed photographs of one cycle of glottal voicing action. The pictures are taken looking down on the glottis; the arytenoid cartilages are out of view at the bottom of the picture. The speaker was a high-pitched adult male: this one cycle required only 4.5 ms. The pictures were taken at a rate of 10,000 frames per second; only every third frame is shown. (Photos courtesy of W. Wathen-Dunn, H. Soron, and P. Lieberman, taken at the Air Force Cambridge Research Laboratories.)

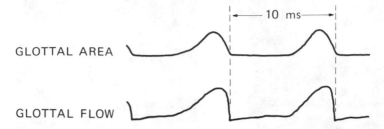

Figure 24.   The upper curve shows an example of how the area of the glottal opening varies in time in phonation and the lower curve shows the corresponding variation of the airflow through the glottis. These curves were generated by a computer model of the vocal folds activated by subglottal air pressure from below. The model was adjusted with typical values of pressure and muscle tension to produce a smoothly sloping spectrum for the glottal flow wave and fundamental frequency of 100 Hz; the period of one cycle is 10 ms. (Curves made at Sensory Communication Research Laboratory, Gallaudet College, by I. Titze and D. Talkin.)

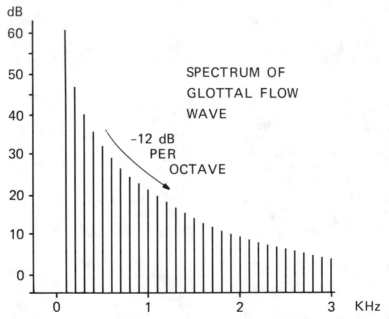

Figure 25.   The spectrum of the glottal flow wave of Figure 24. This is an idealized spectrum, which serves well as a model of the source spectrum for the vowel sounds.

ing, and to individual characteristics of vocal fold behavior. However, an idealized glottal spectrum with a smooth slope of -12 dB/octave is a good, normal basis for describing the spectra of voiced sounds.

The pitch or fundamental frequency of the glottal pulsing depends on the tension on the vocal folds, on the effective mass of the vocal folds, and on the subglottal pressure. The effective mass depends on the size of the vocal folds, which in turn depends on age, sex, and the individual. For example, the vocal folds are progressively larger, as we go from children to women to adult males. This corresponds to a change in voice pitch or fundamental pulse rate going from higher to lower pulsing rates as we go from the smaller vocal folds to the larger ones. Information about the speaker's control of voice pitch by means of tension on the vocal folds is presented in the next chapter.

SOURCE-FILTER THEORY OF VOWEL PRODUCTION

In the formation of vowel sounds the action of the glottis produces the basic source of sound, as was just described; this sound is then propagated, or transmitted, through the pharynx and oral tract to the outside air. We can think of the tract as a filter that emphasizes some of the components of the source sound, namely, those at and near the resonant frequencies of the tract. Therefore we can think of the formation of vowels as the result of a filtering action of the pharyngeal-oral tract on the sound source produced by the glottis. This view of vowel production is called the *source-filter theory of vowel production*. This theory led to the first production of model vowel sounds based on vocal tract shape, as already described in Chapter 3. The source-filter theory helps us explain how the details of vowel spectra arise from the combination of: 1) the spectrum of the glottal sound source and 2) the filtering of this spectrum by its transmission through the vocal tract.

You will recall from our discussion of vowel shaping in Chapter 3 that the vowel resonant peaks depend for their frequency locations on the positions of the tongue and lips. Thus, in order to describe how the spectrum of a vowel is formed, all we need to do is describe the effect on the glottal spectrum of the resonant peaks of the vocal tract. The resonant peaks determine the filtering curve or transmission response of the tract. When we apply this filter curve to the spectrum of the glottal sound source, the resulting spectrum is the vowel sound spectrum.

In other words, it is as if the glottal sound spectrum were passed through a certain filter that determines what the vowel will be. This is illustrated in Figure 26, where diagrams show how the spectrum of the glottal sound source is modified according to filter curves of the oral-pharyngeal tract to form the different vowel sound spectra for several vowels. The fundamental frequency is 100 Hz and thus the harmonics are

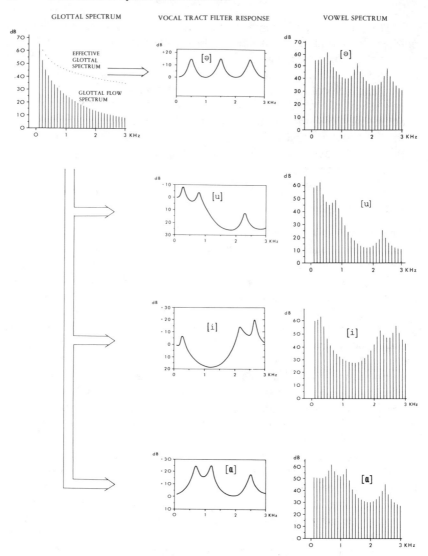

Figure 26.   The production of model vowels according to the source-filter theory. An idealized spectrum sloping −12 dB/octave is assumed as the spectrum of the basic waveform of
glottal airflow. However, radiation of the vowel sound from the mouth is more efficient for
high than for low frequencies, on a slope of about +6 dB/octave. This constant factor is
added to the glottal flow spectrum to give an effective glottal source spectrum sloping −6
dB/octave for all the vowels. It is modified by the filter responses of the vocal tract, shown
for the different vowels, to produce the final vowel spectra on the right. The filter shapes
were calculated from combinations of ideal resonators. (Adapted from Fant, 1960; Stevens
and House, 1961.)

at all the multiples of 100 Hz. The effective glottal spectrum has a slope of -6 dB/octave instead of the -12 dB/octave of the average glottal spectrum; the slope of the effective glottal spectrum is the sum of the -12 dB/octave glottal source spectrum and a $+6$ dB/octave constant factor because of radiation characteristics of the mouth-opening in the human head.

The important things to note in Figure 26 are that the spectrum of the glottal sound source is the same for all the different vowels and this sound spectrum is then changed by the filtering of the vocal tract to produce vowel sounds that have different spectral patterns.

First consider the spectrum envelopes of the vowel spectra, ignoring the individual components. Examine the relations between the formant peaks in the spectrum and the overall slope of the spectrum from low to high frequencies.

The general slope of the spectral envelopes of vowels stems both from the spectrum of the glottal sound source and from the degree of proximity of the formant frequencies. The slope is affected by any formants that are very close to each other. In the case of the vowel [u], for example, the first and second formants are close in frequency and at a low location; the two close resonances reinforce each other and thus raise the low frequency part of the spectrum to a higher amplitude than for the neutral vowel and very high in relation to the third formant of [u]. In the case of the vowel [i] the second formant is close to the third formant, and thus they reinforce each other and raise the high frequency end of the vowel spectrum relative to the middle. However, both F2 and F3 are now very far away from F1, which is in a low position for the vowel [i]. Because of the distance between them, the reinforcing effect of the first formant on the second and third formants is much less. The net result on the spectrum of [i] is that the amplitude level of the spectrum in the region of F3 is still low compared with the amplitude level in the low frequencies, but it is much higher than for [u] and substantially higher than for [ə] and [ɑ]. Thus we see that the particular locations of formant peaks, which are determined by the shape of the vocal tract, will affect not only the location in frequency of the vowel spectrum peaks but also the amplitudes of the peaks in relation to each other and the relative strengths of F3 and higher formants. The amplitudes of components in the F1 region are greater than the amplitudes of components lower in frequency.

In addition to the effect of the tract shape on the vowel spectrum envelope the conditions of glottal action have their effects on the resulting vowel spectrum. There are two main glottal factors: one is the fundamental pulsing rate at the voice pitch frequency, and the other is the amount of vocal effort. The factor of voice pitch affects only the frequency positions

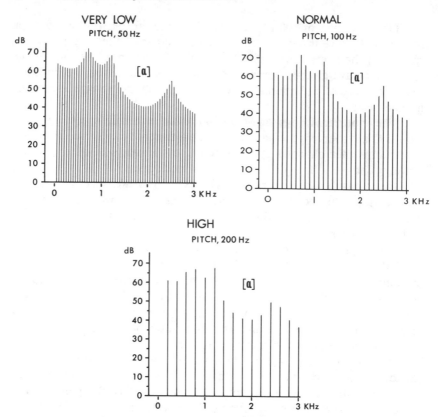

Figure 27.   Effects of voice pitch on a model vowel spectrum. The vowel spectrum envelope is constant but the harmonic spacing changes with fundamental frequency or pitch.

of the individual harmonic components in the spectrum and does not affect the shape of the spectrum. The effects on the spectrum of changes in voice pitch frequency are illustrated in Figure 27. On the left side of Figure 27 is the spectrum for a voice pitch that is lower than the fundamental frequency of 100 Hz that was assumed for the vowels of Figure 26. The low pitch causes the spectrum components to be spaced more closely together, compared with the vowel on the right side of the figure, which has a fundamental frequency of 100 Hz. The low-pitched spectrum on the left is for a fundamental voice frequency of 50 pulses per second. Thus the spectrum components in the vowel are at 50-Hz intervals. A voice pitch as low as 50 Hz occurs for extremely low-pitched voices as sometimes heard in radio announcers. At the bottom of Figure 27 is the spectrum for a high-pitched voice where the voice fundamental frequency is 200 pulses per second. For this vowel the spectral components occur at intervals of 200 Hz and the density of components is thus lower.

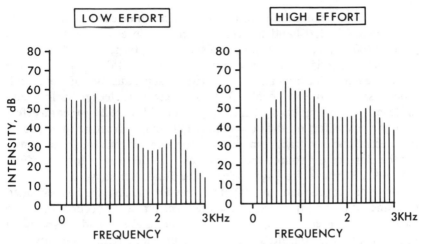

Figure 28. Effects of vocal effort on the vowel spectrum. Note that the overall slope of the vowel spectrum is steep for low effort and more gradual for high effort. The second and higher formants are relatively more intense under high vocal effort. See text for further explanation.

It should be especially noted in Figure 27 that the shape of the spectrum envelope, which is determined by the positions of the formants and their relations to each other, is not changed by changes in the voice pitch. Only the spacing of the component frequencies, that is, the spacing of the harmonics corresponding to the fundamental pulse rate, is changed by changes in voice pitch. How these components are shaped to form the spectrum envelope depends only on the vocal tract shape and not at all on the frequency of the voice pulsing rate.

The glottal wave assumed for Figures 26 and 27 had a smooth spectrum envelope with slope of −12 dB/octave. The spectra of real glottal pulses do not have such a smooth spectrum slope, but the 12-dB slope is a good representation for average speech spoken for specimen or citation purposes. In more relaxed phonation the glottal pulses are more rounded on the corners, causing the glottal spectrum to slope downward more steeply. A typical spectrum slope for this type of phonation is −15 dB/octave; this value would correspond to a relaxed conversational level of vocal effort. If the style of speaking is very forceful, the glottal pulses can have very steep sides and sharper corners, because of higher subglottal pressure on the opening of the vocal folds and higher Bernoulli suction before the closing. With such high effort, the glottal spectrum slope will be more shallow than −12 dB/octave, say about −9 dB/octave (see Fant, 1959; Flanagan, 1958; Mártony, 1965; Rothenberg, 1973).

Figure 28 shows the effect of a change in vocal effort on the vowel spectrum of a model [ɑ] vowel. For the purposes of the figure we assume that there is no change in the voice pitch and no change in the shape of the vocal tract. The left-hand spectrum is for the vowel spoken softly on a pitch of 100 Hz, that is, the glottal pulsing rate is 100 per second and vocal effort is low; the right-hand spectrum is for the same [ɑ] vowel at the same pulse rate but with a high amount of effort and producing a higher amplitude of sound. For low vocal effort the spectrum is steeper in slope and the level is low in amplitude. On the right side of Figure 28 we see an effect of high vocal effort on the vowel spectrum. In constructing these model [ɑ] spectra, the oral tract response was the same as that for [ɑ] in Figure 26; the slope of the source spectrum was −15 dB/octave for low effort and −9 dB/octave for high effort. The fundamental voice pitch frequency was kept the same at 100 Hz. The vocal tract shape has remained the same, as for an [ɑ] vowel, and so the spectrum peaks occur at the same locations. However, for higher effort the voice is louder and the spectrum slope has changed considerably; the spectrum slope is more shallow with higher amplitudes at the high frequencies, and the amplitudes of the formant peaks of the spectrum are higher than for normal effort, but the fundamental component is lower in amplitude. In other words, the increased voice loudness with high effort is due to increases in the amplitudes of the resonant oscillations.

In addition to the effects of glottal pulse shape on the overall slope of the glottal spectrum, the individual spectrum components are affected in amplitude by the general time features of the glottal wave. The time features are the duration of the open portion, the ratio of the open portion to the closed portion, and the degree of symmetry of the opening and closing legs of the pulse. These features cause variations in component amplitudes above and below the average slope of the spectrum. These variations give a scalloped effect to the source spectrum envelope by lowering the amplitude of about every fourth or fifth harmonic. In addition there is often a narrow depression in the source spectrum, somewhere in the region between 600 and 1000 Hz, which is due to absorption of sound by the subglottal spaces. Research on glottal function is currently concerned with relating these aspects of the glottal waveform to various conditions of phonation. Systematic rules about the glottal spectra for various styles and types of phonation should result from this research, but at present we do not have these rules.

Individual anatomic characteristics of the vocal folds and voice training can also affect the spectrum of the glottal pulses. However, at present we do not have enough systematic knowledge to explain how these individual characteristics arise. In general a highly efficient, ''strong'' speaking voice is attributable to a steep offset of the glottal pulse before the closed portion and not to the vocal tract resonances per se; the resonances are more strongly excited by a more efficient shape of glottal pulse. However, professional singers are able to adjust their pharynx to raise the vowel spectrum in the region F3 to F5 (Sundberg, 1973).

SPECTROGRAMS OF VOWELS

Spectrograms[3] of spoken examples of the vowels [i], [ɑ], and [u] are shown in Figure 29 to illustrate the variables in vowel formation. The vowels were spoken by an adult male in words beginning with [h] and ending with [d]. Next to the spectrogram of each vowel is a spectral section taken at one time point during the vowel. The spectrograms and sections were made on a Kay Sona-graph adjusted to apply an upward tilt to the spectrum above 500 Hz of 3½ dB/octave. The sections show the effects on the spectrum envelope of the vocal tract shape differences between [i], [ɑ], and [u]. The sections also show the effects on the glottal source spectrum for low- and high-pitched voices: the voice pitch is reflected in the frequency spacing of the harmonic components, with wider spacing for high pitch than for low pitch. The effects of high vocal effort appear in the amplitudes of F2 and F3 between 1 and 3 kHz, which are seen to be much more intense relative to the F1 region for high effort vs. low effort.

The pitch of the voice can be seen in a spectrogram as well as in the spectrum sections. In the spectrogram there is a pulse of sound energy for each pulse of the glottis, which forms the source of the vowel sound. On the spectrogram each glottal pulse appears as a dark striation running from low to high frequencies. The striations succeed each other in time exactly in synchrony with the glottal pulses. Since the glottal pulses are more widely spaced in time for a low-pitched voice, the spectrogram pulses are farther apart for vowels spoken on a low voice pitch. For the high-pitched voice the glottal pulses and the striations in the spectrogram are more closely packed together, because for a high-pitched voice the glottal pulses succeed each other more rapidly in time.

Spectrograms of all of the vowels and diphthongs are shown in Figure 30, as spoken by an adult male in syllables beginning with [h] and ending with [d], except for [ə], which was spoken in the phrase *a toy* [ətɔɪ]. The speaker used his native General American dialect except for the vowel [a] where he imitated a native of Massachusetts saying the word *hard*. Going across the top row of spectrograms (A), we go through the series of front vowels starting with [i] and going through [ɪ], [e], [ɛ], [æ], and [a]; you will note that the second formant comes down from high to low frequencies through this series of front vowels, and the first formant rises from a low to a high frequency position, through the series. You will also

---

[3]If you are not already familiar with spectrograms, you should review the operation of the sound spectrograph described in Chapter 2.

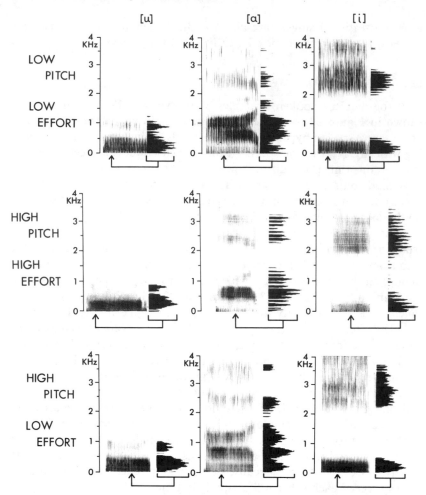

Figure 29.   Spectrograms and spectral sections of natural vowels under different combinations of voice pitch and vocal effort. For the spectral sections each vowel was sampled at the point in time indicated by the arrow. The sections show how the harmonic spacing changes with voice pitch and how the intensity of the components in the higher formant regions increase, relative to the fundamental, with high vocal effort.

note that two of the front vowels, namely, [ɪ] and [ɛ], are shorter in duration than the other vowels. Of course any vowel can be deliberately shortened or prolonged in pronunciation, but, as they occur in naturally spoken English, certain vowels have shorter durations than the other vowels. The average durations of vowels in stressed one-syllable words, spoken by American talkers, was found to be about 230 ms for long vowels and 180 ms for the short vowels (Peterson and Lehiste, 1960). The vowel durations in Figure 30 are similar to these values.

The second row of spectrograms (B) shows the sound patterns of the back vowel series starting with [u] and going through [ʊ], [o], [ɔ], and [ɑ]. You will note in this series that the first and second formant resonances go from low frequency positions to higher frequency positions. In the series of back vowels there is one short vowel, [ʊ].

Figure 30 (C) shows the spectrograms of the three central vowels [ʌ], [ə], and [ɚ]. The short central vowel is [ə]. The diphthongs [ɑɪ], [iu], and [ɔi] and [ɑʊ] are shown in (D); they are longer in duration. Diphthongs are similar to double vowels and they include a glide in articulation from one vowel position to another. In the spectrograms of the diphthongs you can see both the first and second formant frequency positions changing in time as the vocal tract shape changes from one vowel conformation to the other.

NASALIZATION OF VOWELS

Normally the vowel sounds of English are spoken with the velum raised against the walls and back of the pharynx to shut off the nasal passages completely from the pharynx and oral tract. However, speakers of American English often seem to nasalize their vowels slightly by allowing the velum to remain slightly open. Nasalization also occurs in vowels that are adjacent to nasal consonants, especially in the portions of the vowel immediately next to the consonant.

In pathologic speech, such as that of a person who has a cleft palate, which opens the oral tract into the nasal passages, or a person with an undeveloped velum or abnormally sluggish velum action, there may be extreme nasalization of all sounds. Persons who were born deaf sometimes speak with nasalized sounds.

The important acoustic effects of nasalization have been determined through research on vocal tract models (House and Stevens, 1956). Electrical models were built of the cavities of the nasal tract and the oral tract, and the two tracts were connected together through circuits representing greater or lesser amounts of opening between them. It was found that the main effect on a vowel of an opening at the velum is to produce changes in the filter curve of the oral tract. One effect was that the first formant became broader and less peaked than before, because of the damping of the formant resonance by the loss of energy through the opening into the nasal tract.

Another change is to apply negative resonant peaks to the oral tract response. These negative resonances are called *zeroes*. Zeroes are antiresonances; they are exactly the opposite of resonances in their effect on the spectrum. Instead of reinforcing and amplifying the spectrum at and near the resonant frequency, an antiresonance selectively absorbs sound so

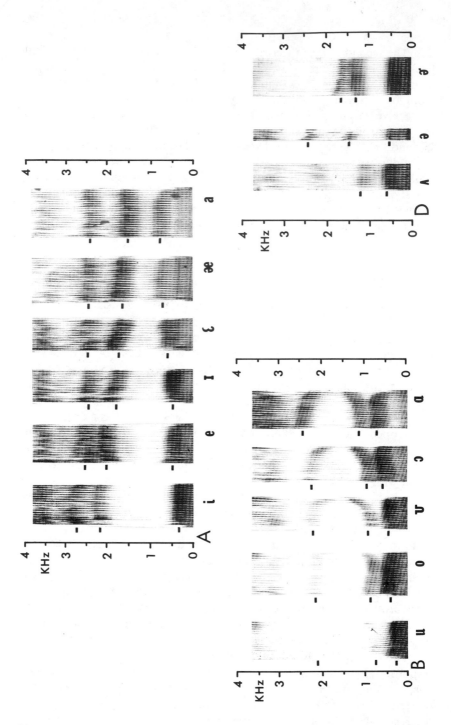

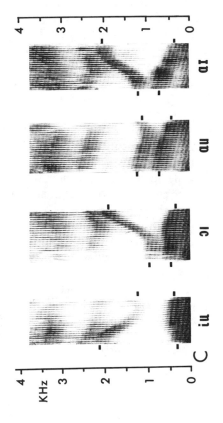

Figure 30. Spectrograms of examples of the vowels and diphthongs of American English. The approximate midvowel locations of formants are in-dicated by the bars beside each spectrogram.

that it greatly reduces the amplitudes of components at and near the anti-resonant frequency. In addition, for each zero there is an extra formant. The amount of these effects depends on the amount of opening between the pharyngeal-oral tract and the nasal tract. That is, the nasalization effects on the spectrum depend on the *amount of coupling* between the two tracts. The amount of coupling also affects the frequency positions of the zeroes and extra formants. The total effect on the spectrum is complex but there are two general effects. First, the presence of a low frequency zero below F1 tends to make the spectral peak in the region of F1 appear to be higher in frequency than it would normally be. Thus the effects of nasalization on F1 are to reduce the amplitude, and to move the apparent F1 in this region to a higher frequency position. The amount of frequency shift in the apparent F1 is 50 to 100 Hz. Second, the nasal coupling can also cause zeroes in the region of F2 and F3, and often this reduces the peakedness of these formants or completely flattens the peaks.

Some effects of nasalization are diagrammed in Figure 31, showing spectrum envelopes for a natural [ɑ] and for the same vowel heavily nasalized. The talker spoke the [ɑ] continuously, maintaining fairly constant positions of tongue and jaw while opening and closing the velum to nasalize and denasalize the vowel. The peaks due to the formants are numbered 1, 2, and 3 for the normal [ɑ]; for the spectrum of the nasalized [ɑ], z's are drawn to indicate spectral regions that appear to be influenced by zeroes in the vocal tract response. In this case it appears that a low frequency zero at about 600 Hz has produced a spectral dip at that frequency and that two higher zeroes have radically altered the normal spectrum at points near the third resonance. The positions of these zeroes may be typical for heavily nasalized [ɑ] but should not be considered to hold for milder degrees of nasalization, nor for other vowels, since the pharyngeal-oral shape and amount of velar opening interact to determine the frequency positions of the nasal formants and zeroes.

SUMMARY

The spectral characteristics of vowels are caused by the combination of the spectrum of the glottal source sound and the resonances of the pharyngeal-oral tract. The source-filter theory of vowel production considers the glottal source spectrum to be shaped, or filtered, by the response of the vocal tract, independent of the glottal action of voicing phonation. Factors that affect the glottal spectrum operate through changes in the pulse form of the airflow through the glottis in forming each glottal pulse. Vocal fold tension affects the fundamental pulsing rate and the airflow velocity causes a suction force (Bernoulli force) between the folds,

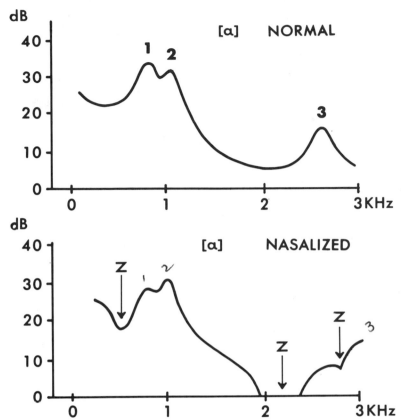

Figure 31.   An example of the effects of vowel nasalization on the vowel spectrum. The spectrum envelopes of a normal [ɑ] and a nasalized [ɑ] are plotted as derived from spectral sections. The first three formants are labeled in the normal vowel; reductions in spectrum level in the nasalized vowel, presumably because of the addition of zeroes to the vocal tract response, are indicated by "z."

which affects the pulse shape. The spacing in frequency of the glottal spectrum components depends on the voice pitch (fundamental pulsing frequency); the slope of the spectrum depends on the pulse shape, which is sensitive to the amount of vocal effort.

The formant resonances of the vowels and diphthongs, and the effects of changes in pitch and vocal effort, are exemplified in spectrograms of natural speech.

Vowel sounds may be nasalized and this causes a reduction in F1 amplitude and the insertion of antiresonances (zeroes) and extra formants in the transmission of the pharyngeal-oral tract, thus altering the normal vowel spectrum.

CHAPTER 5

PROSODIC FEATURES

CONTENTS

Speech has melodic features that are an essential part of each language, essential in that certain melodic patterns of speaking are used consistently to convey differences in meaning and grammar. Melodic features are the patterns of tone, that is, voice pitch patterns, and rhythmic patterns in the durations and intensities of the syllables. These patterns can express many different meanings. Consider, for example, how we use different tonal glides of voice pitch to change the meaning of just one spoken word, the word *yes*. A long, upward-gliding *yes* can mean, *Oh, is that really true? Tell me more.* A shorter up-gliding *yes* means, *OK, I'm listening.* A downward-gliding *yes* means, *Yes, I agree.* A long, drawn-out *ye...s* with a steady voice tone can indicate boredom or impatience.

These are only a few of the things we can mean just by tonal variations of *yes* in certain situations. This type of tonal expression with speech is a form of communication that uses a social code for informal communication. This code is not a formal linguistic property of our language; it is an expressive code.

A song is another example of expressive speech. The melody of a song conveys a mood or emotion that is not a formal part of the language.

From the viewpoint of acoustic phonetics the expressive uses of speech depend on the tonal patterns of the voice pitch and on variations in the syllable stresses and timing to form rhythmic patterns. The expressive melodies and rhythms of speech are fascinating to study scientifically, but we do not have a large body of knowledge about them because speech scientists have devoted their research primarily to the linguistic aspects of speech. Thus our study of the acoustic phonetics of rhythm and tone concentrates on their linguistic functions and is limited to English.

The rhythms and intonations of speech play a strong role in the formal linguistic code for communication. We have all experienced difficulty in understanding a foreign speaker who can articulate well all of the sounds of English but does not speak with English rhythms and intonation. The reason for our difficulty is that the particular sounds of any utterance are formed under definite rules of rhythm and intonation, and these "prosodic" rules are unique for every language. Different languages share many articulations in common, but these are distinctively tailored to fit the prosodic rules of each language. Another example of the importance of rhythm and intonation sometimes appears in the speech of deaf persons. A person who is deaf from birth can be taught to articulate individual speech sounds, but his speech can still be nearly unintelligible if his rhythmic and tonal maneuvers do not follow the normal rules. In the field of artificial speech, for example, in reading machines for the blind and in computer talk-back applications, the correct programming of the prosodics has been found to be necessary for good intelligibility.

The general name for the rhythmic and tonal features of speech is *prosodic features*. They usually extend over more than one phoneme segment and thus are said to *suprasegmental*. The prosodic features are produced by certain special manipulations of the sound sources and the shaping of the vocal tract. The source factors operate through actions of the speech breathing muscles and the vocal folds; the shaping factors operate through the movements of the upper articulators. The acoustic patterns of the prosodic features are found in systematic variations of the duration, intensity, and fundamental frequency (pitch), and in the spectrum patterns of the individual sounds. Our aim in this chapter is to give a basic explanation of how some of these prosodic patterns are produced. We begin with the glottal source, and then proceed to describe other factors.

We are mainly interested in the prosodic features that convey linguistic information. *Stress* and *intonation* are the most important of these. By means of stress we differentiate similar forms that have different meanings; for example, compare the two phrases *That's just in sight* and *That's just insight*. In the first phrase there is a stress on *sight* but *in* is unstressed; in the second phrase this relation is reversed, giving an entirely different meaning. By means of intonation patterns we differentiate grammatical functions; an example is the rising intonation of a question as contrasted with the falling intonation of a statement. One can state *That's just in-*

sight, using a downward pitch glide, or one can query *that's just insight?* using an upward pitch glide. A speaker can also emphasize or accentuate the part of an utterance that he feels to be specially significant. For example, the statement *That's just insight* can be spoken with emphasis on *that, just,* or *insight,* depending on which word the speaker wants the listener to give special attention to.

The manipulation of the glottal source for prosodic features has been studied in some detail in order to define the physiologic and acoustic conditions of stress patterns and intonation patterns (Ladefoged, 1963, 1967; Lieberman, 1967). This work has established some basic mechanisms of prosodics. These experiments are now described, including some details of experimentation that are typical of some the ingenious methods of experimental phoneticians.

GLOTTAL SOURCE FACTORS IN STRESS AND INTONATION

There are two main factors responsible for production of the glottal source variations for prosodic features: 1) the *tension on the vocal folds* and 2) the *subglottal air pressure.* These affect the characteristics of the glottal sound source, especially the pulsing rate (fundamental frequency) but also the source amplitude and the source spectrum.

Subglottal Air Pressure

Increasing force on the lungs causes a corresponding increase in the subglottal air pressure. The increase in subglottal pressure causes an increase in the rate of repetition of the airflow pulses emitted by the glottis; that is, the fundamental frequency increases. It is believed that the increased rate may be caused in two ways. First, the increased elastic stretch on the folds as they are forced farther apart by the increased subglottal pressure can cause a faster closure movement. Second, the lateral displacement of the folds may be kept constant by increased muscle tension and this may increase the stiffness of the folds or reduce their mass, causing them to move at a higher rate. Increased subglottal pressure can also cause a faster rate of inward movement of the folds just before glottal closure, because of an increased Bernoulli effect; this causes a more sudden closure and results in a greater efficiency of pulse excitation of the air in the upper tract. Thus, subjectively, the pitch[1] and loudness of the voice are both increased

---

[1] In acoustic writings on speech the term *voice pitch,* or simply *pitch,* means the fundamental frequency of the vocal fold action in producing a glottal sound source. In the field of hearing, the sensation of pitch is found to depend largely on the fundamental frequency of the sound stimulus. Thus the pitch sensation and the frequency of a sound signal are closely related, but they are not the same thing. In the speech literature, however, pitch and fundamental frequency are used synonymously, and we will use these terms in the same way.

by increases in subglottal pressure, and a sharper timbre or quality will also result if the increase of pressure causes more sudden glottal closures. Everyone experiences these effects when attempting to shout louder and louder in order to attract someone's attention. The loudness goes higher but so do the pitch and timbre of the voice.

There are some familiar examples of the relations between the air pressure on a flexible slit-like opening, such as the glottis, and the characteristics of the pulse wave produced. One example is the noise-making horns used to celebrate New Year's Eve. The harder you blow, the higher is the pitch (frequency) and loudness (amplitude). A similar physical situation exists in speech when a steady note is sung and then outside pressure is suddenly put on the chest of the singer to increase his subglottal pressure. This causes an immediate rise in pitch and loudness. Children sometimes use this effect in play, pushing and pounding on one another's chests to make themselves sing unpredictable songs.

As a first step in the study of intonation and stress Ladefoged measured the relation between the subglottal pressure and voice pitch (Ladefoged, 1963). The chest-push effect was used to measure this relation. The procedure was as follows. The subject intoned a vowel sound in a relaxed manner holding his vocal force relatively constant; the experimenter pushed on the subject's chest, using different amounts of force, causing the subject's voice to rise and fall; the voice sound wave and the subglottal pressure were both recorded during these maneuvers. The subglottal pressure was picked up by means of a small balloon located in the esophagus just behind the trachea of the subject. The balloon was connected to one end of a flexible plastic tube and its placement was accomplished simply by the subject's swallowing the balloon and tube down a short way into the esophagus. The other end of the tube was attached to a pressure-sensing device, which measured the pressure in the tube. This pressure was recorded graphically by a continuous tracing of the increases and decreases in pressure. It was found to be nearly the same as the pressure measured directly through a large hollow needle inserted into the larynx just below the vocal folds.

The voice pitch was measured by deriving the fundamental frequency from the sound wave of the vowel intoned by the subject. The fundamental frequency was measured automatically by an electronic circuit and recorded graphically on the same chart as the recording of subglottal pressure.

The results of these measurements are shown in Figure 32. Each point in the figure shows the fundamental frequency corresponding to a given amount of subglottal pressure. The fundamental frequency is plotted on the vertical scale in Hertz. The subglottal pressure is plotted on

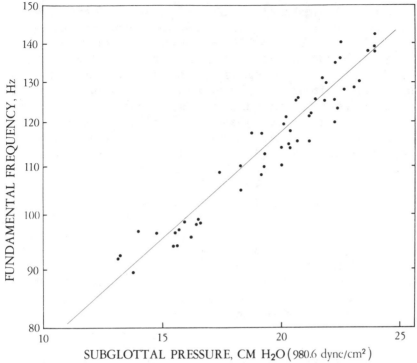

Figure 32.   Relation between voice fundamental frequency, plotted on a log scale, and sub-glottal pressure; measurements by Ladefoged using pushes on the chest to vary subglottal pressure. The group of points between about 90 and 100 Hz are from the speaker's normal phonations, before he was pushed. (Adapted from Ladefoged, 1963.)

the horizontal scale in centimeters of water (cm H_2O; multiply by 9.806×10^2 to obtain the pressure in metric units, dynes per square centimeter, dyne/cm^2). The 16 points clustered on the lower left part of the graph are results without any external pressure on the speaker's chest; they represent the normal, rather forceful low frequency range of this speaker. His normal fundamental frequency ranges from about 90 Hz to 100 Hz and his subglottal pressure ranges from about 13 to 16.5 cm H_2O, a somewhat higher than average range of pressure. The remaining points on the graph show the voice fundamental and subglottal pressure for instances of the peak pressures resulting from the pushes on the chest of the speaker while he was phonating. It will be seen that the higher the subglottal pressure, the higher the fundamental frequency of the speaker's voice. This relation approximates a straight line when the fundamental frequency is scaled logarithmically as it is on this graph; a line is drawn through the points for comparison. The scatter of points around the straight line probably occurs because the speaker's vocal fold tension was not the same each time that his chest was pushed. The change in voice fundamental frequency in Figure 32 averages about 4.5 Hz per cm H_2O; this is based on a total change of about 45 Hz over the 10-cm range from 14 to 24 cm H_2O.

The next step in Ladefoged's study of intonation and stress was to find out how different stress patterns are produced by different patterns of subglottal pressure, depending on whether the stress is located on the first syllable or the second syllable of a word and also depending on whether the word is spoken in a statement or in a question. The words chosen were pairs of two-syllable words in which the word was a noun when the stress was on the first syllable, but the same word was a verb when the stress was on the second syllable. These were spoken in short sentences, for example, *That's a digest* and *He didn't digest;* or *That's a survey* and *He didn't survey.* Each of these sentences could be spoken either as a statement, that is, with a downward contour of intonation on the final word, or as a question, with a rise in intonation.

It was found that the pattern of subglottal pressure for producing the phrase was related to the location of the stressed syllable in the phrase. These effects are diagrammed in Figure 33, where we see the patterns of subglottal pressure and fundamental frequency for the four sentences with the word *digest*. Examine the subglottal pressure pattern under the word *digest* [daɪdʒɛst] spoken as a noun with stress on the first syllable (upper curves of subglottal pressure). Then do the same for *digest* spoken as a verb with stress on the second syllable (lower curves). You will note that the stressed syllable is always spoken with a higher subglottal pressure. The pressure increase on the stressed syllable seems to be greater for the statements on the left than for the questions on the right.

Now examine the intonation patterns above the pressure patterns. These show the voice pitch (fundamental frequency) during the vowels and the duration of each vowel. For the statements, on the left, we see that the general trend for the voice is downward-going from the beginning of the statement to the end. Also we see that the stressed syllable has the longest vowel duration of any in the sentence and that the noun in the statement has a very high pitch on the stressed syllable. On the other hand the verb in the statement has a high pitch on the second, stressed syllable even though it is the last syllable in the sentence.

When the same sentences are spoken as questions, the pitch of the voice rises continuously from the beginning to the end of the question. For the noun in the question neither the duration nor the pitch of the stressed syllable is higher than that of the following unstressed syllable because of the rising intonation contour on the final unstressed syllable. The

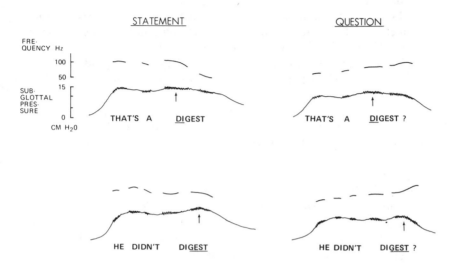

Figure 33.   Relations between contours of voice fundamental frequency and subglottal pressure for statements and questions with two different patterns of word stress. The stressed syllable is underlined and indicated by an arrow under the contour of subglottal pressure. The intonation contours are above the contours of subglottal pressure. It can be seen that the stressed syllables correspond to peaks in the pressure contours and that the intonation contours rise for the questions and tend to fall for the statements. (Adapted from Ladefoged, 1963.)

rising contour is required to express the question. In the verb form of the word in the question the second syllable, i.e., the stressed syllable, has a longer duration and higher pitch.

We see from these comparisons that the patterns of voice pitch and duration, corresponding to stressed versus unstressed syllables, are dependent on whether the general pattern of intonation expresses a statement or a question.

Now examine the subglottal pressure patterns in relation to the intonation curves of the four sentences. The striking thing to note is that the subglottal pressure is relatively constant and does not show a trend corresponding to the intonation contour; that is to say, the subglottal pressure is not generally falling during the statements and it is not generally rising during the questions. What is it then, that controls the voice pitch to produce the rising intonation of a question in contrast to the falling intonation of a statement? It must be the tension on the vocal folds and not primarily the subglottal pressure.

Vocal Fold Tension

The major factor controlling voice pitch is the tension on the vocal folds; muscular control of this tension is applied through small muscles in the larynx. At the time of Ladefoged's study, there were no methods for measuring the vocal fold tension to determine its exact role in control of voice pitch. On the assumption that any changes in pitch not accounted for by changes in subglottal pressure would be due to changes in vocal fold tension, Ladefoged concluded that the overall pattern change in vocal fold tension is somewhat more simple than would be indicated by following all the fundamental frequency changes seen in the acoustic signal. It also appeared that the strongest stress of a syllable in a phrase is produced by a combination of an increase in vocal fold tension and a peak in subglottal pressure.

We can now summarize our main points about stress and intonation as follows: 1) Phonetic patterns for different stress patterns and different intonational expressions are based on an interplay between manipulations of the vocal fold tension, the peaks of subglottal pressure, and the durations of the vowel and consonant articulations. 2) The voice fundamental frequency reflects both the vocal fold tension and the subglottal pressure. When there is an increase in either the vocal fold tension or the subglottal pressure, or both, there is a corresponding increase in the voice fundamental frequency. 3) During the utterance of a phrase, if the changes in voice fundamental frequency caused by changes in the subglottal pressure are taken into account, the resulting "basic" curve, reflecting the effect of vocal fold tension, is a relatively simple curve compared to the curve of changes in fundamental frequency.

We see then that there is a complex interaction between the stress patterns of speech and the intonation or inflectional patterns of speech. The resulting acoustic patterns of vowel duration, pitch, and intensity are also rather complex but there is evidence that the basic factors of subglottal pressure and vocal fold tension operate in relatively simple ways.

Breath Group Theory of Intonation

Experimental work by Lieberman (1967) led him to propose a simple theory of how the basic patterns of subglottal pressure and vocal fold tension are coded to produce the effects of stress and intonation. The theory states that speech is based on two simple actions, the grouping of words into breath groups and the marking of these groups by stress and intonational changes.

Words, phrases, or sentences are grouped into *breath groups*. A breath group is a section of utterance that is produced between two respiratory inspirations (Stetson, 1951, pp. 3, 106, 135). The typical breath group is produced on a pattern of change in subglottal air pressure that rises just before the beginning of the breath group and then remains fairly constant except during the last part of the group, when the subglottal air pressure falls gradually during the final part of the breath group and then falls abruptly to end the group. In most breath groups where the speaker has no reason to emphasize the final word or syllables, his fundamental frequency falls during the final part of the breath group because of the fall-off in subglottal pressure.

Lieberman proposes that this relatively simple manipulation of the breath stream, and a state of rather constant vocal fold tension throughout the breath group, is the basic maneuver for speaking; it is called the *unmarked breath group*. Short statements, such as *That's a digest* or *That's just insight,* are produced by one unmarked breath group. Longer statements would consist of a series of such breath groups.

The unmarked breath group is considered to be the simplest way to produce an utterance with the least amount of muscular effort expended to maintain phonation. In this sense the breath group is universal for all languages, although some languages, dialects, and individual habits may involve simple variations on this "archetypal" breath group.

An example of an utterance spoken as an unmarked breath group is shown in Figure 34. The utterance was the statement *Joe ate his soup,* with the main stress on *Joe.* It will be seen that the fundamental frequency and the subglottal pressure tend to parallel each other. The final syllable *soup* has a fundamental frequency contour, which starts at a high pitch

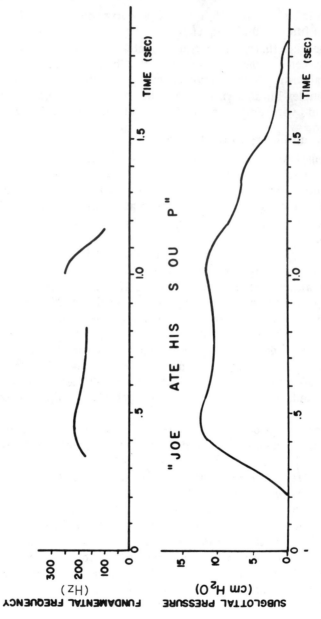

Figure 34. Contours of fundamental frequency and subglottal pressure for an unmarked breath group. (From Lieberman, 1967.)

88

level but falls very rapidly under the influence of the falling subglottal pressure, probably supplemented by a decrease in vocal fold tension.

Relatively simple variations on the basic breath group produce the stress patterns specified by the language and the expressive or emphatic patterns desired by the speaker. For example, to express a question, the speaker may raise his vocal fold tension during the last portion of the breath group and thus maintain his fundamental frequency at a constant level instead of allowing it to fall under the influence of the declining subglottal pressure.

The pattern of syllable stress within the breath group is generally dominated by a momentary increase in the subglottal pressure during the stressed syllable. The rise in pressure produces an increase in the fundamental frequency, in the loudness, in the level of the high frequency part of the vowel spectrum, and is associated with increased duration of the vowel in the stressed syllable (in relation to the other syllables of the breath group).

The main stress of the breath group corresponds to the peak subglottal pressure of the group. The syllable that follows the peak may have a slightly subnormal pressure because of the lower level of elastic recoil (see Chapter 1) by the lungs because there is a rapid reduction in lung volume during the peak stress. This lowering of subglottal pressure following peak stress is usually not compensated by a change in vocal fold tension and therefore the voice fundamental frequency is lower on post-stress syllables.

An example of an utterance spoken as a *marked breath group,* marked for a question, is shown in Figure 35. The utterance was *Did Joe eat his soup?* The breath group is *marked* by the rising fundamental frequency on the final syllable, which occurs despite the falling subglottal pressure. The rise during *soup* must have been caused by an increase in vocal fold tension.

Within a given language there may be variations in the manipulation of vocal fold tension and in the subglottal pressure pattern of the breath group. For example, Lieberman believes that, in contrast to the relatively constant vocal fold tension maintained through breath groups by American speakers, speakers of British English tend to begin a breath group with rather high vocal fold tension, which tends to decrease throughout the breath group. Ladefoged's data in Figure 33 were obtained from a speaker of British English. This speaker's contours of subglottal pressure do not appear to fall greatly and thus his falling intonation on statements may have been realized by a decrease in vocal fold tension.

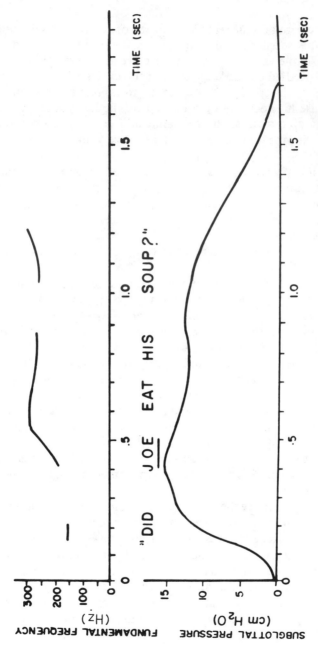

Figure 35. Contours of fundamental frequency and subglottal pressure for a marked breath group. (From Lieberman, 1967.)

Controversy over the Breath Group Theory

The breath group theory of intonation is attractive because of its simplicity, but other research, partly by Ladefoged and his co-workers, has indicated that the production of intonation and stress may be considerably more complex. Vanderslice (1967) asked, "Is it the larynx or lungs that controls pitch?" and Ohala (1977) has recently reviewed the counter-evidence. A primary difficulty is the fact that the subglottal pressure and vocal fold tension are not completely independent of each other. The vocal fold tension has some influence on the subglottal pressure. This is because the vocal fold action controls the flow of air from the lungs, which in turn can affect the subglottal pressure (Ohala, 1974, 1977). For example, a temporary vocal fold adjustment, for a higher pitch and intensity, can reduce the airflow and raise the subglottal pressure; thus the higher pitch may have been caused by the increased vocal fold tension and not by the accompanying increase in subglottal pressure. The conclusion reached by Ohala is that changes in vocal fold adjustments are the primary factor in producing the pitch change in stressed syllables. He is carrying out further studies, measuring the effective degree of resistance of the vocal folds to airflow by monitoring the volume of air in the lungs (Ohala, 1977).

Larynx Muscle Action for Stress and Intonation

The actions of the muscles of the larynx that control the tension and thickness of the vocal folds have recently been studied in relation to stress and intonation patterns. The action of muscles is studied by means of an electrical technique called *electromyography* or EMG. In EMG studies of the larynx the muscle activity is picked up through small electrode wires, inserted through the neck from the outside, to monitor the electrical activity of each muscle. The amount of electrical activity in a muscle is correlated with the amount of tensioning force that the muscle is producing; thus a muscle's EMG activity may be taken as an indicator of the contracting force it is exerting.

The stretching forces exerted on the vocal folds are from two sets of muscles: 1) a set of muscles within the larynx, called *intrinsic laryngeal muscles,* which act directly on the front-back tension of the vocal folds, and 2) a set of muscles in the neck called the *strap muscles.* The strap muscles control the vertical position of the larynx as a whole. The vertical position affects the vocal folds by varying the stretching tension from below. If the larynx is held high, there is more stretching tension on the folds from the tissues of the trachea, which attach to the folds from below. If the larynx is held low this stretching force is less.

In EMG studies of the control of intonation, simultaneous recordings are made of the pitch, the subglottal pressure, and the electrical activity of the intrinsic and strap muscles of the larynx. There have been quite a few such studies, but, because of the somewhat invasive nature of the EMG technique, only a limited number of speakers have been used, and sometimes not all of the muscles were monitored. This research is still in progress and there has been some controversy about how the results should be interpreted. A simplified version of this work follows. The student who wants to go into detail should first read Hirano and Ohala (1969), where the muscles and techniques are described, then Lieberman et al. (1970) and Atkinson (1978). Atkinson's interpretation of the findings, which is a modified version of the breath group theory, is presented here.

Recall that the contour of change in pitch (the intonation contour) varies in downward or upward trend, depending on whether the talker is making a statement or asking a question. The intonation contour also varies in shape, depending on the stress pattern of the words spoken. The stress pattern is determined jointly by the stress patterns of the words and by the intent of the talker, who may selectively emphasize or deemphasize one or more of the words. These same linguistic maneuvers have been used to produce different contours in the studies of the relations between intonation contours, laryngeal muscle action as seen in EMG, and subglottal pressure.

The first general finding is that, in statements, the subglottal pressure seems to be the main controlling factor; in other words the falling pitch contour of a statement is related to a falling contour in the subglottal pressure; this relation is extremely close in the low range of pitch, which tends to occur at the end of the unmarked breath group that is used for a statement having no strong emphasis on the final portion. The subglottal pressure-to-pitch relation is significant for other types of statements as well; in contrast, the relation between pitch and laryngeal muscle activity is weak for statements. For questions, on the other hand, the situation is reversed. The rising intonation contours of questions were found to be accompanied by increasing amounts of activity in the intrinsic laryngeal muscles that stretch the vocal folds. Also, in the part of a question where pitch is high, this relation is more close, and then the subglottal pressure seems to be a weak or ineffective factor in changing the pitch.

The strap muscles of the larynx appear to coordinate with the other two factors to adjust the pitch range in the following way: the strap muscle, which lowers the larynx, is active when the pitch is low, producing a slackness in the vocal fold tension, which is thought to increase the sensitivity of pitch to the subglottal pressure. When the pitch is high the larynx-lowering strap muscle is inactive. By high and low pitch is meant the high and low regions of normally spoken statements and questions. Thus the strap muscles might be thought of as adjusters or facilitators for the use of the high and low ranges of the conversational voice, whereas the intrinsic muscles are primarily responsible for pitch variations in the high range and the subglottal pressure is responsible for variations in the low range.

Both intrinsic muscular and subglottal factors can act together, however. For example, at the end of a breath group the fall of pitch with falling subglottal pressure may be prevented by increased tension from the intrinsic muscles, thus producing a marked breath group where questioning intonation is needed at the end of the breath group. Furthermore, when a syllable in a marked breath group is emphasized by the talker, a syllabic increase in subglottal pressure may be superimposed on a high tension, high-pitched portion of the breath group, or on a low-tension, low-pitched portion; the increased pressure will have more effect, raising the pitch of the syllable, if it is in a low-pitched portion of the breath group.

Intensity and Spectrum in Stressed Syllables

Thus far we have dealt primarily with the voice pitch factor in the stress patterning of speech. Other sound features from the glottal source factors in stress are the sound intensity and the spectral balance between low and high frequency regions. Intensity and spectrum balance are discussed just briefly.

The spectrum balance of a vowel sound can be affected by the amount of vocal effort, as noted in Chapter 4. An increase in vocal effort increases subglottal pressure, and, if the vocal fold adjustments are maintained, the result is a steeper glottal flow wave with sharper corners. The spectrum of this wave has a shape that slopes downward more gradually than the spectrum of the more rounded glottal flow wave produced with lower subglottal pressure. Stressed syllables are spoken with greater vocal effort. Thus, on stressed syllables the source spectrum slopes downward less steeply than it does for unstressed syllables. Increased vocal fold tension might also affect the spectrum balance by boosting the high frequency end of the glottal spectrum. Stressed vowels consequently have relatively more intense amplitude in the region of F2, F3, and higher formants. This effect was demonstrated by Lieberman (1967).

We may *summarize the major sound-source factors* in prosodic features as follows:

1. The fundamental voice frequency (or pitch) of vowels, responding to the amount of subglottal pressure and vocal fold tension, is higher in stressed syllables than in unstressed syllables. In addition, voice pitch shows a contour of variation (intonation contour) over the syllables

of a phrase that corresponds to the grammatical function and structure of the phrase.

2. The intensity of the vowels in stressed syllables is higher than in unstressed syllables.
3. The spectrum balance of vowels is affected by the higher vocal effort on stressed syllables, resulting in relatively more intensity of F2, F3, and the higher formants.

DURATIONAL PROSODIC FEATURES

In addition to the glottal source factors of pitch, intensity, and spectrum, there are important durational variations that arise from prosodic conditions. We have already noted in Figure 33 that syllable stress causes a lengthening of the vowel. Durational features involve the control of the tongue and lip articulations in coordination with the presence or absence of phonation. This coordination is subject to a wide variety of prosodic influences, such as the number of syllables in a word; the location of stress; emphasis; boundaries between words, between phrases, between clauses, and between sentences; and the influence of word importance and meaning/content. These factors in articulation cause certain systematic changes in the durations of vowels and consonants, changes that have been well studied for two important reasons. First, physiologically minded phoneticians needed data that indicate how the temporal patterning of speech is organized by the brain and motor system. Second, the need for good artificial speech in computer talk-back systems, and also in text-to-speech for the blind, has led to an intensified search for specific prosodic rules governing the durations of consonants and vowels. Basic data and initial rules have been published recently by Klatt (1975, 1976) and by Umeda (1975, 1977); Lindblom and his colleagues (Lindblom, Lyberg, and Holmgren, 1977) have studied duration patterns to arrive at principles of motor organization. The following account is based on all of this work.

Syllable Duration and Position in Breath Group

In an early study of durational prosodics, Stetson (1928; 1951, p. 113) measured the durations of syllables occurring in either initial position or final position in a breath group. Final position in the breath group was found to be associated with longer duration. Initial single syllables had a mean duration of 280 ms compared with final syllables of 310 ms. Two-syllable rhythmic units had a mean unit duration of 480 ms in initial position and 600 ms in final position in the breath group.

Vowel Duration Effects

The vowels are greatly affected in duration, depending on the following consonants, the rate of speaking, the syllable stress, the number of syllables in the word, the position of the vowel in the phrase or sentence, the type of word, and the importance or emphasis assigned to the word by the speaker. Umeda (1975) was the first to study a large range of these effects, using extended reading from text. She found that the longest vowels were those in stressed syllables occurring at the end of phrases, clauses, or sentences. These are called prepausal stressed vowels; on the average they ranged from 150 ms for [ɪ] to 212 ms for [ɑ]. In contrast the same vowels in "function" words (that are not usually stressed), such as *in* and *on,* were much shorter, averaging 52 ms for [ɪ] and 97 ms for [ɑ]. The position and word type thus cause vowel duration changes by large factors, as great as two or three to one.

Another major factor in vowel duration is the characteristics of the consonant following the vowel. Vowels are shortened when followed by voiceless stop consonants; a typical amount of shortening was about 20 ms but the prepausal stressed vowels were shortened by an average of 40 ms. A following nasal consonant lengthens the preceding vowel if it is not prepausal and not one of the lax vowels, [ɪ, ɛ, ʌ]. Diphthongs follow rules similar to the vowels except that the nasal consonant lengthening of diphthongs also occurs in the prepausal position.

The importance of a word also affects its duration, especially the duration of the main vowel. Umeda found that a given main vowel is longer in words having a high meaning content, such as nouns and main verbs, than it is in words that carry little content and are more predictable from the context, such as articles and prepositions. Furthermore, when an initially unpredictable word, *father,* occurred repeatedly during a discourse, the main vowel [ɑ] was much longer the first few times the word occurred than later in the discourse.

Consonant Duration Effects

The durations of consonants are also affected by syllable stress, emphasis, the position of the consonant in the word, and grammatical conditions, as shown by Umeda (1977). The duration of the consonant was taken as the constricted or closed time as seen on spectrograms. This was measured for stops, nasals, fricatives, and [l] and [r]; the burst durations after stops were not included as part of the stop durations but were measured separately.

First consider the stop and nasal consonants that occurred between two vowels, i.e., single intervocalic consonants. The average duration for types of these intervocalic consonants ranged from 25 ms to about 90 ms, depending on the location of adjacent syllable stress, of a word boundary, and on the specific consonant. The shortest average durations occurred for [t, d, n] (25, 26, 34 ms), within a word and following a stressed vowel. The longest average durations occurred for intervocalic [p, b, m] (89, 90, 86 ms), initiating a word that was a stressed syllable or a word that began with a stressed syllable. The condition of stop voicing, i.e., voiced [b, d, g] vs. unvoiced [p, t, k], had no effect on the consonant closure duration when the consonant was word initial and stressed; for poststressed stops within a word, the average closures for [b] and [g] were 10 and 8 ms shorter, respectively, than for [p] and [k]; the [t] and [d] in this position are executed by American speakers as very brief flaps with no difference in average duration.

The occurrence of a pause after the consonant had a large lengthening effect on fricative consonants. This is similar to the prepausal lengthening effect seen for vowels, but it did not occur consistently among nonfricative consonants. Consonants following a pause were predominantly [s, ʃ, m, n, l]; these were all shortened in this postpausal position.

As with vowels the duration of consonants is longer in words having a higher content of meaning. The average difference was about 20 ms for [m] and for the stops [t, b, d], and 40 ms for [f].

It might be expected that the degree of change in consonant duration would be proportional to its inherent duration, i.e., that long consonants, such as fricatives, would show more variation than short consonants, such as stops. However, an analysis of the amount of variation in duration of single intervocalic consonants showed no relation to the average duration of the consonant class. Rather the widest variation seemed to be caused by conditions where there could be a wide variety of prosodic influences, such as more or less word emphasis and more or less blending across word boundaries.

The unvoiced stop consonants are accompanied by a release burst of noise during the transition between the opening point of the closure and the point at which the voicing of the vowel begins. The duration of these bursts is also found to depend on prosodic conditions of word boundary, stress, pause, and meaning/content. One major series of conditions causes an increase in both burst duration and closure duration, generated by factors of intersyllabic pause, word boundary, and stress locations relative to the unvoiced stop. However, if the stop is at the end of a word there is little burst duration regardless of different closure durations; if it follows a nasal consonant the burst duration may be normally long or short, but with proportionately much shorter closure duration.

Rules Describing Durational Effects

Klatt (1973) noted that there was a limit to the temporal compressibility of vowels when they are affected by a combination of two shortening factors, namely, when followed by an unvoiced consonant and/or by an additional syllable, compared with the long vowel seen in a monosyllable that ends in a voiced consonant. He later expressed this incompressibility in a formula (Klatt, 1975), which was also applied as a rule to adjust consonant durations for various shortening effects (Klatt, 1976).

Lindblom et al. (1977) and Umeda (1977) have also proposed rules expressing lengthening and shortening effects for vowels and consonants. The Lindblom rules are the most general; they are mathematical statements of the operation of three principles: 1) the greater the number of subunits in a unit of speech, the shorter is each subunit, 2) each subunit is shorter up to a limit of compressibility, and 3) the number of subunits following a given subunit has a greater shortening effect than the number of preceding subunits. These principles are seen to operate for both small and large subunits, i.e., for vowels and consonants as subunits of syllables, for syllables as subunits of words, and for words or phrases as subunits of sentences. Word-final and phrase-final (prepausal) lengthening are thus accounted for as being less shortened, by principle (3).

Going even further, Lindblom et al. (1977) proposed a tentative theory of motor organization of any sequence of syllables that invokes only two principles to account for the various durational phenomena seen. One principle puts a limitation on the number of units that can be held in motor memory waiting to be performed. The other principle involves economy of effort for performing the transitions between adjacent units. For more on this theory, see p. 163 in Chapter 10.

Rules like these are currently being used to improve the intelligibility and naturalness of artificial speech produced by computer from keyboard-typed sentences. They also have important implications for further research on how the brain organizes the production of speech and controls the speech movements. Furthermore, these rules may have considerable potential for application in speech training and therapy.

ORAL TRACT SHAPING FACTOR

Thus far in our study of prosodic features we have described two factors in prosodic variations. First, the voice source is the origin of changes in pitch, intensity, and spectrum, depending on the prosodic stress patterns of words and phrases; second, the articulatory movements of the vowels and consonants produce differences in the durations of vowels and consonants depending on stress patterns and position in sentence or phrase.

These two factors, i.e., the voice source variations and the timing of articulatory movement, are the most important factors for the prosody of English.

In addition, there are some systematic differences in oral tract shape depending on stress and emphasis; the shape differences result in vowel formant differences. In English these are highly correlated with differences in pitch, intensity, and duration, and the formant differences do not seem to be as noticeable as the intensity differences (see Chapter 11); thus the oral tract shape differences do not seem to be of primary importance in the communication of English stress patterns. Nevertheless, these articulatory shaping differences are an interesting feature of some languages, and they have been studied because they are important for understanding the motor organization of speech. Let us look at these effects briefly.

The effect of stress on oral tract shape is audible if one listens carefully to words like *ob*ject vs. ob*ject* spoken in sentences like *That's an object* and *He didn't object*. In *ob*ject the [ɑ] of the first syllable sounds strongly [ɑ]-like in quality and has formant frequencies similar to those of a specimen [ɑ] vowel; however, in ob*ject*, the "[ɑ]" is very different in quality; it sounds more like the neutral vowel; in fact the formant frequencies are shifted toward the positions for the neutral [ə] vowel. Another such pair of words is *re*ject vs. re*ject* in *A reject is bad* and *To reject is bad*. A similar effect occurs in Swedish between certain pairs of words where the stress patterns are the only word-differentiating factor. In general the effect is for an unstressed vowel to have a partially neutralized, reduced vowel quality.

This effect, where the unstressed version of a vowel has more neutral formant positions than the stressed vowel, is called *vowel reduction*. There are languages that do not show vowel reduction in unstressed vowels. A review of acoustic studies of vowel reduction in different languages is given by Lehiste (1970, pp. 139–142).

There are several acoustic studies of vowel reduction in English and Swedish. Tiffany (1959) used 20 American talkers speaking short test sentences; Lindblom (1963) used a Swedish talker speaking selected syllables in a "carrier" phrase that had different stress patterns. These studies measured the formant frequencies and durations of the stressed and unstressed versions of nearly all the vowels of English and Swedish, keeping the adjacent consonants constant. The results of the Swedish study showed very consistent reduction of the duration of the unstressed vowel relative to its stressed version and displacement of the frequency of F2 toward a more neutral position. For example, the F2 of long stressed [ɪ] in the syllable [dɪd] was about 2200 Hz, but in the short unstressed [ɪ] F2 was shifted downward (toward the neutral position of 1500 Hz) to about 2000

Hz; in the syllable [dɔd] the long stressed [ɔ] had a low F2 of about 850 and the F2 of short unstressed [ɔ] was shifted upward to 1150 Hz. The displacement of F2 toward neutral was fairly regular in that it was correlated to a significant degree with the amount of decrease in duration relative to the long stressed version of the vowel. On the other hand, in the American study some of the vowels showed the expected neutralization of F2 but others did not; the duration and pitch changes were quite consistent: there was longer duration and higher pitch on the stressed versions of all the vowels.

There are several differences between these two experiments that might have produced the discrepancy in F2 neutralization, but perhaps the most important difference is that meaningful sentences were employed in the American study in contrast to the somewhat artificial carrier phrases of the Swedish study. Furthermore, the stress variations in the American study were produced by the talkers by means of emphasizing or not emphasizing the words containing the test vowels, that is, by attempting to signal the importance attached to key words. In the Swedish experiment the talker may have been operating more as a strictly rhythmic producer of stress and thus the extent of his articulatory movements toward a given vowel position might have been more consistently subject to foreshortening on the shorter vowels. In a later Swedish experiment (Stålhammar, Karlsson, and Fant, 1974) the long Swedish vowels, spoken in connected speech, showed small neutralization effects, but the short vowels showed larger, more consistent neutralization.

Gay (1978) carried out a study of vowel reduction where both the rate of utterance and the stress were systematically varied. The talkers were American phoneticians and they were instructed to try to maintain vowel identity in the unstressed versions of the vowels and not to reduce them all the way to neutral. The unstressed vowels were found to be shorter and lower in pitch than their stressed versions, for both rapid and slow speech. There was some neutralization in formant frequencies in the slowly spoken unstressed vowels compared with the formants of rapidly spoken stressed vowels of about the same duration as the unstressed vowels. However, the rapid rate of speaking per se did not produce formant neutralization; the rapidly spoken stressed vowels, although shorter than the slowly spoken stressed vowels, were not neutralized in formant frequencies; the same was true of the unstressed vowels. This tends to indicate that the mechanisms controlling the articulators operate differently in producing rate changes and stress, even though both affect vowel duration. Slis (1975) found that stress produces an earlier movement toward the initial consonant of a stressed syllable compared with an unstressed syllable.

On the whole it appears that the oral tract shape of a vowel may be affected not only by the stress pattern but also by the vowel system of the particular language, and even by the momentary necessity of the speaker to communicate a word as clearly as possible. The intention of the speaker as a factor in vowel shaping is implied by one of the duration findings of Umeda, mentioned earlier, and by the low degree of vowel reduction by Gay's speakers, who were instructed to maintain vowel identity in their unstressed syllables.

SUMMARY

The rhythms and intonations of a language are formed under definite rules and these prosodic rules are an important aspect of the code of every language. The prosodic features are produced by special manipulations of the glottal sound source and the timing of articulatory movements. The source factors operate through actions of the speech breathing muscles and the vocal folds; the timing factors operate through the movements of the upper articulators. The two main factors in the glottal source variations for prosodic features are: 1) the tension on the vocal folds and 2) the subglottal air pressure. These affect the fundamental frequency, the amplitude, and the source spectrum. Increasing the subglottal air pressure increases the fundamental frequency or pitch of the voice and also the intensity. The pressure increase is produced by increasing the expiratory forces on the lungs.

The relations between the subglottal expiratory mechanism for controlling intonation and the mechanism of the muscle tension on the vocal folds have been studied experimentally to explain the acoustic effects for the features of stress and intonation. The intonation contour for a statement generally shows a down-going pitch, which may be correlated with a decrease in subglottal pressure toward the end of the statement. However, superimposed on this may be variations in the pitch due to the syllable stress of the utterance and the speaker's emphasis. For expressing a question, the pitch contour rises during the utterance because of increased vocal fold tension and, again, the stressed syllable will have a higher pitch than the other syllables. The stressed syllable generally corresponds to a peak in the subglottal pressure to raise the syllable pitch.

A breath group theory of intonation has been proposed, which states simply that the intonation contour will naturally always fall toward the end of a breath group because of the lower subglottal pressure just before taking a new breath of air. Then this basic breath group contour can be marked as a question through an increase in vocal fold tension. The theory assumes, in its simple form, a high degree of independence of the two factors, vocal fold tension and subglottal pressure, in determining pitch. Some investigators believe that the vocal fold tension factor is the dominant factor, not the breath group cycle. A recent study of the vocal fold tension through electromyography indicated that the breath group theory had to be modified such that the intonation contours are controlled primarily by vocal fold tension in the high-pitched parts of a contour and by subglottal pressure in the lower pitched parts of a contour. The vertical position of the larynx is thought to be an adjustment factor in determining which control factor dominates, the vocal fold tension or the subglottal pressure.

Another glottal source factor related to stress and intonation is the sound intensity and the spectral balance between the low and high regions of the glottal source spectrum. Increased subglottal pressure will increase the intensity of the glottal source sound and raise the high frequency part of the source spectrum relative to the low frequency part. Thus, stressed vowels are found to have a higher amplitude in F2 and the higher formants than unstressed vowels.

In addition to the glottal source factors just discussed, there are important durational variations that arise from prosodic conditions. In general the syllable is longer in final position in a breath group. Within breath groups, at places where pauses may occur at the end of phrases and clauses, it is found that the vowels are longer. If a word is an unstressed function word, the vowels are shorter. The characteristics of consonants that follow a vowel have a strong effect on the preceding vowel duration. In particular vowels are shortened when followed by voiceless consonants. The importance of a word also affects its duration, especially in the duration of the main vowel of the word. Consonant durations are also affected by factors of the syllable stress and the position of the syllable in the utterance, in similar ways to those effects on vowel duration.

Rules describing the prosodic effects on the durations of vowels and consonants have been formulated by phoneticians who are interested in these rules for synthesizing correct speech expression and for explaining the motor organization of speech production. In general, these rules express the fact that the greater the number of subunits in a larger unit the shorter is each subunit up to a limit of compressibility. Another general rule is that the number of subunits that follow a given consonant or vowel has a greater shortening effect than the number of preceding subunits. One theory explains these rules on the basis that only a limited number of units can be held in the motor memory waiting to be performed and, second, that a principle of economy of effort applies for performing the sequence of units.

In addition to the two general production factors in prosodic variations, namely, the voice source in its pitch, intensity, and spectrum slope
and the articulatory movements of the vowels and consonants in the various durational patterns, there are some systematic differences in the oral
tract shape for a given vowel or consonant depending on stress and emphasis. These are thought to be secondary to source, spectrum, and durational differences. If a vowel is in an unstressed syllable, the formant frequencies tend to be reduced toward a more neutral vowel. This effect is
called vowel reduction and it is normally a strong effect in English because of vowel articulations that fall short of the target vowel position on
the brief, unstressed syllables. Measurements of vowel formants in
stressed and unstressed English syllables normally show considerable
vowel reduction in the unstressed syllables, but a trained speaker can, if
desired, form the unstressed vowels without the neutralization of articulation.

CHAPTER 6

CONSONANT FEATURES, GLIDES, AND STOPS

CONTENTS

We now turn to a study of the acoustic patterns of consonants. The main acoustic features of consonants and how each feature is produced are described, beginning with the classification of consonants according to their articulatory features. Next consonant production and vowel production are compared, and the acoustic patterns corresponding to each of the different articulatory features are described. The glide features are explained and compared with diphthongs and stop consonants. In subsequent chapters the features of nasals, stops, and fricatives and voicing and place of articulation are described.

ARTICULATORY FEATURES OF CONSONANTS

Phonetic study of the consonants has developed a classification of consonants according to their articulatory features. Certain acoustic features correspond to the articulatory features, and in turn the acoustic features are the basis for the perceptual distinction of one consonant from another by a listener. The relations among articulatory, acoustic, and perceptual features form a theory of distinctive features. A theory of distinctive features constructs category systems for phonemes; the categories are intended to cover all languages. Each feature category is derived by joint consideration of three levels of linguistic analysis: the perceptual level, the acoustic level, and the articulatory level. Thus the purpose of distinctive feature theory is to provide a single consistent framework for specifying the phonology, i.e., the communicative sound structure, of any language (Chomsky and Halle, 1968; Jakobson et al., 1967).

Table 2. Articulatory classification of consonants

Place of articulation	Manner of articulation					
			Stop		Fricative	
	Glide	Nasal	Voiced	Unvoiced	Voiced	Unvoiced
Front						
Bilabial	w,ʍ	m	b	p		
Labiodental					v	f
Middle						
Dental					ð	θ
Alveolar	j,l	n	d	t	z	s
Palatal	r				3	ʃ
Back						
Velar	w,ʍ	ŋ	g	k		
Pharyngeal						h
Glottal			ʔ			

Distinctive feature theory has been highly useful in the study of speech communication. However, the purpose here is more limited. We deal only with English, and primarily with physiological and acoustic phonetics. Thus, the description of the acoustic patterns of consonants follows a classification according to articulatory features rather than distinctive features. The articulatory features of consonants are of three types: 1) features of manner of articulation, 2) the voicing feature, and 3) features of place of articulation. The manner and voicing features are types or states of articulation that can occur with any place of articulation; the voicing feature is either voiced or unvoiced; the manner features are glide, stop (plosive), nasal, and fricative. There are three subsidiary types of glide articulation: semi-vowel [w, j], lateral [l], and retroflex [r]. There are three general places of articulation—front, middle, and back— and at each general place there are two or three subsidiary places. The English consonants are shown in Table 2 arranged in rows corresponding to place of articulation and in columns corresponding to voicing and manner of articulation.

You may already be familiar with articulatory classification of consonants from a study of general phonetics. If not, you should memorize the classification because it is so commonly used in discussing consonants and it forms the basis for our study here.

CONSONANT PRODUCTION COMPARED WITH VOWEL PRODUCTION

Consonants differ from vowels in two main ways: 1) in vocal tract shaping and 2) in sound sources. The *sound source* for vowels is always periodic, but a consonant may be produced with a periodic sound source, an aperiodic sound source, or a combination of periodic and aperiodic sources. Aperiodic sources of consonant sound are caused by constrictions in the vocal tract. Consonants often include aperiodic sound because the tract constrictions for many consonants are so narrow that the airflow of the breath stream becomes turbulent. Turbulent airflow generates an aperiodic sound. The periodic sound source for consonants is the airflow fluctuations resulting from the periodic movements of the vocal folds, just as for vowels.

The *vocal tract shaping* of consonants constricts the tract to a larger degree than for vowels. The stop consonants, such as [p, b, t], obstruct the breath stream completely during a portion of the articulatory gesture. The fricative consonants, such as [ʃ, s, z], are formed with a very narrow constriction. Even the glide consonants, [w] and [j], constrict the oral tract more than do the corresponding close vowels, [u] and [i].

The constriction differences cause important general differences in sound pattern between consonants and vowels. The openness of the oral tract during vowels gives them the general characteristic of strong, voice-pulsed sound. In contrast the constrictedness of consonants causes them to have weaker voiced sound, aperiodic sound, or absence of sound. These differences are discussed briefly now, and later in more detail for the various types of consonants.

The stop or plosive consonants [p, t, k, b, d, g] are produced by a movement that completely occludes the vocal tract. During the occlusion there is either complete silence or only weak, low frequency sound. There is a complete silence for an unvoiced stop; during the occlusion of a voiced stop there is only the sound of the very lowest harmonics as long as voicing is maintained during the occlusion. As we shall see later, certain conditions often suppress the voicing.

When the occlusion of a stop consonant is released to form a following vowel, a transient and, for unvoiced stops, a burst of noise-like sound occur during the release. Thus, in contrast to the continuous, strong, voiced sound of vowels, the stop consonants have an interval that is silent, or nearly so, followed by a release burst of sound.

The continuant, nonplosive consonants are the glides [w, j, r, l], the nasals [m, n, ŋ], and the fricatives [s, ʃ, f, θ, z, ʒ, v, ð]. These are produced by movements that form partial constrictions of the vocal tract. Partial constriction causes either a reduced voiced sound during the constriction or, for fricatives, a noise-like, aperiodic sound caused by a turbulent sound source. The voiced sound produced during the constrictions of the glides and nasals is weaker than for vowels, especially in the region of F2 and above. Usually the noise-like sounds of the unvoiced fricatives [s, ʃ, f, θ] have more energy at middle and high frequencies, above 2 kHz, than at lower frequencies; in contrast, voiced sounds always have more energy in the low frequencies, below 1 kHz, than at higher frequencies.

GLIDE CONSONANTS AND DIPHTHONGS

The following description of consonant features concentrates first on the manner features, then on the voicing feature, and finally on the place features. This order is the order of importance of the features in their phonemic function in English (Carterette and Jones, 1974; Denes, 1963). We can begin our study with glide consonants, taking advantage of the fact that glides are similar to the vowels that we have already studied.

The remainder of this chapter concerns the articulatory actions for the glide features and their corresponding acoustic features: first the contrast between glide consonants and diphthongs and voiced stops, and then the differences among the voiced glides [w, j, r, l]. The unvoiced glide [ʍ] is discussed in the chapter on voicing.

The semivowel glide consonants, [w] and [j], when combined with vowels, are similar to diphthongs; the differences are that the glide consonants are produced with a constriction that is greater than the closest vowels and the articulatory movements to and from the glide constriction are faster than the movement between the two vowels of a diphthong.

Let us examine how the glide consonants are produced. The production of a consonant involves four important physiological factors: 1) the constricting effect of the consonant articulation on the oral tract, 2) the subglottal air pressure, 3) the air pressure in the mouth, and 4) the state of the vocal folds. Figure 36A shows the action of each of these factors in the production of the phrase *a Y* [əwɑɪ]. This phrase contains the glide [w] and the diphthong [ɑɪ] for comparison.

Each of the first four numbered rows in Figure 36 represents the movement, state, or pattern of one of the four factors. The last row (5) shows a spectrogram of the sound patterns of the phrase marked with lines to show how the sound patterns are related to the four production factors. The articulatory factors are schematic; the spectrogram was made from the utterance of an adult male speaker.

In row 1 the basic phases of the oral tract movement are traced. These are as follows: open during vowels, transitional closing from vowel to consonant, constricted phase of the consonant, and transitional opening from consonant to vowel. The movements shown are schematic; the forms of movement shown are based partly on inferences from acoustic patterns and partly on high speed motion pictures of lip and tongue movement (Fujimura, 1961; Houde, 1968; Kent and Moll, 1969; Perkell, 1969; Truby, 1959).

In row 1 of Figure 36A, the oral tract is initially in an open position for the neutral vowel [ə]. About 60 ms after the start of the vowel, the lips and tongue begin to move toward constriction for [w]. The transition time from open to narrow constriction is about 75 ms; the constriction lasts about 100 ms; the opening transition is about 75 ms. The total duration of the consonant movement is about 250 ms. During the period of narrowest constriction, the amount of constriction changes only slowly, compared with the rapid transitions to and from the constriction. After the opening transition of [w], the diphthong [ɑɪ] lasts about 350 ms. The oral tract is more constricted during the [ɪ] portion than during the [ɑ] portion. These durations are fairly typical for the utterance in a citation style of a short vowel, glide consonant, and a stressed diphthong.

The open phases of vowels can vary considerably in duration, depending on regional accent, on the identity of the vowel, on the consonants with which it is coarticulated, and on whether it is stressed or unstressed, or receiving special emphasis. For the various consonants, the closed time, or the constricted time, is generally in the range of 75 to 150 ms; longer times can occur on fricative consonants. On the average the duration of the period of constriction per consonant in rapid, fluent speech is about 100 ms.

Keeping in mind the basic open-constricted movement cycle, as sketched in row 1, we can explain how these movements will affect the sound patterns. First there must be speech sound generated by sound sources. Rows 2 and 4 indicate how these sound sources are produced and how they fit in with the open-constricted movement cycle to produce the phrase *a Y*.

The subglottal air pressure and the vocal fold action produce sound that is modified by the open-to-constricted cycle of the oral tract movement. In Figure 36 the articulations are coordinated in time, as shown schematically in rows 1 through 4; the corresponding sound patterns are shown in the spectrogram below. Before phonation of the [ə] begins, the vocal folds are brought close together (row 4) and the subglottal pressure begins to rise (row 2). When this pressure is high enough the vocal folds begin their opening and closing action to produce the basic sound source for the vowel [ə]. This voicing action continues until, at the end of the phrase, the subglottal pressure becomes too low to produce any vocal fold action. The pressure variations generated by the pulses of glottal airflow are seen as the small oscillations in the subglottal pressure. The average subglottal pressure is rather constant through the vowel [ə] and through

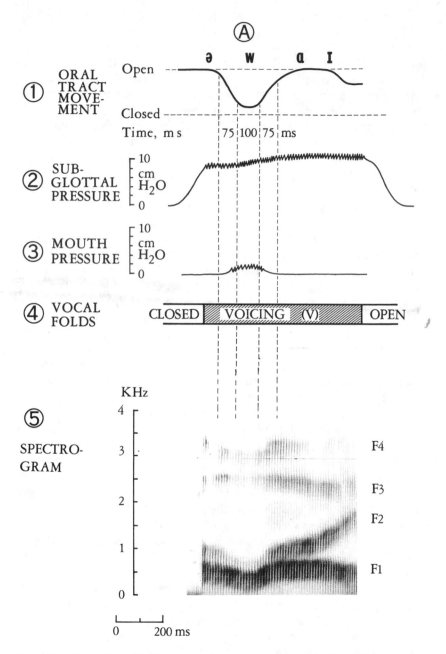

Figure 36.   The patterns of articulation, air pressure, and phonation in relation to the spectrographic acoustic patterns for the phrases *a Y* [əwaɪ] and *a buy* [əbaɪ]. A full explanation of

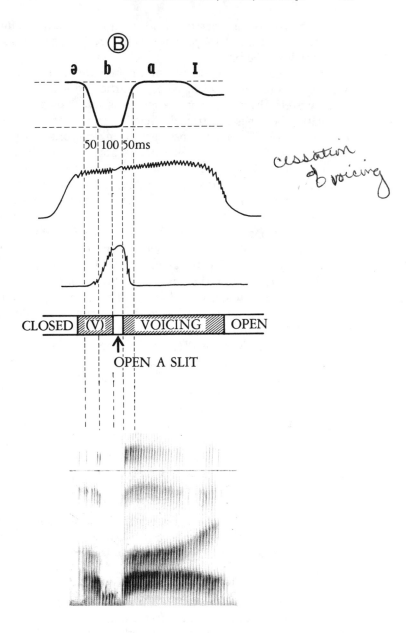

ə   b   ɑ   ɪ

50 100 50ms

cessation of voicing

CLOSED (V) VOICING OPEN

OPEN A SLIT

each numbered line, 1 through 5, is given in the text. The acoustic patterns are of actual utterances and the other patterns are drawn schematically to illustrate typical conditions for such utterances. The pressure unit cm H_2O is equal to 9.806×10^2 dyne/cm^2.

part of the consonant constriction. It then rises to a maximum and falls off again during the [ɑɪ]. This rise is what produces the stress on the second syllable of the phrase.

Row 3 indicates the amount of air pressure in the mouth relative to atmospheric pressure as zero. When the articulation is fairly open, as it is for all vowels, the pressure in the mouth is zero; however, whenever the articulation becomes constricted, there is a rise in the air pressure behind the constriction. The state of pressure during consonant constrictions depends on specific patterns of articulation, and this pressure is extremely important in generating certain sound patterns for the consonants. For the consonant [w] there is a considerable amount of lip constriction, and thus there is a small rise in pressure. The rise is small because the lips do not close completely.

The spectrogram shows how the sound patterns of the phrase are related to the articulation events above. When the voicing excitation of the oral tract begins, F1 is located at about 500 Hz, F2 at 1000 Hz, and F3 at 2500 Hz. The low F2 position may be due to a slight back constriction by the tongue. The formants drift downward from these positions for about 60 ms until the lips and tongue begin to move rapidly toward the [w] constriction. Then both F1 and F2 turn down in frequency because of the increasing constriction at the lips and the more back-constricted tongue; these changes in F1 and F2 frequencies are what we would expect according to the F1 and F2 constriction rules of Chapter 3. As the transition continues and the constriction becomes greater, the frequency positions of F1 and F2 become lower and lower. These changes in the formant locations are the formant transitions for [w]. As indicated by the dashed vertical lines, the formant transitions are correlated in time with the changes in constriction in row 1, which cause the formants to move to lower and lower frequencies with more and more constriction during the onset of the [w] consonant and to rise again as the lips open and the tongue moves toward the [ɑ] position. The lip constriction also causes F3 and F4 to go down in frequency and to be greatly reduced in intensity; F1 and F2 are also lower in intensity during the narrowest part of the constriction. During and after the opening transition from the constriction, the tongue articulation moves to [ɑ] then to [ɪ], causing F2 to rise farther and F1 to fall again for the [ɪ].

The timing of the formant transitions is an important aspect of the glide consonant sound. The basic transition, caused by the movement into and away from the constriction, takes about 75 ms. This is seen most directly in the F1 transition, because the frequency of F1 is more closely related to the amount of constriction. If the vowel formants are located far from the glide consonant formants, then the F2 transitions may require more than 75 ms while the F1 transition lasts only about 75 ms.

The glide [w] differs in three ways from the vowel [u]. First, the lips constrict more for [w] than for [u]. This causes lowered intensity of F1 and F2, and great reduction of the intensity of F3 and the higher formants. Second, [w] may be formed in front of any tongue position; the tongue position is affected by the adjacent vowels. A slight back constriction of the tongue may accompany the [w] constriction at the lips. The vowel [u], on the other hand, requires a narrow back tongue constriction in addition to lip constriction. Third, the speed of oral tract movement is faster in producing [w] than in movements between two vowels; this is seen by comparing the speeds of F1 transition in Figure 36. The F1 transition on the opening of [w] into [ɑ] is much faster than the F1 transition from [ɑ] to [ɪ]. These differences are typical of the differences between glide consonants and diphthongs.

GLIDE AND VOICED STOP

Now that we have seen how the glide consonant [w] is produced, and how it is different from vowels and diphthongs, we need to compare it with other consonants. First, we compare [w] with [b]. The consonant [b] is a voiced stop produced at the same place of articulation as [w], i.e., by a constriction of the lips. Figure 36B is a schema of the production of [b], in the phrase *a buy,* for comparison with the production of [w].

We see that the vocal folds are again closed at first and that the subglottal pressure rises in time. When the subglottal pressure is high enough, vocal fold voicing action begins, thus producing the source sound for the vowel [ə]. This pulsing continues throughout the vowel and through the transitional phase from open to constricted. So far all is similar to [w]. The similarity ends, however, at the point where the constriction of the lips to form the [b] reaches an amount of constriction sufficient to impede and then block the breath stream. Then the air pressure in the mouth immediately begins to rise, as shown in row 3. After the lips close completely, the mouth pressure continues to rise; it approaches the level of the subglottal pressure. During part of the rise in mouth pressure there is still enough pressure drop across the glottis to maintain vocal fold voicing, although at a decreasing pulse rate (because of the decreasing pressure drop across the glottis). Finally the pressure drop is not large enough to cause vocal fold movement and there is a period of complete silence. The silence lasts about 25 ms until the lips begin to open in the transition from the completely closed state toward the following vowel.

As soon as the lips are even slightly open the dammed-up air in the mouth begins to flow very rapidly through the lips, and soon the mouth pressure goes back down to zero, the atmospheric base line; the release of this pressure takes only 10 to 20 ms. This release of the pressured air in the mouth produces two sounds: an abrupt transient of increased sound pressure followed by a very brief burst of turbulent sound. The turbulent sound occurs when there is sufficient air velocity, through the barely parted lips, from the brief airflow outward in response to the higher than atmospheric air pressure inside the mouth.

During all this time the vocal folds are still held together in a position ready for voicing, probably forming a slit; as soon as the air pressure in the mouth has dropped far enough, there is a sufficient difference between the mouth pressure and the subglottal pressure for voicing action to resume. In other words, as the mouth pressure goes down because of airflow through the opening lips, and the pressure drop across the glottis becomes large enough, the vocal fold voicing begins again for the following vowel. Voicing then continues throughout the rest of the transition to the vowel and during the vowel phase.

As the vowel continues, the subglottal pressure curve reaches a maximum, giving the stress to the [aɪ], and then begins to decline especially toward the end of the vowel.

Now examine the sound patterns of the phrase *a buy* in row 5 of Figure 36B. Note that the formant transitions are very similar to the transitions for [w] except that they seem to be cut short by the closure of the lips. Theoretically, F1 reaches zero frequency at the moment of complete lip closure, and thus the F1 transition of [b] can reach a lower frequency than that of [w]; this is sometimes seen when a voicing pulse happens to occur during the final 10 ms or so of the closing movement of the lips.

While the lips are completely closed there is no sound present except weak sound in the very low frequencies, at the fundamental frequency, and perhaps at the second harmonic; these frequencies are low enough to be transmitted at low intensity through the closed lips and the cheeks. The sound in the region of F2 and above is completely suppressed by the closure of the oral tract; indeed F2 and the higher formants are partially suppressed and lowered in frequency during the last phase of the transitional part of the consonant movement because of the progressively smaller lip opening.

At the end of the closed phase when the lips part and the mouth pressure releases through the lips, the release transient and a very brief, 10-ms burst of turbulent sound are seen in the spectrogram. Just before this pressure release, during the latter part of the closed phase, the vocal fold voicing has stopped and there is complete silence. After the release burst has dissipated enough of the mouth pressure, voicing begins again and there are corresponding vertical striations in the spectrogram, one for each airflow pulse emitted by the glottis. The lips continue to open and the tongue has already moved toward the [ɑ] position. As the lips continue to open F1 rises, producing a transition to a level of about 650 Hz for the [ɑ], and the F2 frequency also rises to about 1150 Hz. The reappearance and upward transitions of F3 and F4 are also seen. After the transition interval is over, the formant frequencies remain at rather steady locations until the formants begin moving toward the [ɪ] part of the diphthong.

Now compare the two consonants [w] and [b]. We see that their sound patterns differ mainly in that sound is very weak or absent during the complete closure of the [b] and there is a release-burst of sound upon opening, whereas for [w] there is strong low frequency sound present throughout and no transient burst with the opening movement. These differences arise in the oral tract movement: the [b] movement closes the tract rapidly and completely but the [w] movement goes only as far as a narrow constriction and then begins to open again. Because the [b] closes completely, three acoustic features of a voiced stop are produced: 1) weak or absent low frequency sound, 2) a brief burst of air pressure release just before voicing begins again for a following vowel, and 3) a rapid F1 transition. The transition is typically 50 msec for a stop vs. 75 msec for a glide.

The formant transitions associated with [w] and [b] are very similar in direction. This is because the transitions are produced by constricting the oral tract at the lips.

GLIDE AND STOP AT MIDDLE PLACE

We now examine the production of the glide [j]. This glide is produced by a movement of the tongue to form a constriction at the front of the palate.

In Figure 37 we have schematized the factors in production of the glide [j] in contrast to the voiced stop [d], using two phrases, *a yacht* in Figure 37A and *a dot* in Figure 37B. The constrictive movements for [j] and [d] are similar to those of [w] and [b] in Figure 36; in other words, the tongue makes a glide-consonant movement toward and away from the palate for [j] that is very similar to the movement of the lips in forming [w]; and for [d] the tongue makes a stop-consonant movement to and away from the alveolar ridge that is very similar to the movement of the lips for [b].

Also the same patterns of manipulation of the subglottal pressure, mouth pressure, and vocal fold action occur for [j] and [d] as for [w] and [b].

Therefore, the sound patterns seen in the spectrograms of [j] and [d] are similar to those seen in the spectrograms of [w] and [b] except for a difference caused by the difference in the place of constriction. This difference is seen largely in the transitions of F2. According to the formant constriction rules for F2, constriction at an alveolar or front palatal posi-

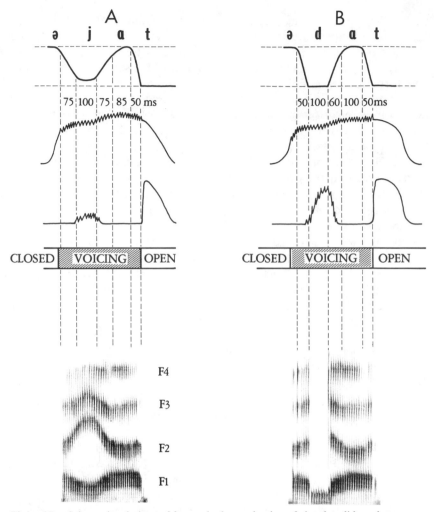

Figure 37.   Schematic relations of factors in the production of alveolar glide and stop con-sonants, exemplified in the spoken phrases *a yacht* [əjɑt] and *a dot* [ədɑt]. A full explanation of each line, 1 through 5, is given in the text for Figure 36 and this figure. The pressure unit cm H_2O is equal to 9.806×10^2 dyne/cm^2.

tion causes F2 to rise in frequency, but constriction of the lips causes F2 to decrease in frequency. For F1 the constriction has the same effect at both locations: a lowering of the F1 frequency during the transition from vowel to consonant and a rise in F1 frequency during the transition from conso-nant to vowel. The F2 transitions in *a yacht* and *a dot* show a rapid rise in frequency during the onset of the consonant constrictions and a rapid fall in frequency at the offset into the stressed vowel [ɑ].

The words *yacht* and *dot* end with the consonant [t], which is an alveolar unvoiced stop. The production of this consonant is explained later. Here, however, we can see that [t] has formant transitions in the same direction as those of the other alveolar consonant [d], as we might expect. Also notice that the mouth pressure rises suddenly during the [t] occlusion and voicing stops completely; the reasons for this are discussed later.

LATERAL AND RETROFLEX GLIDES

The lateral alveolar consonant [l] and the retroflex palatal consonant [r] are very similar to glide consonants in the speed of movement, in the degree of oral tract constriction, and in the action of the vocal folds. Phoneticians sometimes classify [l, r] as liquids rather than glides. However, liquid is an auditory term not necessarily related to articulation. Thus, we have classified [l, r] as glides, based on their transition speed. These two consonants differ from each other, and from the other glides, in the manner in which the tongue is shaped to form the constriction. For [l] the tongue tip makes contact with the alveolar ridge but is shaped to leave lateral openings, one on each side of the contact area. For [r], the tongue is flexed back and curved upward (retroflexed) so that the tip forms a moderate constriction at the palate.

The acoustic effects of [l] and [r] articulation can be seen in the spectrograms of Figure 38, where they can be compared with [w] and [j]. The transitions between the vowels and the consonant constrictions have a similar duration for all four consonants, as seen especially in the F1 transitions. The amplitude is low during the constrictions, especially for F2 and higher formants, because of the greater constriction compared with the more open vowels.

The frequency courses of the formant transitions differ among the four consonants, especially in F2, F3, and F4. First compare the formant transitions of [r] and [l]. For the movement to the [r] constriction there is a large F3 transition downward to about 1300 Hz, because of the increasing constriction of the oral tract at the middle of the palate by the retroflexed tongue tip; there is also a slight downward transition in F2 and F4. For the movement to the [l] constriction there is a slight downward transition in F2 but little or no transition in F3 or F4. These aspects of [r] and [l] contrast with [j]. For [j] there are upward transitions of F2, F3, and F4 going from [ə] to the constriction and downward again for the [ɑ]. For [w] F2 makes a large downward transition to the constriction, but F3 is not affected in frequency; F4 makes a smaller downward transition than F2.

The F1 transitions are similar for all the glides, and the transition duration is about 75 to 100 ms. The [l] has two discontinuities in the spec-

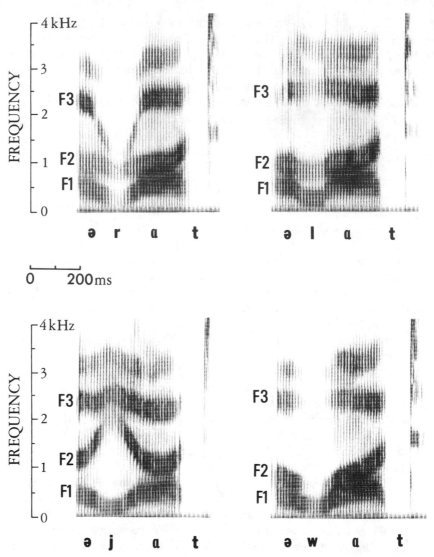

Figure 38. Spectrographic acoustic patterns of the glide consonants exemplified in the phrases *a rot* [ərɑt], *a lot* [əlɑt], *a yacht* [əjɑt], and *a watt* [əwɑt]. See text for description of the important acoustic differences and similarities between these consonants.

trum and amplitude, which are seen especially in the F1 and F2 regions; this is because the tongue tip makes, holds, and then releases its contact with the alveolar ridge. The other glides [r, w, j] are not articulated with a tongue-tip contact and therefore their formant transitions change smoothly in time without discontinuities.

The F2 transitions of [w] and [j] are in opposite directions because of the opposite effects on F2 frequency of the labial constriction for [w] compared with the alveolar constriction for [j]. The F3 transitions for [j] are opposite the direction of those for [r].

The formant pattern of [l] during the constriction is prominent in the region of F3 and F4, in contrast to the other glides. The formants of [l] vary in location depending on the adjacent phonemes, as is described later.

Palatal glides can easily be trilled. Trills are not phonemic in English but they are often part of the vocal repertoire of children. A trilled [r] or [l] is produced by a vibration of the tongue tip toward and away from the palate, causing a rapid alternation in the spectrum between a pattern for a very narrow constriction and the pattern seen for the untrilled glide. Probably a Bernoulli suction effect between palate and tongue is a factor in producing trilled consonants. The alternation rate of trills is usually in the range of 20 to 30 per second, and thus two to three trill cycles may occur during a glide constriction of 100 ms (1 / 10 second).

EFFECTS OF UTTERANCE POSITION

The examples of [w, j, l, r] thus far have been in an intervocalic position, i.e., between two vowels. A consonant may also occur initially at the beginning of an utterance or finally, at the end. Spectrograms of initial and final glide-like consonants are shown in Figure 39. The patterns of the initial glides are very similar to the constricted and releasing phases of the intervocalic glides in Figure 38; also the patterns of the final glides are like the onset-constriction patterns of the intervocalic glides. The constricted phase of the initial glide consonant may be more brief than for the intervocalic glide because sound-source production by the glottis may not start at the very beginning of the oral tract constriction. In the examples of final position, [r] and [l] are more diphthong-like and drawn out in duration of the constriction because phonation is not shut off but merely allowed to gradually die out; the formant transitions are slower and the discontinuity seen for initial [l] is not seen for final [l] for one of the speakers.

The position of a glide consonant is often adjacent to another consonant, forming a compound consonant or consonant cluster. Then the glide consonant articulation strongly affects the adjacent vowel.

SUMMARY

For acoustic phonetic study the consonants are classified according to their articulatory features rather than according to distinctive feature

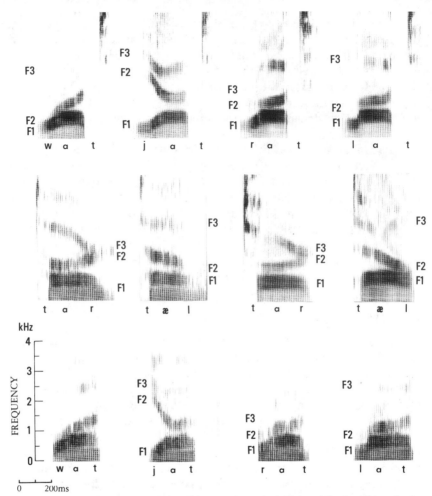

Figure 39.   Acoustic patterns of the glide consonants in initial and final positions in the words *watt* [wɑt], *yacht* [jɑt], *tar* [tɑr], and *tal* [tæl]. The important points to note are described in the text. Two different male speakers spoke each word; the speaker for the top row of spectrograms has very even, regular glottal pulses and highly resonant formants, compared with the speaker in the bottom row, who was the author.

theory. The articulatory features of consonants are of three types: features of manner of articulation, voicing, and place of articulation.

Features of the articulation of glide consonants are: 1) a speed of articulation that is faster than that for diphthongs but slower than that for stops, 2) a degree of constriction that is greater than that for vowels, and 3) occurrence of lateral and retroflex forms of tongue articulation. The acoustic patterns of glides show formant transitions of intermediate

Table 3. Main features of glide consonants compared with voiced stops and diphthongs

Features	Diphthongs	Glides	Voiced stops
Timing			
Oral articulation	Slow	Medium-fast	Fast
Type of constriction	(No narrow constriction)	Brief constriction	Brief closure
Spectral			
Intensity during constriction	(No narrow constriction)	Strong	Weak
Spectrum during constriction	(No narrow constriction)	Low frequencies strong up to about 600 Hz; midfrequency energy weaker than in diphthongs	Very low frequencies; fundamental alone, lowered in pitch; no energy in F2, F3 and higher regions
Formant transitions	Slow formant transitions between the two component vowels	Medium-fast transitions appropriate to place, lateral opening, or retroflexion	Rapid formant transitions

speed, weak amplitude of F2 and higher formants during the constriction phase, and characteristic F patterns depending on lateral (F2), retroflex (low F3), labial (low F2), or alveolar (high F2) constriction characteristics.

A summary of the main articulatory and acoustic features of diphthongs, glides, and voiced stops is given in Table 3.

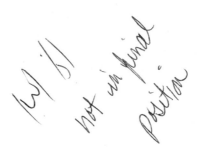

CHAPTER 7

CONSONANTS: NASAL, STOP, AND FRICATIVE MANNERS OF ARTICULATION

CONTENTS

This chapter contains a description of the articulation and acoustic features for three more manners of articulation that produce phonemic distinctions among the consonants of English: nasal, stop (or plosive), and fricative. These three manner-features are extremely important. Together they account for about 80% of all the consonantal distinctions (Denes, 1963).

The nasal consonants have some acoustic similarities to glides, so the nasal manner of articulation is described before discussing how nasals differ from glides. The nasals are also compared with voiced stops. Fricative consonants are then described, especially as compared with stops.

NASAL CONSONANTS

The nasal consonants [m,n,ŋ] are articulated by a combination of two movements: 1) movement of the tongue or lips to completely occlude the oral tract and 2) lowering of the velum. Velar lowering introduces an opening from the pharynx into the nasal passages; this opening is called the velopharyngeal port or simply the *velar port*. The oral occluding movements for the nasals are similar to those for the corresponding voiced stops [b,d,g] in that the constricting movement of the tongue or lips is rapid and a complete oral occlusion is formed. Because of this similarity some linguists classify the nasals as stops having the feature of nasalization.

During the oral occlusion of a nasal consonant the sound produced by the glottal action of phonation is propagated through the velar port

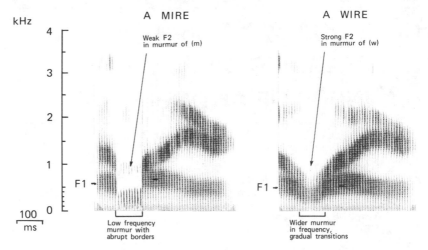

Figure 40.   Spectrograms of *a wire* [əwaɪr] and *a mire* [əmaɪr] to compare the transitions and constriction murmurs between glide and nasal consonants. The transitions are more abrupt for the nasal. The strongest part of the murmur ranges up to about 800 Hz for the glide but only to about 300 Hz for the nasal.

and the nasal passages, and out through the nose. This sound from the nose is called a nasal murmur; its spectrum is dominated by low frequency sound determined mostly by the main resonance of the large volume of the nasal passages constricted by the small nose openings. The nasal passages of a speaker remain constant in shape and size for the different nasal consonants. For this reason the murmur spectrum does not differ greatly among [m,n,ŋ].

NASAL-GLIDE-STOP DIFFERENCES

Figure 40 compares the nasal and glide consonants showing spectrograms of the phrases *a wire* [əwaɪr] and *a mire* [əmaɪr]. The spectrograms show differences between nasal and glide consonants in the transitions to and from the consonant constrictions and also during the murmurs of the constriction intervals. The strong low frequency portion of the nasal murmur is similar to that in the glide constriction intervals except that in the nasal murmur it is limited to the region below about 300 Hz, whereas the strong low frequency energy in the constriction of glides ranges up to about 800 Hz. The nasal murmur has abrupt borders compared to the more gradual transitions of the glide constriction from vowel to constriction and back to vowel. The abruptness of onset and offset of the nasal murmur results from two circumstances: 1) the oral occlusion is sudden in onset and offset and 2) the nasal port is already wide open at the onset of the occlusion and remains so throughout.

There are important differences between nasals and glides in the spectrum of the murmur sound above the low frequency part. The nasal murmurs are much less intense above 800 Hz than are the murmurs of the glides, and the pattern of formant frequencies in this upper region is not consistently definitive among the nasals [m,n,ŋ] as it is among glides.

We next compare the nasal and voiced stop consonants. The nasal vs. stop acoustic differences are somewhat complicated but they can be easily understood if the production factors are kept in mind. There are three main acoustic differences between voiced stops and nasals: 1) the stops have release bursts but the nasals do not; 2) the nasals have stronger intensity of the constriction murmur; and 3) the vowels adjacent to nasals are nasalized, but not for stops. The movement of the oral tract for nasals is similar to that of stops, with rapid transitions, abrupt onset and offset of occlusion, and an occlusion interval of about 100 ms. However, during the occlusion interval of nasals there is present the relatively strong, low frequency sound of the murmur compared with weak or absent sound during stop occlusions. The murmur and nasalization patterns can be compared in Figure 41. Let us now see how all these acoustic differences are produced.

Release Bursts and Murmur Intensity

During the closed period of voiced stops, the vocal folds continue to open and close, emitting pulses of subglottal air into the closed oral cavity. As this continues, the air pressure in the mouth increases until it is high enough to stop phonation or until the release of the oral closure. At the moment of release the oral pressure is higher than the atmospheric pressure. Thus, upon release, there is a burst consisting of a transient (momentary), step-like increase in the pressure of the air in front of the lips and following formant resonances; then phonation starts for the following vowel sound. In contrast, the release of a nasal consonant is not accompanied by a burst because, due to the open state of the velar port, there has been no build-up of air pressure in the oral-pharyngeal cavity during the oral occlusion.

The first event in the burst is the step-like, instantaneous increase in sound pressure; this is followed by damped oscillations at resonant frequencies (formants) determined by the location in the vocal tract of the sound source (the step change) and the vocal tract shape at that moment. The voiced stop release bursts are brief, lasting only 10 to 20 ms. The release burst of the [b] in Figure 41 was visible on the original spectrogram but cannot be seen in the reproduced figure.

The nasal murmur during the oral occlusion of the nasals is more intense than the constriction murmurs that are seen during voiced stops; the reason is that much more sound can radiate through the nostrils during

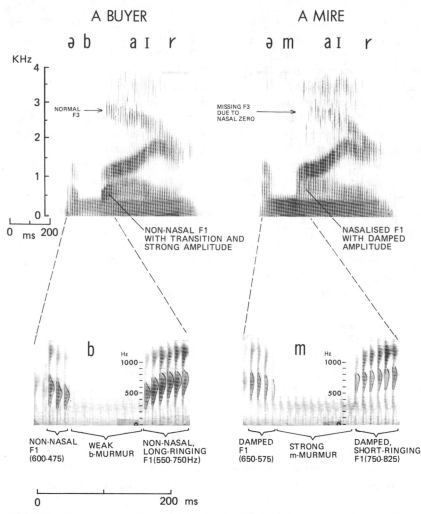

Figure 41. Spectrograms of *a buyer* [əbaɪr] and *a mire* [əmaɪr] to compare the acoustic patterns of nasal vs. voiced stop consonants. In the upper spectrogram, the stop has a very weak murmur during the occlusion interval and a release transient and the nasal has a strong murmur and no release transient. Nasalization adjacent to the nasal causes differences in the vowel spectrum compared with that adjacent to the stop. In the bottom spectrograms, the murmurs and transitions in the vowels are presented on an expanded time scale. The expansion makes visible the individual formant-ringing intervals of the vowel. These ringing intervals have been outlined on the spectrogram and look like "lozenges," which are straight on the left leading edge and round on the right trailing edge. Because nasalization damps the ringing of F1, the lozenges are thinner (shorter ringing time) near the nasal than the stop. The time expansion was accomplished on a Kay Sona-graph (late 1950s model) by making the original recording on "reproduce" speed, which gives a 3:1 time expansion and 3:1 frequency compression relative to the normal procedure. The frequency scale was then re-expanded on reproduction using an accessory, the Kay Scale Magnifier Sr., Model S.

the nasal consonant than can radiate through the walls of the closed vocal tract during the voiced stops.

Thus there are two main differences distinguishing nasals and voiced stops that stem from the articulatory conditions during the oral occlusion, the absence or presence of a release burst and the intensity of the murmur.

On the release (or opening) of the oral occlusion of nasals the oral opening movement is a little slower compared with releases of stops. This difference is due to the air pressure in the mouth during stop closures compared with the lack of this pressure on nasals because of the open velar port and nose. The pressure of air behind the stop closure causes a slightly faster opening movement just after the release than is seen for the nasals (Fujimura, 1961).

Nasalization of Vowels Adjacent to Nasal Consonants

The movement downward of the velum for a nasal consonant begins well before the beginning of oral tract movement toward occlusion, and thus the opening of the velar port is already accomplished by the time the oral tract becomes closed; also the velar port remains open during the release and opening of the oral occlusion. The lead and lag of velar opening and closing, preceding and following the oral tract occlusion, are typically about 100 ms. This causes nasalization of portions of vowels for about 100 ms preceding and following nasal consonants.

The effects of the leading and lagging nasalization are seen in Figure 41 by comparing the vowels adjacent to the stop in *a buyer* with the vowels adjacent to the nasal in *a mire*. Nasalization of vowels introduces extra resonances and antiresonances into the response of the oral tract because of the tuning effects of the velar opening and connected nasal cavities. It should be emphasized that these nasalization effects are mainly caused by changes in the response of the oral tract, not by added sound coming out of the nose, a sound that is negligible because of its low amplitude in the frequencies above about 500 Hz, relative to the vowel sound. In mathematical descriptions of the response of the vocal tract, the resonances (or formants) are called *poles* and the antiresonances are called *zeroes;* these terms are used in describing the effects of nasalization on the vowel spectrum.

Nasalization introduces a pole at a very low frequency, which intensifies the fundamental, and a zero at a frequency just above the pole, which reduces the energy in the spectrum above the fundamental, in the F1 region. If the normal oral tract F1 is low in frequency the zero can cancel the F1 resonance, leaving a flat spectrum. If F1 is normally high, the zero reduces the spectral energy in an area between the fundamental and F1. The zeroes often show in the spectrogram as light patches or light areas in the

F1 region, and these can be seen in Figures 41 and 42. Nasalization also introduces zeroes in the regions of F2 and F3.

In areas of the spectrum where zeroes are present the spectrogram has missing or depressed harmonics, and there is an overall broadening in frequency bandwidth and reduction in intensity of the oral formants relative to those seen near the stop consonant closures where there is no nasalization. These effects are clearly visible, especially in the expanded sections of the spectrograms in the lower half of Figure 41. The F1 intensity is weaker adjacent to the [m] than the [b], the F1 transitions are less extensive (starting and ending frequencies of the F1 transitions are given in parentheses on the spectrogram), and the resonant ringing of F1 is damped out more rapidly. In the expanded spectrograms the ringing period of the formant forms a lozenge-shaped pattern, which has been hand-outlined on the spectrogram for each formant pulse; it will be seen that the formant-ringing lozenges are thinner near the [m] than near the [b].

The frequency locations of the poles and zeroes due to nasalization depend greatly on the amount of opening of the velar port. The velar port changes in size, from small to larger before the oral occlusion and from large to smaller during the opening of the occlusion. These changes in amount of velar opening cause changes in the frequency locations of the poles and zeroes, making the spectral effects of nasalization extremely variable, depending on the time course of velar movement and the particular combination of vowel and consonant.

The F1 formant transitions of nasal consonant articulation are often somewhat overridden by the changing pole-zero pattern from nasalization. This is seen in Figure 41, comparing the F1 transitions adjacent to the closures of [b] vs. [m]. The F2 transitions in Figure 41 are not so much affected by nasalization as are the F1 transitions.

Figure 41 also shows a case of suppression of F3 by a zero, where after the [b] the F3 of the following vowel starts immediately upon release of the [b] occlusion; on release of the [m] occlusion, however, F3 is apparently suppressed because it is seen only after a delay of about 50 ms.

Initial and Final Nasals and Stops

Initial and final nasal consonants are similar to the intervocalic nasals in timing and spectral pattern. Examples are shown in the spectrograms of Figure 42. When a syllable begins and ends with a nasal consonant the lag and lead of nasalization cause the entire vowel to be nasalized. Compare *mom* and *bob* in vowel pattern; note that the formants are weaker throughout the nasalized [ɑ̃] of *mom* compared with the [ɑ] of *bob*. A weak or blank area below F1 indicates the presence of a zero in the oral

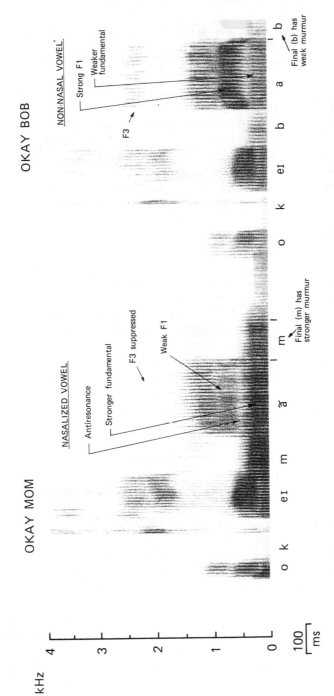

Figure 42. Spectrograms of *Okay Bob* and *Okay Mom* to compare initial and final voiced stop and nasal consonants. The lag and lead of the velar opening for the nasal consonant causes complete nasalization of the [ɑ̃] in *Mom* in contrast to the "normal" [ɑ] in *Bob*. The important effects of the nasalization are noted in the spectrograms and discussed in the text.

127

tract response caused by nasal coupling. This zero reduces the amplitude of F1. A pole of lower frequency than this zero increases the amplitude of the fundamental compared with its amplitude in the unnasalized vowel.

FRICATIVE CONSONANTS

The fricative consonants are similar to the stop and nasal consonants in the general timing of the open-constricted cycle of articulation. The difference is that, instead of being produced with a complete occlusion of the oral tract during the consonant gesture, fricatives are produced with a narrow constriction. The breath stream, passing through the constriction, becomes turbulent because of friction of the airstream on the walls of the constriction; this generates a hissing sound, which is the hallmark of the fricatives. The main differences between the sound patterns of the alveolar voiced fricative, stop, and glide are compared in Figure 43. In the spectrograms we see that the vowel formant frequencies and their transition are similar for the [d] and [z]. This is because of the similarity of the tongue articulations. However, during the fricative constrictions for [z] there is a strong, continuous, turbulent sound between 4 and 5 kHz but a complete silence in this high frequency region during the occlusion of the [d].

The high frequency turbulent sound during the constriction of the [z] is caused by turbulence of the airstream as it passes through the narrow constriction between the tongue and the alveolar ridge. Air turbulence produced in this way, by various kinds of narrow constrictions in the vocal tract, is the typical source sound for all fricative consonants. At the source it is a random noise having a spectrum with approximately equal amplitude, on the average, at all frequencies. The amplitude at each frequency varies randomly, from moment to moment in time. This randomness can be seen in the spectrum of the [z] sound in Figure 43; the spectrogram of a sound with randomly varying amplitudes at each frequency of the sound has a mottled appearance as compared with the striated appearance of periodically pulsed sounds, such as vowels. However, a closer examination of the [z] sound reveals that there is also a partial periodicity of amplitude. This is often seen in voiced fricatives because the vocal folds are held fairly close together throughout the consonant constriction and the airflow through the folds causes them to vibrate toward and away from each other, more or less as in vowel phonation, and this modulates the airflow supplied to the fricative constriction above, thereby modulating the turbulence amplitude produced.

The overall spectrum shape of the fricative sound received outside the mouth is determined by the size and shape of the oral cavity in front of

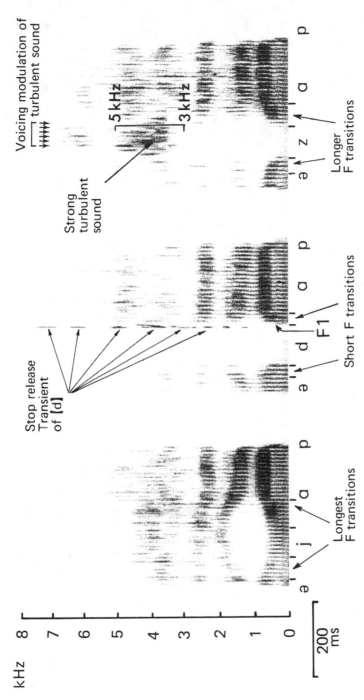

Figure 43. Spectrograms of *a yap* [əjɑp], *a dap* [ədɑp], and *a zap* [əzɑp] for comparison of the acoustic patterns of glide, stop, and fricative. Acoustic features are noted on the spectrogram and further discussed in the text.

129

Table 4. Summary of main features of nasals, glides, voiced stops, and voiced fricatives

Features	Nasals	Glides	Voiced stops	Voiced fricatives
Timing				
Oral articulation	Rapid	Medium	Rapid	Rapid
Velar articulation	Brief closure duration Velar port opening leads oral closing Velar port closing lags oral opening	Brief closure duration Velar port remains closed	Brief closure duration Velar port remains closed	Brief closure duration Velar port remains closed
Spectral				
Murmur intensity	Strong	Strong	Weak	High frequency turbulence
Murmur spectrum	Low frequency resonance of nasal passages up to about 300 Hz; very weak above this	Low frequencies strong up to about 800 Hz; midfrequency pattern stronger than nasals; different F patterns among glides but not among nasals	Very low frequencies (fundamental alone); no energy in F2, F3 or higher regions	Strong in high frequencies (above 2.5 kHz)
Formant transitions in adjacent vowel	Nasalization during the transitions, may obscure expected transitions; F1 of adjacent vowels is weakened	Long formant transitions appropriate to speed, place, and retroflexion (r articulation only)	Short formant transitions	Somewhat longer formant transitions than for stops
Overall spectral changes	Abrupt onset and offset, without a release transient	Gradual, smooth changes	Abrupt and with a release transient	Change from periodic to random turbulence that is amplitude modulated; no release transient

130

the constriction. The spectrum of fricatives is usually much more intense in the frequencies above about 2.5 kHz than at lower frequencies. The spectra of fricatives are discussed in more detail under the topic of the shape and place features of consonants (Chapter 9).

The formant transitions in F1 and F2 during the closing and opening movements should be compared between [z] and [d]. It will be seen that the transitions are slightly longer and slower for [z] than for [d]. Perhaps this difference is because the tongue must form a certain shaped narrow passage against the palate in order to produce the fricative turbulence of [z], and this adjustment requires a controlled slowing down of the constricting movement compared with the movement for [d], which can attain occlusion simply by collision with the palate; there is some evidence from an x-ray study that this may be the case (Perkell, 1969).

Note in the figure that the release of [d] has a sharp transient containing energy up to 7.5 kHz followed by brief formant ringing at F1, F2, F3, and F4, and a silent gap of about 15 ms before the first vocal fold pulse of the vowel and its very strong F1; this delay in voicing may have occurred because the last half of the occlusion period was de-voiced, indicating a high mouth pressure that had to be dissipated before vowel voicing could begin. A similar release gap in voicing does not appear after the [z].

Figure 43 also includes a spectrogram of the phrase *a yap* so that the alveolar glide [j] can be compared in rate and extent of formant transitions with [d] and [z]. The transitions have been marked on the spectrograms. It will be seen that the transitions of [j] are more extended than those for [d] and [z].

There is an additional manner of fricative articulation, called affricate, which includes the consonant sounds [tʃ], as in *church,* and [dʒ], as in *judge;* sometimes affricates are considered to be unitary phonemes, the sounds of which are symbolized by [č] and [ǰ]. The affricates are produced like fricatives that are preceded by an occlusion instead of a more open articulation. The occlusion is formed at the same place as the ensuing constriction for the friction part, which is usually of shorter duration than in a fricative.

SUMMARY

Table 4 summarizes the articulatory and acoustic features of all four manner distinctions among consonants: nasality, glide, stop (plosive), and fricative.

CHAPTER 8

CONSONANTS: THE VOICED-UNVOICED CONTRAST

CONTENTS

The phonemes /b,d,g,z,ʒ,v,ð/ are said to be voiced in contrast to the phonemes /p,t,k,s,ʃ,f,θ/, which are unvoiced. In phonology the corresponding distinctive feature is called voicing. The term *voicing* refers to the vibratory action of the vocal folds, which produces voicing periodicity in the speech wave, as explained in Chapter 4. Voicing is usually present during the constriction of voiced consonants and absent during the constriction of unvoiced consonants. This difference is controlled by the muscles of the larynx, which hold the vocal folds in either a closed or open position. The position of the folds also produces other acoustic differences (other than presence or absence of voicing) that distinguish voiced vs. unvoiced consonants.

To illustrate how the essential sound differences arise between voiced and unvoiced consonants, a schematic picture of the action of the oral tract articulators together with the subglottal pressure pattern, the mouth pressure, and the position of the vocal folds was constructed. Figure 44 shows this picture for [b] and [p] using the phrases *a buy* and *a pie*. Note that the first line, showing the oral tract movement, is similar for the two phrases, but the closure movement is a little faster for [p] than for [b]. The transitional movements for [b] and [p] are complete in about 50 ms. The subglottal pressure curve too is the same in general. However, in the mouth pressure there is an important difference during the occlusion: the pressure rises slowly for [b] but rapidly for [p]. This is because of the difference in vocal fold position during the occlusion.

It is in the difference in vocal fold action that we find the origin of the voiced-voiceless distinction. This difference produces the main acoustic differences between the voiced and unvoiced stops. In row 4 it can be seen that during the closed phase of the consonant [p] the vocal folds are in a wide-open position in contrast to [b], where they remain closed in a posi-

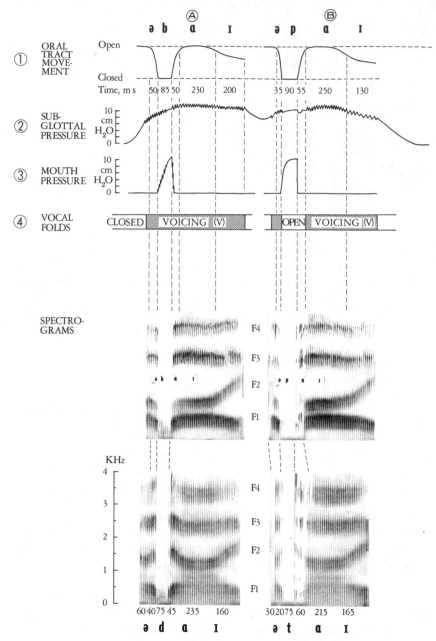

Figure 44.   Schematic oral tract movements, subglottal pressure contours, and states of the vocal folds, comparing voiced and unvoiced stop consonants in the phrases *a buy* [əbaɪ], *a pie* [əpaɪ], and *a dye* [ədaɪ]/*a tie* [ətaɪ], together with spectrograms. The strength and duration of the release bursts of the unvoiced stops are greater than for the voiced stops [b] and [d], because of the difference in the state of the vocal folds, closed or open, during the consonant occlusion. Further differences are explained in the text.

tion to produce voicing. The wide-open position on [p] affords little or no resistance to the flow of air into the mouth and so the mouth pressure rises rapidly to become equal to the subglottal pressure. Also, because the vocal folds have been opened wide at about the same time as the lips close, there is no vocal fold pulsing at all during the closed phase because the vocal folds are too far apart; furthermore, there is little or no pressure drop across the glottis because the mouth pressure is virtually the same as the subglottal pressure.

ACOUSTICS OF CONSONANT VOICING

At the end of the closed phase of [p], when the lips just begin to open to form the following vowel, the high mouth pressure is released and a strong flow of air travels from the trachea through the open vocal folds and out through the small lip opening. The release of the high mouth pressure and the subsequent rush of airflow from the trachea through the mouth and out through the narrow lip opening causes an intense transient sound, essentially a step-like change in pressure, followed by turbulent sounds (friction and aspiration) before the vowel begins. We call the transient and following friction and aspiration, all together, the burst of the consonant.[1]

During the burst interval of [p] the vocal folds start to move back toward the voicing position and, when the mouth pressure reaches a low enough level through the dissipation of the burst-flow, the voicing action of the vocal folds begins again for the following vowel.

The lip-opening transition continues during the friction and aspiration phase before voicing begins for the following vowel. The part of this transitional phase that is voiced is thus shorter than it is for the voiced consonant [b], because the first part is occupied by friction and aspiration. The release interval for [b] shows a weak transient before the first voice pulse but no friction or aspiration, because the vocal folds are held together, thus preventing any strong flow of air from the trachea.

The sound pattern during the unvoiced burst usually shows the second formant position rather strongly and also the transition of the second formant as the lips open more and more; the first formant energy does not appear strongly until the vocal tract is again excited by voice pulses. The

[1]During the [p] release the subglottal pressure shows a dip of about 1 cm H_2O, which is not seen on the release of [b]; this dip is probably due to the fact that the vocal folds are still wide apart, allowing a high airflow to occur. At this point in time the mouth and trachea are connected through a rather wide-open glottis; just before this, at the moment before the lips open, the mouth pressure and subglottal pressure are equal and there is no airflow out of the trachea; when the lips suddenly move apart a high flow occurs from the trachea but the relatively massive chest and lung tissues cannot move inward quickly enough to maintain the subglottal pressure, and this would cause the pressure to fall momentarily until the chest catches up and the glottis closes for voicing the vowel.

lack of first formant energy during the burst is believed to be due to sound absorption in the region of F1 by the trachea and lungs.

In the spectrogram for the phrase *a pie* in Figure 44, note that the F2 transitions associated with [p] are very similar to those associated with [b]. This reflects the fact that the movement of the lips is similar for the two consonants.

It is the control of the sound source of the pulsing state of voicing vs. complete silence and the strong, noise-like airflow on release that distinguishes the voiced from the unvoiced stop consonant. In the case of the voiced consonant, vocal fold pulsing continues for some time during the closure and the burst on the release is short and weak, whereas for the unvoiced consonant there is complete silence (no vocal fold pulsing) during the closure and the burst on release is strong, of longer duration, and the F1 energy does not appear until the beginning of the following vowel. In speech perception these consistent differences in sound pattern are used by listeners to perceive the voiced-voiceless distinction between stop consonants.

The alveolar stop consonants [d,t] are produced just like the labial stops [b,p] in that the actions of the vocal folds, the subglottal-mouth pressure effects, and the general form of constricting movements are the same. The vocal folds remain close together in a position for voicing during the occlusion of [d], as they do for [b]; for [t] the vocal folds are pulled open at the start of the occlusion and then brought back together during the opening transition, just as we saw for [p].

The subglottal pressure curve is also the same. The mouth pressure during the occlusion quickly rises to equal the subglottal pressure for [t] as for [p], but for [d] the mouth pressure rises more slowly, just as for [b], and does not reach equality with the subglottal pressure before the release of the occlusion occurs.

The form of the constriction movement is about the same for all of the stop consonants; transition from open to occluded and from occluded to open takes place in about 50 ms, and the duration of the occlusion is about 100 ms. The contact of the tongue with the palate covers a greater area and has a slightly longer duration for [t] than for [d]; the tongue contact of [t] extends backward somewhat from the alveolar ridge whereas [d] has a narrower region of contact along the ridge.

Now examine the sound patterns of [d] and [t] in the phrases *a dye* and *a tie* in the bottom row of Figure 44. In their source characteristics, the sound patterns of [d] and [t] are the same as the corresponding patterns of [b] and [p]. That is, for the voiced stops the periodic sound source operates throughout the consonant, as long as the transglottal pressure conditions permit, that is, as long as there is enough pressure drop across the glottis to cause vocal fold vibration. Sometimes the pressure drop is low and voicing stops (called de-voicing). On release of the voiced occlusion a weak and brief transient burst occurs, which sometimes produces a very brief, turbulent noise source. The transient excites the resonances of the oral tract and the brief noise burst may also exhibit these resonances.

For the unvoiced stops, the wide open state of the vocal folds does not permit periodic voicing. There is no sound source operating during the occlusion (complete silence), and then at the release there is a transient followed by strong noise from the turbulence at the narrowest part of the constriction as it is just opening. Because the vocal folds only begin to close after the release of the occlusion, there is a strong turbulent flow of air during most of the opening transition of the oral tract; the turbulent sources on releases of [t] operate for 40 ms or more and excite the resonances of the oral tract shape. Finally, when the vocal folds are sufficiently close together, voicing action can resume for the following vowel and voicing striations are seen in the spectrogram.[2]

All of these effects of the source conditions and the corresponding features in the sound patterns that differentiate voiced from unvoiced consonants are the same for all the stop consonants.

The difference in vocal fold adjustment for voiced vs. unvoiced stops is the main cause of the acoustic differences. However, there are other articulatory differences that also contribute to the voicing distinction. We have noted that the tongue contact extends farther back for [t] than for [d]. The duration of the closed interval is usually slightly longer for unvoiced stops than for voiced stops. In addition the larynx position is higher for unvoiced consonants than voiced consonants, which would tend to make the mouth pressure higher and to stretch the vocal folds to produce a slightly higher pitch in adjacent vowels. Furthermore a higher tension may consistently exist in one or more of the articulating factors of unvoiced stops and an enlargement of the mouth cavity may occur during the occlusions of voiced stops.[3]

---

[2]A detailed discussion of the acoustic factors in stop production is given by Fant (1973, Chapter 7). To summarize: the unvoiced bursts have three sound sources, transient, frication, and aspiration; frication is produced by turbulence at the consonant constriction; aspiration is produced by turbulence at the glottis. We may speculate that the aspirant turbulence is produced as the glottis becomes narrower during its closure toward the voicing position.

[3]Some linguists prefer the terms *lax* or *lenis* for voiced and *tense* or *fortis* for unvoiced, referring to evidence that the constrictions of unvoiced consonants are articulated with more force or tension than for the voiced consonants. This is true, but the present author believes this may be only a secondary, synergistic effect, necessary to contain the higher air pressure in the mouth that occurs on unvoiced consonants because of the wide-open posture of the vocal folds; the primary factor is believed to be the open or closed posture of the vocal folds as described in the text. However, the issue should not be considered closed: Malécot (1970) provides an interesting review and Slis (1975) proposes a neuromuscular theory of stop-voicing phenomena, which states that the acoustic features of unvoiced stops and tense (long) vowels are due to stronger neural commands to the articulators than for the voiced stops and lax (short) vowels.

The voicing contrast of stops is produced as just described in English and some other similar languages, such as German, Swedish, and Dutch. In some other languages, however, there are phonemic stop contrasts not used in English, such as pre-voiced and unaspirated unvoiced; these are produced by mechanisms of vocal fold adjustment, articulator tension, and timing coordination, which are different from those we have given. For an advanced discussion of some of the possible mechanisms, see Fujimura (1972).

The oral shape conditions and the corresponding formant patterns differ between stop consonants that are articulated at different locations in the oral tract, as we would expect. A main difference appears in the frequency transitions of F2. For the labial stops we saw that, other conditions being equal, F2 is lowered in frequency by the labial constriction. For the alveolar stops F2 is raised by the constriction. Further description of pattern differences related to place of articulation are given in Chapter 9.

In formal citation we can distinguish pairs of words like *weather* and *whether*, *witch* and *which*, although these contrasts are usually not well marked in informal speech. The second of each of these word pairs begins with a voiceless version of [w] that is symbolized as an upside-down w [ʍ]. The voiceless source of sound is produced by a wide-open glottis and a back constriction sufficient to generate a turbulent sound which is shaped in spectrum by a glide-like movement of the lips from constricted to open. During the glide transition to the following vowel the vocal folds move from the open position to a close position for voicing. In Figure 45 we can compare [w] and [ʍ] in the phrase *or whether the weather will change.* The sound spectrum at the first part of the noise phase of [ʍ] in *whether* is concentrated in the low frequencies, but as the lips begin to move toward a more open position the noise sound contains higher frequencies; this transition is similar to the opening transition of the [w] in *weather*.

PHYSIOLOGICAL STUDIES OF CONSONANT VOICING

The state of the vocal folds, held together for voiced or held apart for unvoiced, is a major factor in the voicing feature of consonants. How is this accomplished in speech production? Hirose and Gay (1972) studied the actions of the muscles in the larynx that control the position of the vocal folds. The activity of the vocal fold positioners was recorded from electrodes inserted in two muscles: 1) an abductor muscle that is anatomically arranged to pull the vocal folds apart, the posterior cricoarytenoid muscle (PCA), and 2) an adductor muscle that pulls the folds together, the inter-

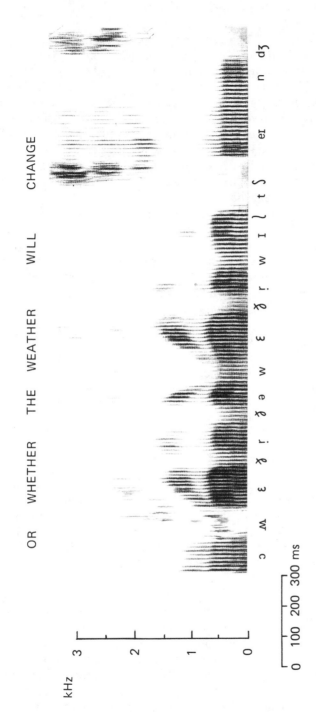

Figure 45. Spectrogram of the phrase *or whether the weather will change* to illustrate differences between unvoiced [ʍ] and voiced [w].

139

arytenoid muscle (IA). The subject spoke phrases that contrasted in the voicing of consonants, such as /əpʌp/, /əbʌp/, /əpɪb/. Each phrase was spoken a number of times and a computer was used to add up the muscle activity signals received from small electrodes in each muscle (averaged EMG activity). It was found that the adductor IA was active during vowel phonation and during voiced consonants but the abductor PCA was active during unvoiced consonants. Furthermore the IA and PCA tended to be reciprocal in action: as PCA activity increased to produce an unvoiced consonant, the IA activity decreased. Thus the abductor does not have to overcome the active tension of the adductor to pull the vocal folds apart for unvoicing the consonant.

Flanagan and his co-workers (Flanagan et al., 1976) studied the activity of PCA and IA together with the actual movements of the vocal folds. The glottal opening was observed and recorded by passing light from above the glottis to a photocell beneath. Very accurate time recordings of the glottal opening and the muscle actions that occurred upon speaking single phrases were made by digital recording. These revealed that, for an intervocalic unvoiced consonant, the abductor PCA muscle began activity 20 to 30 ms in advance of the glottal opening and continued to act while the glottis was open, until (at about 40 or 50 ms before the following vowel) the IA muscle activity began, starting to move the folds back together, and the PCA muscle ceased acting. This brief study indicates that the muscles controlling the vocal fold positions are very precisely activated in time to produce the voicing differences between consonants.

VOICED VS. UNVOICED FINAL CONSONANTS

When final consonants occur in a pre-boundary position, that is, immediately before the end of a word, phrase, or sentence where a pause may occur, the vowel preceding the consonant is considerably longer if the consonant is voiced than if it is unvoiced. The pre-boundary vowel lengthening effect of voicing the final consonant is large, being on the order of 50 to 100 ms. The effect is largest if the vowel is the last one in the utterance.

An illustration of these effects is given in Figure 46 showing spectrograms of the sentences *Take a cap in the cab* and *Take a cab on the Cap* (a peninsula on the French Riviera). Each sentence was spoken fluently without any pauses. The durations of the consonant constrictions and the preceding vowels are given in ms on the spectrograms. The vowel before the phrase boundary [b] in the second sentence is 220 ms in duration but the vowel before the phrase boundary [p] in the first sentence is only 170 ms, giving a lengthening effect of 50 ms due to the voiced consonant. For

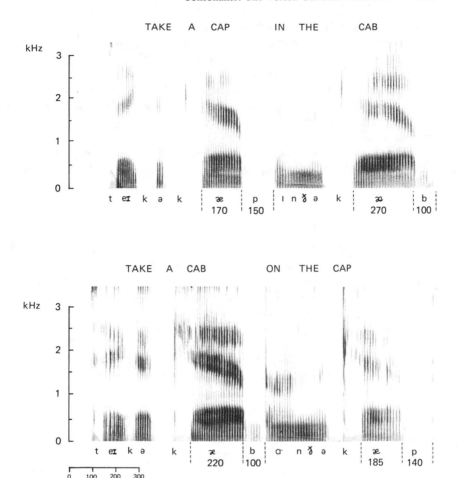

Figure 46.   Illustrating duration differences in vowels and consonants associated with the voiced/unvoiced stop features.

the utterance final vowels, the [æ] of *cab* in the first sentence and the [æ] of *Cap* in the second sentence, the lengthening is 85 ms, a very large durational difference.

The durations in the first and second sentences of Figure 46, including release bursts of the intervocalic [p] and [b], respectively, show a 50-ms shortening effect of voicing, a fairly large difference due to the phrase-final position of these consonants; it is equal to the amount of lengthening of the vowel preceding the voiced [b]. It is as if there is a tendency toward equal syllable length between *cap* and *cab,* and thus the

vowel duration of *cap* loses the amount gained by the following consonant. However this is not the case when the two syllables are final in the
utterance, where the shortening of consonant closure is 40 ms but the
vowel lengthening is much greater, 85 ms.

Vowels before syllable-final consonants that are not pre-boundary
also show a lengthening effect depending on voiced vs. unvoiced consonant, but it is a much smaller difference, being on the order of the difference in duration of closure.

The timing coordinations between the vocal folds and the upper articulators that produce the voicing effects have been described by Slis and
Cohen (1969) and Slis (1975).

VOICED AND UNVOICED FRICATIVES

The production of the voiced/unvoiced contrast in fricatives is very similar to that of the stops: the vocal folds are held wide apart during the constriction interval for unvoiced fricatives and close for voiced fricatives.

The vocal folds often vibrate during voiced fricative constrictions
and the resulting periodic modulation of the airflow can be seen in corresponding periodicity in the amplitude of the frication sound.

The characteristics of voiced and unvoiced fricatives are illustrated
in Figure 47 showing spectrograms of the clauses *the base of the bays* and
the bays at the base. Each clause contains two phrases, one of which is at
the end of the utterance with voiced [z] and unvoiced [s] in phrase-final
boundary positions. This allows us to compare the durations of the pre-
boundary sounds at both utterance positions as we just did for the stops
[b] and [p]. The durations of the fricative constriction intervals and preceding vowels are given on the spectrograms.

First it should be noted in Figure 47 that the vocal folds do not always
vibrate during the voiced fricative: the utterance-final [z] in the first
clause shows no little or no low frequency sound and no correlated periodicity in the higher frequencies, whereas the intervocalic [z] in the second
clause shows pronounced periodic low frequency sound and a considerable amount of periodicity in the middle and high frequencies of the turbulent frication. The mid- and high frequency periodicity is difficult to
discern because it is superimposed on the random amplitude fluctuations
of the turbulence; therefore the pulses of the low frequency sound have
been marked on the spectrogram at middle and high positions to make it
easier to look for the pulse correlations.

The durations of the constrictions and the preceding vowels show
strong effects of the consonant voicing, similar to those seen for the stops.
The lengthening of the vowel by the voicing of the following consonant is

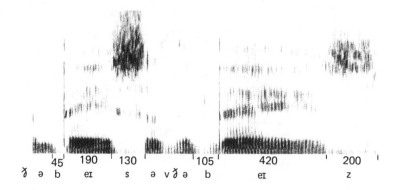

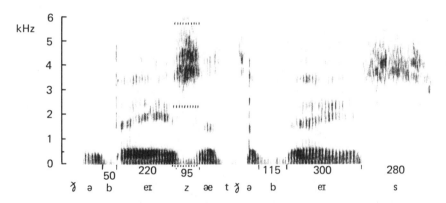

Figure 47.   Illustrating characteristics of voiced and unvoiced fricatives in different positions in utterance. Durations and frication-periodicity are indicated on the spectrograms.

120 ms in utterance-final position and 30 ms in the non-final but preboundary position. The shortening of the consonant constriction by voicing is 80 ms in utterance-final position and 35 ms in non-final. Lengthening of the syllables due to utterance-final position is very large: 330 ms longer than in non-final position for the syllable *base* and 360 ms longer for *bays*.

PHYSIOLOGICAL STUDIES OF FRICATIVE VOICING

In order for a long frication sound to be produced, as seen in fricatives, a continuing supply of high airflow is necessary. This tends to be incompatible with voicing phonation because the vocal folds are held together throughout the constriction, restricting the flow. Experimenters have studied this problem, measuring the air pressure behind the constriction and the degree of adduction of the vocal folds for stops and fricatives.

Table 5. Summary of the main features of the voiced/unvoiced contrast in stops and fricatives

Feature	Voiced stops	Voiced fricatives	Unvoiced stops	Unvoiced fricatives
Timing				
Preceding vowel	Long preceding vowel when in pre-boundary position	Long preceding vowel when in pre-boundary position	Shortened preceding vowel when in pre-boundary position	Shortened preceding vowel when in pre-boundary position
Constriction	Brief oral closure	Brief oral constriction	Longer oral closure	Longer oral constriction
Release	Brief release transient, 10–20 ms	No transient on release	Strong release transient and aspiration, 30–70 ms	No transient on release
Spectral				
Constriction	Very low frequency sound during closure, but this may be absent (de-voiced)	Very low frequency sound during constriction and correlated fluctuations in mid- and high frequency regions; these two features may be absent	Silence	Strong mid- and high frequency sound
Release	Weak transient on release of closure but no aspiration	No transient on release	Strong release transient; following oral resonances during aspiration showing formant transitions in F2 and F3	No transient on release

144

Comparing the amount of air pressure behind the constriction, it is highest for unvoiced stops and next highest for unvoiced fricatives, voiced fricatives, and voiced stops, in that order (Collier et al., in press). Thus the air pressure in the mouth is higher for voiced fricatives than for voiced stops; the higher pressure is probably necessary for the airflow for the friction sound. There is some evidence that the vocal folds are held more open during voiced fricatives than during voiced stops (Sawashima, 1968; Sawashima and Miyazaki, 1973). This would seem necessary to allow enough airflow to produce a frication sound. Sometimes there is no voicing during voiced fricatives; then the only contrast with unvoiced fricatives is durational shortening and weaker frication for the voiced fricative.

Collier et al. also studied the action of the muscles controlling the position of the vocal folds in voiced and unvoiced fricatives and stops in Dutch. They concluded that voicing was accompanied by less activity in the abductor muscles than the activity seen on unvoiced consonants, confirming the results for stops in English mentioned previously (Hirose and Gay, 1972). However, there was less activity in the adductor muscles (they pull and hold the folds together) on the fricatives than on the stops, indicating that the folds are positioned farther apart for fricatives than for stops, apparently to allow more airflow.

SUMMARY

The features of consonant voicing are summarized in Table 5.

CHAPTER 9

CONSONANTS: FEATURES OF PLACE OF ARTICULATION

CONTENTS

Up to this point in our study of the consonants we have covered the features that arise from the manner of articulation and the source of sound. In manner of articulation we have covered the features of glide, nasal, stop, and fricative manners, and in the source of sound we have covered voiced sources and unvoiced sources. A consonant may be articulated at any place in the vocal tract at which a constriction can be formed. Almost any manner or source can be employed with any place of constriction. Thus the possible patterns of the acoustic characteristics that result from these many different combinations are varied and can be somewhat complex. The major effects that have been found are described in this chapter.

The place of articulation affects the shape of the vocal tract, so we would expect that many of the differences between places of articulation will be seen in differences in the formant patterns. Furthermore, in forming consonant constrictions the vocal tract shape has to change from open to constricted at different places, causing transitions in the formant frequencies. Thus the place features of the consonants are associated with transitional changes in spectral patterns in contrast to the manner and source features, each of which is rather constant in spectral pattern and therefore characterized by sudden on-off changes in the gross features of the spectrum. However, the complete pattern of a speech sound depends on the source as well as its relation to the vocal tract shape. Some of these relations are discussed in this chapter: first, the transitions in the formants that are related to the distinction between labial place of articulation and alveolar place, then the ways in which the formant transitions for different places of stop consonants vary with different vowels, and finally the ways in which different places of articulation of the fricative consonants result in different spectrum patterns of the frication sound.

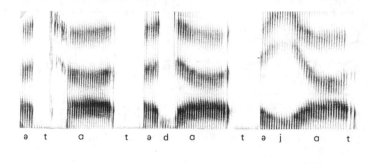

ə   t   ɑ   t   ə   d   ɑ   t   ə   j   ɑ   t

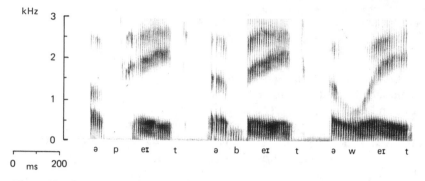

kHz 3
     2
     1
     0
0 ms 200

ə   p   eɪ   t   ə   b   eɪ   t   ə   w   eɪ   t

Figure 48.   Spectrograms for comparing initial alveolar and labial stops and glides. Note that alveolar vs. labial place are differentiated by the direction of transition in F2.

FORMANT TRANSITIONS OF ALVEOLAR VS. LABIAL CONSONANTS

It will be recalled from Chapter 3 that alveolar constrictions cause F2 frequency to rise and labial constrictions cause F2 frequency to fall, and the frequency change of F2 is dependent on the amount of constriction. When an alveolar consonant is articulated the closing movement goes from open to more constricted and the opening movement goes from constricted to more open. Therefore, with an alveolar consonant we would expect that F2 frequency would rise in frequency during the closing movement and fall in frequency during the opening movement, and for a labial consonant F2 frequency would rise during the opening movement and fall during the closing movement. These effects are illustrated in Figure 48, showing spectrograms of the alveolar stops and a glide in the phrases *a pate, abate, await*. These phrases were selected so that a neutral vowel precedes each consonant; note that the F2 frequency of this vowel rises during the closing movement to the alveolar consonants in the top row of the figure but F2 falls before the labial consonants in the bottom half of the figure. Upon the opening to the vowel following the consonants, F2 falls in frequency after the alveolar consonants in the top row and in the bottom row F2 rises toward the following vowel upon the opening movement from the labial consonants. It will also be noticed that the F3 frequency tends to parallel the transitions in F2 frequency. Comparing the unvoiced stops with the voiced stops, it can be seen that the transition in F2 frequency is visible during the aspiration period of the release burst of the unvoiced stops.

CONSONANT PLACE: TRANSITIONS WITH DIFFERENT VOWELS

As we have seen, the distinction between labial and alveolar place of articulation is very simply indicated by the direction of transition of the second formant. However, when we consider vowels other than the [ɑ] and [eɪ] combined with all three places of stop articulation—labial, alveolar, and velar—the distinctions become more complex. We can best appreciate these differences by examining some further illustrations. In the spectrograms of Figure 49, the consonants [b], [d], and [g] are combined with three front vowels [i], [ɛ], and [æ], and the transitions of F1, F2, and F3 have been traced. For the labial and dental stops the F2 transitions differ in direction with the vowels [i], [ɛ], and [æ], in the same way that they did with the [ɑ] of the previous figure, namely, that the direction of transition of F2 on opening is upward for the labials and downward for the alveolars. On the other hand, with the velar stop [g] the transition of F2 is also downward on the opening of the consonant as it was for the alveolar stop. Here we must examine F3 to see a definite difference. The F3 opening transition from [g] tends to be divergent from the F2 transition instead of parallel to it, as it was for the alveolar stop. This is especially noticeable in the lower row of Figure 49 on the vowels [ɛ] and [æ]. On the [ɛ] initially, the F3 transition is flat and then rising toward the middle of the vowel to give a divergent pattern.

It can also be seen in Figure 49 that the release burst varies between [b], [d], and [g] in such a way as to be a differentiating factor among the three places of articulation. Examine carefully the release bursts for their frequency extents and frequency locations. It will be seen that the labial bursts cover a fairly wide frequency band from about 1500 Hz upward, but that they are very weak, consisting only of a transient without any aspiration at all. The release bursts of [d] on the other hand are much stronger and, following the release transient, they have strong energy, which is located in a range above 2000 Hz. Finally, for [g] the release bursts are rather strong, but the strongest energy in them is located at about 2000 Hz and is not spread out as much as it is for the alveolar [d]. Thus, comparing the spectra, the labial burst is diffuse and weak, the alveolar burst is diffuse and strong, and the velar burst is compact and strong.

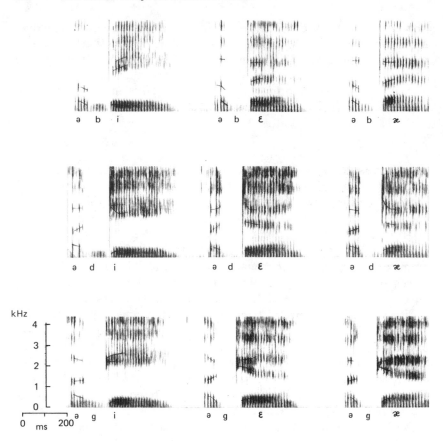

Figure 49. Spectrograms for comparing initial labial, alveolar, and velar voiced stops followed by front vowels. Note that velar place is distinguished from alveolar by an F3 transition that is divergent from the F2 transition and by release transients that are very compact in spectrum.

The same stop consonants are combined with back vowels in Figure 50. The F2 transitions exhibit the same difference between [b] and [d] as they did with the front vowels, namely, that for the labial [b] the F2 closing transition is downward in frequency and the F2 opening transition is upward in frequency, whereas for the alveolar [d] the situation is just the opposite, the closing F2 transition is upward in frequency and the opening F2 transition is downward. The frequency of F3 can be seen to move more or less in parallel with F2 for the alveolar consonant [d]. For the velar consonant [g] the F2 transitions are similar to those for [d], with the opening transition downward in frequency and the closing transition upward. The frequency of F3 upon the opening transition is either constant or diverging upward from the F2 transition. The consonant release bursts before

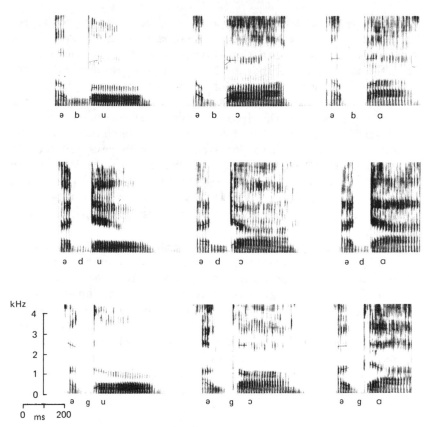

Figure 50. Spectrograms comparing initial labial, alveolar, and velar voiced stops followed by back vowels. Here velar place is distinguished by flat or upward F3 transitions and very strongly resonant transients.

the back vowels show a similar difference between [b] and [d] to that seen with front vowels, that is, the [b] bursts are weak and the [d] bursts are strong in energy at F2 and above. However, the [g] bursts are not compact in frequency as with the front vowels; they show downward F2 opening transitions from low F2 starting positions because of the back constriction. The F2 starting position is strongly resonant in the release burst; in contrast, the [b] bursts do not show the low F2 starting frequency at all. Comparing the F2 bursts and the starting F2s between [d] and [g], it is seen that, for the same vowel, the F2 starting position is much lower in frequency for [g] than it is for [d].

These features of place of voiced stops are also seen in unvoiced stops, but the opening F2 transitions take place largely during the long aspiration intervals of the release bursts.

Fant (1973) has described the production factors leading to the spectral differences at the release of stop consonants depending on different places of consonant constriction. Immediately after the opening transient, the airflow relieving the mouth pressure passes through the still narrow constriction, generating a frication turbulence noise. The size and shape of the cavity in front of this noise source determine the spectrum pattern of the frication. The alveolar [t] and [d] have a small front cavity, which acts as a high pass filter and concentrates the transmitted turbulence energy in the higher frequencies compared with the case for the velar constrictions for [k] and [g], which have a larger cavity in front of the constriction and thus have a main concentration of energy in the burst at a lower frequency. The [p] and [b] consonants have no front cavity in front of the release point and this causes a diffuse spectrum in the release frication.

After the opening movement has proceeded far enough, the constriction no longer produces a sound source and then the source shifts to the glottis. For unvoiced consonants an aspirant source is generated by the airflow through the still open glottis; the resultant aspiration phase shows formants determined by the shape of the oral-pharyngeal tract, at first without F1 because of the open glottis. For voiced consonants the release frication, which is generally weaker because of the lower air pressure in the mouth, is followed by voicing phonation.

The glottal stop [ʔ] is made at the back-most place of articulation and should show the oral formant structure in its release burst.

PLACE FEATURES OF NASAL CONSONANTS

In the nasal murmur that occurs during the oral occlusion intervals of [m, n, ŋ] the spectrum pattern is determined mainly by the sound transmission of the pharyngeal-nasal tract, secondarily affected by the closed oral cavity. The oral cavity may now be viewed as a side branch of different lengths depending on the place of occlusion. The length of the oral side branch is greatest for [m], shorter for [n], the shortest for [ŋ]; this length affects the frequency of an antiresonance (zero) in the transmission of the pharyngeal-nasal tract, which consequently affects the spectrum of the murmur. The frequency of the zero tends to be inversely related to the length of the oral side branch and is at about 800 Hz for [m], 1500–2000 Hz for [n], and about 5000 Hz or above for [ŋ]. The murmur spectrum is strong in amplitude below about 500 Hz and relatively weak above 500 Hz. Thus the differences in murmur features, mainly the location of the zero corresponding to nasal place of articulation, are not very prominent. The formant transitions in adjacent vowels are considered to be more distinctive than the differences in murmur spectrum (Fant, 1960; Fujimura, 1962; House, 1957; Malécot, 1956).

The formant transitions of the nasal consonants would be similar to those of the stops articulated at the same place, except for the fact that nasalization occurs in the intervals preceding and following nasal consonants. As explained in Chapter 7, this nasalization inserts variable zeroes, in the transmission of the oral tract, in the region of F1 and F2. This greatly complicates the description of the formant transitions, but consistent place differences in the transitional spectra must exist because listeners were found to correctly identify these transitions as [m, n] or [ŋ] (Malécot, 1956, Table 5).

PLACE FEATURES OF FRICATIVE CONSONANTS

It will be recalled that the fricative sounds are produced by forming a constriction through which the strong airflow becomes turbulent and produces a random, noise-like sound; this frication sound has random fluctuations in amplitude and covers a broad range of frequencies (like a white noise). This is the source sound for fricatives. The place at which the constriction is formed and the shape and size of the front cavity between the constriction and the air outside the lips have a frequency-filtering effect on the source sound in much the same way that vowel shape acts as a filter to form the vowel spectra from the source sound produced by the glottis. The back cavity, behind the constriction, does not strongly affect the fricative spectrum.

One general filtering rule that determines the spectra of the different fricative sounds is that the low frequency resonances of the shaping cavity are at frequencies inversely related to the size of the cavity (Heinz and Stevens, 1961). These lower resonances are the strongest fricative resonances. Figure 51 illustrates this principle with a spectrogram of a specially chosen phrase (spoken by an adult male) that includes all of the unvoiced fricative consonants followed by a back vowel; the phrase is *How Shaw saw it thaw for him.* For the first fricative in the phrase, [h], the sound source is at the glottis and thus the front cavity is the largest of the five fricatives. In the spectrogram the frequency location of the strongest part of the fricative sound has been marked with brackets. Notice that, as the front cavity becomes smaller, that is, as we go from the largest [h] to [ʃ] to [s] to [θ] to [f], the position of the strongest resonances moves upward in frequency. The strongest resonances are in a region around 1 kHz for [h], 3 kHz for [ʃ], 4 kHz for [s], 5 kHz for [θ], and a range from about 4½ to 7 kHz for [f]. The [f] sound also has weak low frequency turbulences that extend all the way down to about 1 kHz as indicated by the first

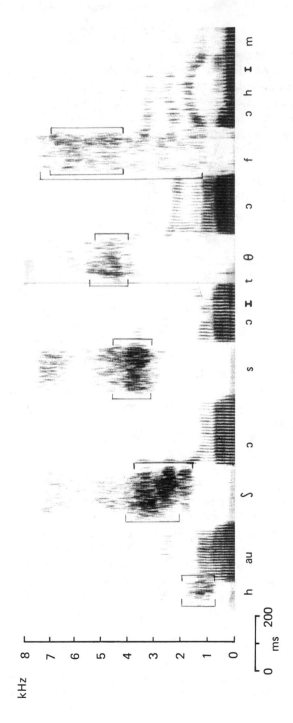

Figure 51. Spectrogram of a special phrase having a series of fricative consonants going from large to small front cavity. The main resonant frequencies of the fricatives are bracketed and are seen to rise in frequency as the front cavity becomes smaller and smaller.

154

left-hand bracket in the spectrogram next to [f]. For female and child speakers the sequence from lowest to highest resonances is shifted upward because of the smaller size of the oral tract.

The spectrum pattern of the [h] sound varies because of two factors. First, the vowel shape to follow the [h] is beginning to be formed before the production of the frication; this shape will change for different vowels and thus affect the spectrum of the [h]. Second, for the close front vowels the source of the [h] turbulence may be at a velar or upper pharyngeal location rather than low in the pharynx or at the glottis. Then the cavity in front will be rather small and the intense part of the frequency spectrum will be located in the region of F2 and F3 of the following vowel, which will be at a much higher location than for the [h] before [a] seen in Figure 51.

In the last syllable of the phrase in the spectrogram (Figure 51), a "voiced [h]" is seen at the beginning of the *him*. This sound appears to be completely voiced at a very low frequency and the F1 and F2 resonances are like those of the following [ɪ]. However, the formants appear to be excited irregularly compared with the vowel. This is probably because the glottis is held only partially closed for the voiced [h] instead of completely closed as for a vowel.

The different voiced fricative consonants, [ʒ, z, v, ð] and voiced [h] are produced at similar locations to the unvoiced ones that we have just discussed and, therefore, their frequency spectra are also governed by the size of cavity in front of the constriction. The friction sounds of voiced fricatives are usually somewhat weaker in intensity than in the unvoiced fricatives because the vocal folds are held closer to a voicing position and the total airflow available for producing turbulence at the constriction is therefore lower than for the unvoiced fricatives, where the vocal folds are held wide apart.

SUMMARY

A summary of the main acoustic features of the places of consonant articulation is given in Table 6.

Table 6. Summary of spectral features corresponding to place of consonant articulation[a]

Consonant class	Place of articulation						
	Labial	Dental	Alveolar	Palatal	Velar	Pharyngeal	Glottal
Glide Constriction/vowel transition	[w] Low F2/upward F2		[j] High F2/downward F2	[j]			
Voiced stop Transient/vowel transition	[b] Diffuse, weak/upward F2		[d] Diffuse, high frequency/downward F2		[g] Compact mid-frequency/diverging F2 and F3		[ʔ] Transient formants same as following vowel
Unvoiced stop Transient/frication-aspiration	[p] Diffuse/upward F2		[t] Strong, high frequency/downward F2		[k] Strong, compact, mid-frequency/diverging F2 and F3		
Nasals Murmur/vowel transition	[m] Zero c. 800 Hz/nasalized upward F2		[n] Midfrequency zero/nasalized downward F2		[ŋ] High frequency zero/nasalized diverging F2 and F3		
Fricatives Frication (strong for unvoiced, weaker for voiced)/vowel transitions	[v, f] Diffuse spectrum, strongest around 5–7 kHz/upward F2	[ð, θ] Diffuse spectrum strongest in frequencies around 5 kHz and above/downward F2	[z, s] Strong spectrum at 4 kHz and above/often no vowel transitions	[ʒ, ʃ] Strong spectrum at 3 kHz and above/often no vowel transitions		[h] Weak spectrum, 1 kHz and above having formants of following vowel/no vowel transitions	

[a]All transitional features are considered only as seen on consonant release. Two phases of each consonant type are described, separated by a slash. For example, for the glide type the two phases are the constriction and the following transition into the vowel, characterized for [w] by low F2 frequency and upward transition of F2, respectively.

CHAPTER 10

THE FLOW OF SPEECH

CONTENTS

> I do not believe that a division of the flow of speech...has the slightest justification...
>
> E. W. Scripture, 1902

This chapter is about the flow of speech. We have already seen how consonants and vowels flow into each other in the transitions. Now we look briefly at further types of interaction in the flow of articulations and we also examine some properties of fluent speech.[1]

Speech articulations typically overlap each other in time, causing the sound patterns to be in transition much of the time. The vowel formants are usually in transition on the way to or from the midvowel positions. The bursts of noise of consonants also show changes in spectrum under the influence of adjacent articulations. As an example, examine the spectrograms of the sentence in Figure 52: *The branch droops and strikes the steel track.* First note in the top spectrogram that the second formants of the vowels are almost always in transition; F2 rarely stands still. The first formant also moves up and down because of the consonant constrictions,

---

[1]The smooth flow and coordination of the articulatory movements of speech are so basic to its production that the author is not happy to relegate this topic to the last production aspect to be discussed. Nine chapters have taken speech apart and now this one tries to put it back together again. This can be done only to a small extent, not because of the deficiencies in acoustic science, but because the basic knowledge of exactly how speech movements are organized is not highly developed and thus we are not able easily to relate the speech movement flow to the acoustic flow. Some researchers are concentrating on this problem (see Harris, 1977; Lindblom et al., 1977; MacNeilage, 1970) and at some future time it will be possible to organize acoustic phonetics properly, from the movement flow as a basis. This approach would be more natural, should be more comprehensive, and it could simplify explanations of how spoken messages are perceived and understood (see the following chapter). In the meantime, rather than wait for a complete motor theory of speech production, great progress can be made, as in the past 50 years, using the analytic concepts of acoustics and linguistics. These concepts presently work best when things are held still to study the segmental spectral patterns, which are then seen to change with the flow. If we could begin with the flow, then transitions and so-called coarticulatory effects would be the primary patterns, not the fixed vocal tract shapes with which we began our study of vowels in Chapter 3.

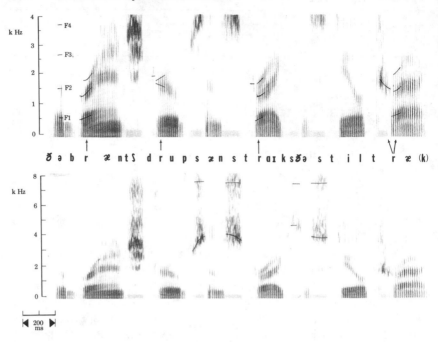

Figure 52.   Spectrograms of *The branch droops and strikes the steel track,* illustrating effects of coarticulation on the spectra of [r] sounds (top spectrogram) and [s] sounds (bottom spectrogram). The [r] sounds are strongly influenced by the following vowel, as can be seen from the lines tracing the indicated formants. In the bottom spectrogram the main resonances of the [s] sounds have been traced and it will be seen that the sound following [s] had a large effect on this resonance.

and to different positions for the vowels. The third formant goes through extensive changes on the [r] sounds, where the formants are traced with lines in the top spectrogram. All of the [r] sounds begin with F3 at a very low position, about 1.6 to 1.8 kHz, with the following [u] and [ɑ] causing lower starting frequencies for F3 than the [æ]. The F3 transitions are all upward toward the normal F3 position of about 2.5 kHz. The starting position of F2 in [r] varies greatly with the following F2 position for the vowel. These are coarticulatory effects on the spectrum patterns of [r].

The [s] sounds in Figure 52 are more fully displayed in the lower spectrogram where the frequency range is extended to 8 kHz. The main resonances of the [s]'s are traced with lines. The upper resonances, above about 5 kHz, are relatively steady in frequency, but there are frequency transitions in the lower resonances. The [s] in *droops* has a large upward transition in its lower resonance. The transition is rapid in the first 50 ms and goes from 2.9 to 3.8 kHz; this transition occurs because the [s] begins while the lips are still only partly open in transition from the [p] position, and thus the [s] cavity is strongly rounded but rapidly becoming less rounded as the lips open rapidly over a period of about 50 ms. The first [s] in *strikes* is influenced by the following [t] and [r] articulations and has a downward transition from 3.9 to 3.6 kHz; the second [s] has a steady resonance at 4.5 kHz. The [s] in *steel* has a steady low resonance at 3.75 kHz.

COARTICULATION

Coarticulation is the term used to refer to the influences of the articulation of one sound on the articulation of other sounds in the same utterance. For a further example compare the spoken words *seep* and *sweep*, in Figure 53. In *seep* the [s] has very little sound energy below 3.5 kHz but in *cosweep* the [s] energy extends down to about 2 kHz. This is because of the coarticulation of [w] with [s]; the [w] is formed by close rounding of the lips and the rounding begins during the [s] in anticipation of the [w]. Lip-rounding lowers the resonance of the mouth cavity in front of the [s] constriction and causes more low frequencies in the source sound to be transmitted out of the mouth than in *seep*, where the lip open area during the [s] is larger and the mouth cavity in front of the [s] constriction is more open. In fact a careful look at the [s] in *sweep* shows that for the first 50 ms it was nearly the same as in *seep*, with a main resonance at about 3.7 kHz vs. 4.0 kHz for *seep*; however, during the last 60 ms the low frequency resonance of the [s] in *sweep* moves downward about 500 Hz under the influence of the coarticulation with [w].

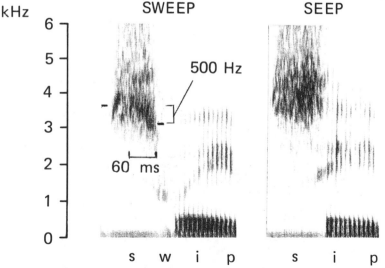

Figure 53.   Spectrogram of the coarticulatory effect on the [s] spectrum of anticipatory lip-rounding for the following [w] in *sweep* for comparison with the [s] in *seep*. The lip-rounding causes a 60-ms lowering of about 500 Hz in the frequency of the lower [s] resonances.

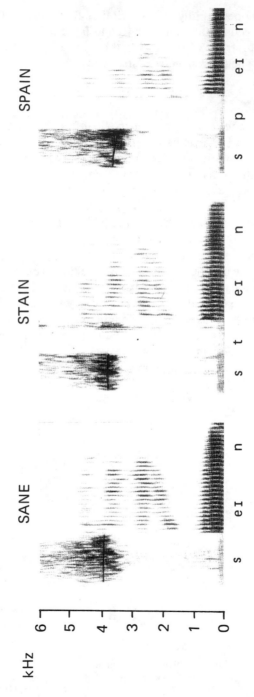

Figure 54. Spectrograms of *sane*, *stain*, and *Spain* for comparing the effects of following sounds on the spectrum of [s] in initial position. The center of the lower resonance of [s] has been marked; it is about the same in *sane* and *stain*, but has a downward transition before the [p] of *Spain*.

160

A similar effect is seen with other labial consonants. Compare the [s] sounds in the words *sane, stain,* and *Spain* in Figure 54. In *sane* and *stain* the [s] sounds are limited to frequencies above about 3.5 kHz, but in *Spain* the low frequency edge of [s] sweeps downward just before the [p] closure, as the lips move rapidly together. The effect is similar to the effect of [w] on [s].

Coarticulation also affects final consonants, as can be seen in Figure 55, where we compare the words *cease, seats,* and *seeps.* In the final [s] of *seeps* a coarticulation effect is seen because of the preceding articulation of [p]. The [s] constriction is prepared during the interval when the lips are closed; when they start to open, the [s] sound begins, but because of the initial presence of lip constriction, the [s] energy begins with a spectrum pattern extending much lower in frequency than in *cease* or *seats.* As the lips open farther the low frequency edge of [s] moves upward for about 40 ms until, for the final 120 ms, it has about the same spectrum as the other final [s]'s.

These are examples of the coarticulation of two adjacent consonants. In the preceding chapter we saw how the place of articulation of a consonant affects the formant transitions of the adjacent vowels. There are also some coarticulation effects between a consonant and the preceding vowel. In other words, coarticulation is the rule in speech production; sounds unaffected by adjacent ones are exceptions.

How does coarticulation take place? Obviously, the movements of tongue and lips are free to overlap in time, but also the tongue articulation for a vowel-consonant-vowel sequence can vary depending on the positions that the tongue must attain, the "target" positions, of the vowels and consonants. Let us examine some explanations of how articulations might interact.

There are two main factors behind coarticulatory effects: 1) the specific vocal tract shapes to be attained and 2) the motor program for performing the sequence of speech units: consonants, vowels, syllables, and phrases.

One major aspect of speech motor programs seems to be that they are anticipatory. That is, the movements for a sequence of sounds, syllables, and words seem to be pre-planned so that earlier parts of the utterance are affected by what is soon to come. This was seen earlier in Chapter 5 on prosodic features, where the evidence on consonant and vowel duration shows that these durations are shortened depending on the number of elements to follow within each hierarchical subunit of the utterance: consonant cluster, syllable, word, or phrase. In a sense, this anticipatory procedure might be expected to be a good way to program a sequence for communicative effectiveness, given the breath group structure of speech.

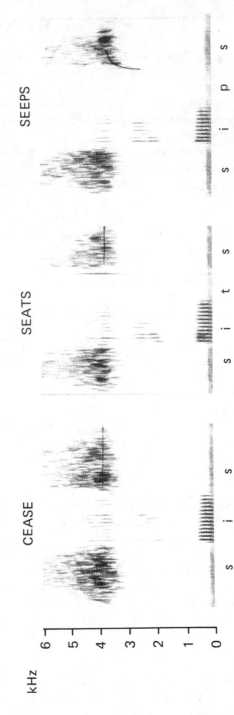

Figure 55. Spectrograms of *cease*, *seats*, and *seeps* for comparing the effects of preceding sounds on the spectrum of [s] in final position. The center of the lower resonance has been traced on the final [s]'s; it is about the same for *cease* and *seats*, but has a large upward transition after the [p] in *seeps*.

If there were no tailoring of early items depending on the number of items to follow, given the limited breath expenditure available before another breath must be taken, then it would frequently happen that proper phrasing and flow of utterance would have to be interrupted. An arbitrary interruption would disturb intonation contours and lead to misinterpretation by the listener of grammatical, and even phonemic, structures. Alternatively, if there were no tailoring of early items, the later items would have to be crowded in and spoken too rapidly for clarity.

A general theory of motor programming has been suggested by Lindblom et al. (1977), based on a previous principle derived by Klatt (1973, 1976). The theory is called the short-term memory (STM) model. The model proposes that there is a short-term storage of the final instructions for speech movements; the contents of the storage are continually changing as instructions leave the store to discharge the actual movements, and new instructions enter for later discharge in proper sequence. The size of the store is limited; because of this there must be economy of storage space and thus every segment in store may be compressed in duration whenever a new segment is entered. However, there is a limit on this compressibility because of the time required for effective target reaching of articulations and the transition times between targets; for example, the gestures for stop consonants must reach full occlusion to produce audible stop-gaps and release bursts; the gestures for fricatives must reach a close constriction before an audible turbulence can be generated.

Consequences of the limits on compressibility are that the vowels and consonants of early monosyllabic words are shortened more in anticipation of increased numbers of later segments than are the segments of early bisyllabic words; similarly early trisyllabic words suffer less shortening than bisyllabic words. This is because storage is in terms of numbers of syllables and less of the limited capacity is necessary for a word with fewer syllables. There is continual readjustment for economizing the allotted storage space depending on the number of phonemes, syllables, words, and phrases in the sentence.

The STM model for motor programming accounts quantitatively for the general amounts of shortening seen and its limits. However, the final segments of an utterance are generally less subject to shortening than earlier segments, suggesting that the earlier segments, which will soon be played out of storage, can sacrifice more space to those on their way in. This is another example of the operation of the anticipation principle. Further studies are needed to measure this effect and incorporate it in the theory.

As mentioned in Chapter 1, the most fundamental unit of speech seems to be the syllable. On the articulatory side, the syllable is produced by the alternation between open and constricted phases of the upper vocal tract. If the syllable is basic to articulation, then the effects of coarticulation would be secondary ones, explainable in terms of the organization of the syllable (Stetson, 1928, 1951). In other words, all the coarticulatory influences of a consonant on nearby consonants and vowels would depend on the particular way in which that consonant gesture and constriction must be carried out as dictated by the organization of the syllable cycle in which it functions as a constriction.

Kozhevnikov and Chistovich (1965) adopted the syllable as a unit for speech production studies of coarticulatory effects within and between syllables (1965, pp. 123–142) and as a basis for a motor theory of speech perception (see Chapter 12). A syllabic view of the organization of speech is currently being developed as a method for synthesizing speech by computer at the Haskins Laboratories (Mattingly, 1977).

A recent study of coarticulation of the consonant and vowel movements of the tongue has indicated that the syllabic length unit of motor organization is a consonant-vowel unit (Gay, 1977). The movements of the tongue were studied by making x-ray motion pictures. It was found that the anticipatory tongue movements for the second vowel of a VCV sequence never began until the consonant closure had been attained. Also substantial movement toward the second vowel target occurred during the consonant occlusion and this had a large effect on the position and shape of the tongue upon release of the occlusion. On the other hand the vowel preceding the consonant had little effect on the position of the tongue at the moment of closure. In other words there seems to be a great deal of coarticulation between consonant and following vowel as a unit and little or no carryover coarticulation of a vowel on a following consonant. What the vowel that follows a consonant is going to be has a large effect and what the consonant is going to be has an effect on a preceding vowel, but what the last vowel was has little effect on the coming consonant. Another way of putting it is that the timing of anticipatory adjustments is geared to start the adjustments mainly during consonant constrictions. Thus the programming for syllables seems to go in simple CV units. Further confirmation of this finding would establish a very important principle.

EFFECTS OF RATE OF UTTERANCE

The speed of speaking is another important aspect of the flow of speech. Speed of articulation can vary greatly depending on the different styles and dialects of different speakers. Furthermore, a given speaker may articulate very rapidly if he is in a hurry and his message is more or less redundant to the situation.

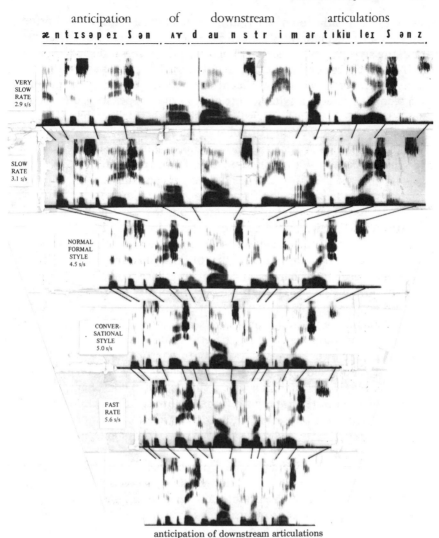

anticipation of downstream articulations

Figure 56.   Spectrograms showing the compression in time of the phrase *anticipation of downstream articulations* spoken fluently at different rates. The rates are given in syllables per second (s/s). The lines between spectrograms connect equivalent points in the stream of each utterance, to illustrate the amount of compression.

These variations in rate of articulation cause appropriate compression or expansion in time of the sound patterns. Examples are shown in the spectrograms of Figure 56. The author spoke the phrase *anticipation of downstream articulations* at six different rates of fluent utterance. The slowest rate is in the top of the figure and the fastest rate is at the bottom, with the intermediate rates ranged in order in between. For the slowest rate, the style was exceedingly deliberate, with each word spoken almost as if isolated from the adjacent words, but without pauses and with words joined in a normal-feeling and fluent manner; 13 syllables were spoken in 4.5 seconds, yielding a syllable rate of 2.9 syllables per second (s/s). The next slower rate was a little faster but still rather deliberately slow (3.1 s/s). The next rate was the formal style rate of this talker (4.5 s/s). The fourth rate was normal conversational (5.0 s/s); this rate is based on only 12 syllables because of the omission of the [ə] vowel in the "-tion" syllable of *anticipation.* The fifth rate was fast conversational (5.6 s/s). The fastest rate was judged to be the fastest clear articulation possible (6.7 s/s).

First note that the change in rate from the most deliberate to the "fastest clear" articulation is rather large, a factor of 2.3:1. What segments have shortened to achieve this compression? It might be expected that, since consonant movements must often attain a specific occlusion or narrow constriction, changes in rate of utterance would tend to be absorbed more by the vowels than the consonants.

To answer this for the utterances of Figure 56, the durations of all of the consonant constrictions and vowels were measured and the percentages of compression were calculated between different pairs of rates. Going from the slowest to normal rate, both consonants and vowels were compressed 33% and this did not change greatly depending on the class of long vs. short vowel or occlusive vs. nonocclusive consonant. Between normal and the fastest rate, however, the vowels were compressed 50% but the consonants only 26%; the short vowels were compressed more than the long (64% vs. 43%) and the occlusive consonants more than the nonocclusive (36% vs. 26%).

One type of consonant compression occurs between consonants that are adjacent across a boundary between two syllables within the same breath group. Examples are double consonants, like the *pp* in *top pole,* and abutting different consonants, such as *pk* in *dropkick, dp* in *tadpole,* and *dk* in *sidekick.* At slow and moderate rates of utterance, the two consonants can be articulated separately, although the first consonant may not be released before the following one reaches occlusion. At faster rates of utterance the articulation of the first consonant advances more into the following one, and at a very fast rate there remains only the single consonant at the beginning of the second syllable.

Stetson (1928, 1951) demonstrated this effect in an extensive series of articulatory recordings. He measured the durations of double (e.g., *pp*) and abutting (e.g., *pk*) consonants, and the durations of their syllables, under different rates of utterance. The rate was varied by two methods:

1) by speaking slowly and then gradually faster in successive repetitions of the test words and 2) by speaking normally but with some of the syllables stressed and others unstressed. A typical slow rate was 2.5 syllables per second (s/s) with a corresponding syllable length of 400 ms: at this rate both consonants were articulated as two separate consonants but with no release of occlusion between. When the rate was increased, at a mean rate of 4 s/s (250-ms syllables) the majority of these consonants had become single, the first member of the pair having been absorbed into the second (Stetson, 1951, Figure 51, p. 69).

The same type of "singling" of double consonants across the syllable boundary also occurred for unstressed syllables in which a final consonant was prescribed and a following heavily stressed syllable absorbed the previous final consonant into its own initial consonant; the majority of these unstressed syllables were 250 ms in duration; that is, they occurred at a momentary rate of 4 s/s (Stetson, 1951, Figure 109, p. 117); this was the same rate at which singling occurred when caused by gradually increasing the rate of utterance of a series of syllables with equal stresses. The normal rate of prescribed single-consonant syllables had a mean of about 5 s/s, compared with the slowest "singles from doubles" of 3.5 s/s (1951, Figure 110, p. 118).

The occlusion durations of single consonants were typically 100 to 140 ms (Stetson, 1951, p. 63). The occlusion durations of the double consonants had a mean of 200 ms for same-member articulation, e.g., *pp, dt,* but only 150 ms for two-member articulations, such as *dp, bd,* where the consonant movements can overlap (1951, Figure 65, p. 78). Thus the two consonants were similar in timing to two overlapped single consonants with the degree of overlap being greater when it was possible anatomically.

SUMMARY

The articulations of speech overlap each other and this causes the formant patterns to be in transition much of the time. The spectrum patterns of consonants are affected by anticipatory adjustments for the following consonant or vowel. These phenomena are called coarticulation. The motor program for performing a sequence of sounds, syllables, and words appears to anticipate the number of remaining units to be performed and shortens the just-to-be performed in proportion to that number, but retaining the reachability of the consonant constrictions and the identifiability of the stressed syllables.

Studies of the movements of the tongue between coarticulated consonant and vowel suggest that the syllable unit of coarticulation is consonant-vowel (rather than vowel-consonant) because the anticipatory movement for a vowel does not begin until the consonant occlusion has been attained.

Rapid rates of utterance cause more overlap of articulations and a consequent shortening (compression) of the durations of consonants and vowels. Very fast utterance appears to shorten the vowels more than the consonants, perhaps because the consonants must attain constriction positions that are sufficient to produce noticeable spectral discontinuities.

CHAPTER 11

ACOUSTIC CUES
IN SPEECH PERCEPTION

CONTENTS

Up to this point we have studied how phonation and articulatory movements produce a flow of sound patterns. These patterns communicate with listeners. Thus the final link in the speech chain is a perceptual process leading to a representation of the speaker's message in the listener. How does the listener decode the stream of speech sound to reconstruct the speaker's message? What aspects of the sound flow are the important ones?[1]

---

[1]The acoustic study of speech perception began early in the nineteenth century with Willis' (1829) and Helmholtz's (1859) studies of vowel sounds; it was further nurtured by other physiologists and by physiologically oriented phoneticians; note, e.g., Alexander Graham Bell's physiological modeling approach to designing an efficient telephone in the 1870s (Bruce, 1973); Hermann's (1894) definition of vowel formants and their independence of voice pitch. During the first half of our century there was much further progress, particularly at Bell Laboratories (formerly Bell Telephone Laboratories), and now this problem has gained the experimental attention of a large "speech community" consisting of specialized scientists and engineers working in more than 50 laboratories around the world.

Much of this research has been motivated by needs of the voice communication industry and by military requirements. If we knew how to send only the essentials needed for correct perception of speech, the channel capacity needed would be about 20 times less than the capacity of a telephone line. In other words, 20 conversations could be encoded on each line.

In addition, many linguists, phoneticians, and psychologists have studied speech perception just to find out more about how speech works; the history indicates that this basic approach was a very efficient way to advance voice communication technology—for example, linguistic principles (Jakobson et al., 1967) have been extremely important in guiding the engineering studies that led to the current high level of speech technology.

continued

Some of the speech perception research that has attempted to answer these questions is described in this chapter. A full coverage of speech perception is not intended. There is a vast literature of studies. A personal selection, along historical lines, has been made to illustrate some of the important problems, the ingenious methods used to study them, and the resulting facts about speech perception. These studies led to some surprising theories of speech perception, which are discussed in the next chapter.

CUES FOR PERCEIVING SPEECH

In research on speech perception the basic problem is to discover which aspects of the sound pattern are the essential ones, the ones used by listeners to identify a given unit of speech. The essential stimulus patterns in perception are called *cues*. Speech cues are the necessary acoustic patterns of speech that are sufficient to cause a person to correctly perceive a given sentence, phrase, word, syllable, or phoneme.

In research on the acoustic cues to the phonemes, the analysis of vowels and their perception was studied first, both in the early work of Helmholtz and in the more recent work. So this chapter begins with recent studies of vowel perception and later moves to some of the research on consonant perception.

Cues to Vowels

As we saw in our chapter on the shaping of vowels, the different tongue shapes and positions are reflected in the frequency positions of the formants, especially the first and second formants, F1 and F2. The formants of vowels were observed in the first acoustic studies using the sound spectrograph, which was developed at Bell Laboratories in 1943, for studies of military voice messages. The first tube model of vowel formant frequencies was formulated at Bell Laboratories (Dunn, 1950). Bell workers were also successful in synthesizing vowels using the concept of the formant (Joos, 1948, p. 83; Miller, 1953). Thus it was suspected that the formant

---

The past 40 years of speech research have involved a very important interaction between perception studies and the acoustic modeling of speech production. The acoustic modelers found it highly efficient to check their models by listening to them (Dudley, 1936). In fact, it might be argued that modeling is the most efficient approach to the understanding of any complex system. Modeling was used very effectively by some of the early workers: Willis, Helmholtz, Bell, and Paget. Recently the most advanced workers proceed with computer modeling of speech (Carré, Descout, and Wajskop, 1977).

Acoustic modeling of speech led to a highly beneficial interaction with perception research because the models were, in turn, used to produce sounds for further, more extended experiments on speech perception that used precisely controlled acoustic cues. After World War II this interactive method of speech research grew very rapidly and produced much of the acoustic knowledge about speech presented in this book. In addition a great deal was learned about speech perception.

frequencies were the essential cues that listeners use to perceive the vowels of speakers, but this idea needed to be verified for natural speech.

Bell researchers (Peterson and Barney, 1952) carried out a systematic measurement of the formants of English vowels as spoken in test words by American men, women, and children. Each word differed only in the vowel; for example, *heed, who'd,* and *hod* were the test words for [i, u], and [ɑ]. In addition to measuring the formant frequencies of each word Peterson and Barney measured the perception of the vowels by randomizing all the words on tapes and playing them back for adult listeners to identify. As might be expected, some of the vowels were not identified correctly, because of pronunciation differences, dialects, and the different formant ranges of men, women, and children. However, the vowels given as substitutes tended strongly to be those having vowel formant frequencies that were adjacent to the intended vowel.

This tendency was later analyzed by Shepard (1972) using statistical scaling of the degree of confusion between all pairs of the vowels. The degree of confusion between any two vowels indicates the extent to which they are perceptually similar. These similarities were scaled and plotted; the plot revealed three dimensions of vowel similarity, as shown in Figure 57, where the vowels are symbolized as balls in space. As will be noticed, the three dimensions arrange the vowels in order of F1 frequency (horizontally), F2 frequency (vertically), and F3 frequency in depth (which is indicated by the size of the ball).

Thus it appeared that the formant frequencies do indeed furnish the cues in speech that listeners use to identify the vowels as spoken by a large pool of talkers, because when a listener misidentified the vowel intended by a speaker he chose a vowel having formants that are close to those of the intended vowel.

In the meantime a group of scientists at the Haskins Laboratories developed a device called the speech Pattern Playback, an apparatus for the study of speech perception that enabled the experimenter to produce synthetic speech from a schematic spectrogram (Cooper, 1950). Based on the actual spectrogram the experimenter drew schematic traces in time of the formant positions and mounted the drawing on the Pattern Playback, which would then scan across the drawing in time to produce a synthetic version of the sound pattern represented by the original spectrogram.

An experiment with the Pattern Playback was carried out to determine just how listeners would identify as vowels the many possible combinations of formant frequency patterns that could be easily produced by the Pattern Playback (Delattre et al., 1952). Part of the experiment presented single-formant sounds at different formant frequencies to listeners who were asked to identify each sound as one of the English vowels.

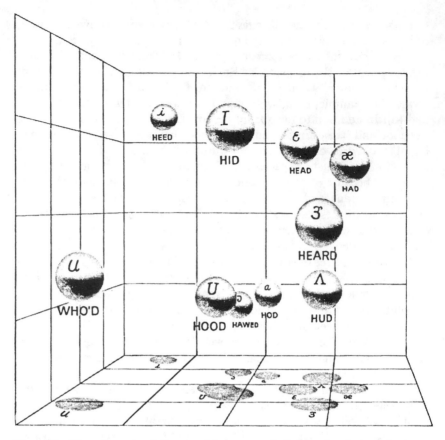

Figure 57.   Three-dimensional diagram of the perceptual relations of spoken vowels, determined by analyzing listeners' confusions among the vowels. Each vowel is represented by a ball. The perceptual similarities among the vowels were converted to distances along each of three dimensions as indicated by the analysis. The closer any two vowels are together, the more similar in perception they will be. It will be seen that the perceptual similarities cause the vowels to line up along formant dimensions, the horizontal dimension being F1, the vertical dimension F2, and the depth dimension (size of the ball) being F3. (Figure courtesy of R. Shepard.)

When the formant was very low, [u] was given as a response and, as the formant frequency increased through the low range, up to 1200 Hz, the series of back vowels [u, o, ɔ, ɑ] was heard by the listeners. When the formant frequency was increased further, the series of front vowels [ɛ, e, i] was heard by the listeners. In another part of the experiment, two-formant sounds were presented. The listener's responses for a given vowel were most unanimous when the F1 and F2 frequencies were similar to the F1 and F2 frequencies for the natural vowels, and there was greater unanimity over the front vowels than had been found with the single-formant sounds.

Thus it appeared that the frequencies of F1 and F2 were the necessary and sufficient acoustic cues in vowel perception.

However, as we have seen in our study of vowel acoustic shaping, the form of the vowel spectrum in the vicinity of F2 is highly dependent on the proximity of F2 to F1 or, alternatively, to F3. Also, when F2 is near F3, then both F3 and F4 tend to be stronger in amplitude. Thus it is possible that F3 and F4 can play a considerable role in determining the exact vowel quality that is heard. Carlson, Fant, and Granström (1975) described some studies to explore this possibility using synthetic vowels. The listener controlled a two-formant vowel stimulus in which he could adjust the frequency of F2 for the closest match to a fixed reference vowel, which had four formants set at average values for the vowel as seen in natural speech. For example, for a reference vowel for [i], the formants were $F_1/255$, $F_2/2065$, $F_3/2960$, $F_4/3400$ Hz; then for the listener's adjustable two-formant vowel, F_1 was 255 Hz and F_2 was adjustable over a wide range. The listener's mean setting of F_2 for best matches to the four-formant reference [i] was at 3210 Hz, a point between F_3 and F_4. Similarly, for other front vowels, the matching F_2 was well above the "natural" F_2 of the four-formant vowel. On the other hand, for the back vowels, the matching F_2 was at the "natural" F_2.

To explain these results Carlson et al. built an electronic model of auditory analysis, a bank of special filters, that incorporated the characteristics of the ear. The model was found to produce two major peaks in its output spectrum for each four-formant reference vowel, and the higher peak had a frequency location close to the listeners' matching F2 in the adjustable two-formant vowel. They conclude from these studies that the perceptual process for vowels consists of the extraction from the auditory input of two frequency locations as characterizing each vowel, the upper extracted location being determined by both F2 and F3.

Another factor in vowel perception is the different lengths of the vocal tracts of speakers, which causes the frequency spacing of formants to vary, as we saw in Chapter 3. How do listeners compensate or normalize for this situation? The longer the vocal tract the lower would the fundamental pitch tend to be, and the formant spacing would be closer in frequency. Fujisaki and Kawashima (1968) found that listeners depended on both the cue of pitch and formant spacing in vowel perception with different vocal tract sizes. This process of normalization was further studied by Summerfield and Haggard (1975), using reaction time of listeners for identifying vowels. The results indicated that the formant normalization was a highly automatic process.

The acoustic effects of nasalization of vowels were early modeled by House and Stevens (1956), as described in Chapter 4. House and Stevens also used their model to study the perception of the nasalization of vowels. Corresponding to the main acoustic effects of nasalization, the perception of nasalized vs. non-nasalized vowels, synthesized with the model, was found to depend on the damping of F1 and its apparent displacement upward in frequency.

Acoustic Cues to Place of Articulation of Consonants

The perception of stop consonants, using synthetic speech from the Haskins Pattern Playback, was studied by making variations of the frequency of the release bursts and of the formant transitions (Cooper et al., 1952). First consider the release burst as a cue to perceiving [p, t] or [k]. In the production of these consonants, the frequency spectrum of the release burst for [t] and [k] depends on the size and shape of the cavity in front of the tongue. For [k] the cavity shape is very different depending on which vowel follows. For [t] the front cavity is small and does not change greatly for different following vowels. These differences produce spectral differences in the release bursts of these consonants. Do listeners use these differences in burst frequency as cues for perceiving [p, t] and [k]?

The Haskins burst study synthesized 84 stop vowel syllables, using seven vowels [i, e, ɛ, a, ɔ, o, u] with 12 different burst frequencies covering the range 360 to 4320 Hz. The syllables were played back at random to listeners who identified the initial part of each syllable as [p, t] or [k]. The results are shown in Figure 58. The burst frequencies are arrayed vertically and the vowels are arrayed horizontally. Each vertical frequency indicated is a burst frequency used in the experiment; the formant frequencies for each of the vowels are shown as thick horizontal bars above the corresponding vowel. The density of the symbols indicates the number of times the listeners responded with each consonant. It will be seen that [t] was the predominant response for the high frequency bursts, 3240 to 4320 Hz, with any vowel. When the burst was a little above or at the second-formant frequency of the vowels [e, ɛ, a, ɔ, o, u] it was heard as [k]; when the burst was below the second formant of [i] or [e], or above the second formant of [o] or [u], it was heard as [p]. The two lowest bursts were heard as [p] with [ɛ] and [a]. Thus it turned out that the perception of these bursts as consonants depended on the burst cue and vowel together.

The next Haskins Laboratories experiment was to study the effect of the transitions in formants as cues to the identification of consonants. It will be recalled that the voiced stop consonants [b, d, g] all have upward transitions of the first formant into a following vowel, but that the direction of second formant transition depends on the place of articulation. In the Haskins study of formant transitions as cues to the perception of stop consonants, 11 different F2 transitions, including upward, downward, and flat, to the steady F2 frequency of the vowel (for each of the seven

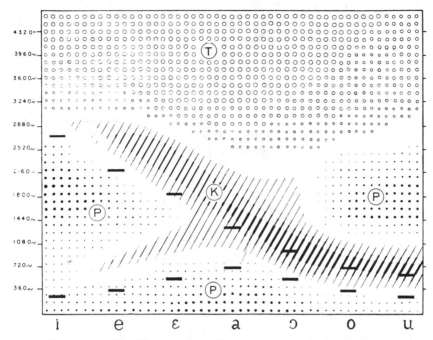

Figure 58.   Listeners' identification of [p, t, k] in response to synthetic syllables made up of a noise burst followed by a two-formant vowel. Different burst frequencies and formant frequencies were employed, as indicated on the vertical scale. The formant frequency levels are marked with heavy bars for each combination (and vowel represented). The size of the symbol in the response plot represents the oftenness of listeners' responses of each consonant as labeled in the figure. (From Cooper et al., 1952.)

vowels), were synthesized to provide 77 synthetic syllables. Listeners were required to identify [b, d, g, p, t] or [k]. The experiments showed that the first formant transition was indeed a strong cue for the perception of a voiced stop consonant and that the second formant transition produced [b] judgments for upward transitions, [d] judgments for flat transitions to mid- or high second formants and for downward transitions to vowels with low second formants, and [g] judgments for downward transitions to high second formants.

The Haskins researchers concluded that the acoustic cues for a phoneme were relational in that the burst and vowel transition cues for a given consonant were different depending on the following vowel. Thus it did not appear that there would be an invariant relation between the phoneme and its acoustic pattern.

As further acoustic knowledge was gained about the production of stop consonants, particularly by Fant (1973) and Stevens (1975), it appeared that there were invariant acoustic cues to place for stop consonants in the first 10 to 30 ms after release of the closure in the early part of the transition to the following vowel. For [b] and [p] the burst and transitions are spread out in spectrum in the low frequency region and the burst is weak; for [d] and [t] the burst is strong and spread over the mid- to high spectral region; but for [g] and [k] the burst is strong and compact, i.e., concentrated in a relatively narrow region of the spectrum in the middle or higher frequencies. These early burst cues are acoustically independent of the following vowel, although the later aspirant parts of the burst are not, because the F2 transitions from a given place are different for different vowels.

Interaction of Burst and F2 Transition as Cues

Recent experiments on the perception of the burst cues and the formant transition cues to place have attempted to determine exactly how these two different types of cues may interact. Do the bursts actually function as invariant cues, by themselves, or do the F2 transitions also play an essential role? Further work at Haskins Laboratories indicated that the consonant release bursts may not be sufficient cues, in and of themselves, for the perception of place of articulation of the stop consonants (Dorman, Studdert-Kennedy, and Raphael, 1977). This experiment was carried out with naturally spoken syllables from which both the bursts and the formant transitions of the following vowel were separated from the original syllables and attached in various combinations to a different spoken syllable beginning with the same vowel. All the syllables were spoken in the phrase "The little [test syllable] dog." The results indicated that the bursts and transitions together were most effective as cues to place of stop consonant articulation when the burst frequency and the starting frequency of the F2 transition were close in frequency. This closeness, a kind of spectral continuity, occurs for the transitions seen for [b] before rounded vowels, for [d] before close front vowels, and for [g] for close vowels. For other combinations the burst was not a very effective cue. Thus the invariant cue to place of articulation depends on consistency of the spectrum match between burst and vowel onset. This experiment is open to criticism because of the use of a non-neutral articulation in the last syllable of the carrier phrase before the test syllable. The final [l] of *little,* because of coarticulatory effects, would be expected to influence the spectrum at the start of the vowel of the vowel-consonant syllable to which were attached the separate bursts and transitions taken from other test syllables.

Blumstein, Stevens, and Nigro (1977) carried out an experiment with bursts and formant transitions to study the operation of special auditory detectors in speech perception. These detectors are postulated mechanisms in the auditory system that appear to be set to respond to the patterns of bursts, transitions, and other acoustic features to signal the occurrence of articulatory features. Such feature detectors had previously been postulated on the basis of the fact that a kind of perceptual fatigue, or adaptation, takes place when one acoustic feature is presented repeatedly. The adaptation of the feature is evidenced by the fact that it causes a test stimulus to be perceived as if the fatigued feature were absent from the stimulus (Eimas and Corbit, 1973). They found, for example, that when a downward second-formant transition is repeatedly presented that is a cue for [d] in [da], and then immediately a [da] syllable is presented having a flat F2 transition, it is heard as [ba], whereas it was heard as [da] when presented by itself, without any preceding series of adapting [da]'s having the downward transition.

In the study by Blumstein et al. (1977), the consonant bursts and formant transitions were synthesized for [b, d, g] in combination with different vowels. Then as adapting sounds for repetition before a test syllable, the bursts and transitions were presented in new combinations and in their normal combinations. If the feature detectors for the bursts and transitions were separate detectors, then their effects on adaptation should depend only on whether or not that feature is present in the test stimulus. However, if the feature detector depends on receiving both the proper burst and transition in determining perception, then adaptation with either a burst or transition would always be partially effective, whichever cue (burst or transition) is present in the test stimulus. The results favored the latter conclusion indicating that the feature detector indeed is tuned to sense proper burst-transition patterns together and therefore does not seem to consist of two separate detectors for burst and transition characteristics.

Cues to Fricative Place of Articulation

In discussing the production of the fricative consonants and describing their spectra it was seen that [s] and [ʃ] are strong and well differentiated by spectral concentrations in the mid- and high frequency range between 2.5 kHz and 6 kHz, whereas [f] and [θ] are weak and more diffuse in spectrum. These differences seem to be reflected in the perception of the fricatives, because a study by Harris (1958) indicated that [s] and [ʃ] were perceived correctly independent of information from the transition to the adjacent vowel, but [f] and [θ] were confused unless the corresponding transitional information was also present. The voiced fricatives [z, ʒ, v, ð] showed a similar difference in perceptual cues between [z, ʒ] and [v, ð].

Cues to Manner and Voicing of Consonants

An experiment by Liberman et al. (1956) employed synthetic syllables from the Haskins playback to study the cue of speed of formant transitions for initial consonants. Rapid transitions were found to be a cue for the stop consonants [b] and [g], and slower transitions between the same frequencies caused the listeners to hear [w] or [j] depending on whether F2 made an upward or downward transition.

The cues for differentiating the glide, retroflex, and lateral consonants, [w, j, r, l], were studied by synthesizing formant patterns with the Haskins Pattern Playback and playing the patterns to listeners for identification (O'Connor et al., 1957). It was found that formant patterns like those we have seen in spectrograms (Chapter 6) caused the listeners to hear the appropriate consonants. For example, a low frequency position of F3 and its associated upward transition to a vowel-like position caused the perception of a syllable beginning with [r].

The voiced/voiceless contrast between initial stop consonants was found to be cued by the release burst and the transition of F1. In the first studies only voiced formants were used. When there was an F1 transition, a voiced stop was heard and when there was no F1 transition, a voiceless stop tended to be heard (Cooper et al., 1952).

In later studies of the perception of stop voicing in initial position, the F1 transition was gradually removed by progressively cutting back (delaying) its onset relative to the onset of F2 and F3. It was found that F1 cutback of 40 to 50 ms was sufficient to completely change stop perception from voiced to unvoiced if the following vowel was [e] and, with [æ] or [ɔ], to cause most of the responses to be unvoiced. When F2 and F3 were noise excited during the cutback interval instead of excited by "voicing phonation," F1 cutback of 30 to 50 ms caused the stops to be heard as unvoiced in nearly all cases (Liberman, Delattre, and Cooper, 1958). Thus, when the acoustic patterns of aspiration and delayed voicing after the consonant release of initial stops are appropriately simulated, as would be implied by the difference in production of closed vs. open vocal folds during the occlusion interval, then the perception of voiced vs. unvoiced stop is consistently cued. In further studies of stop voicing this cue has been called voice onset time (VOT) (Lisker and Abramson, 1967).

The voicing contrast for intervocalic stops may be cued by differences in F1 transition, duration of the occlusion, and differences other than VOT or aspiration, as discussed recently by Lisker (1978), who concluded that all such cues are related to a single articulatory difference: closed vs. open vocal folds during the occlusion.

The nasal consonants [m, n] were found to be perceived when a low frequency broadband murmur preceded the formant transitions appropriate for a nasal consonant. The synthesized syllables consisted of a constant nasal murmur followed by vowels having no F1 transition and various F2 transitions. When the nasal murmur was followed by an upward transition in the second formant, a syllable beginning with [m] was perceived; if the second formant transition was downward, a syllable beginning with [n] was perceived; and if the second formant transition was upward, to a high second formant, a syllable ending in [ŋ] tended to be perceived (Liberman et al., 1954). The nasalization of the adjacent vowel was found to be a differential cue for nasal vs. voiced stop by Pickett (1965), using synthetic syllables generated by a synthesizer having both oral and nasal tract analogue circuits.

Categorical Perception of Speech Cues

In the earlier Haskins work with the second-formant transition as the cue to place of articulation of the stop consonants [b, d], and [g] it was noticed that, when a series of syllables was generated by using different starting points for the F2 transition, stepped over the series in small steps from low to high starting points, the perception of the stop consonants was found to go in distinct jumps between the low-starting group, heard as [b], the middle-starting group, heard as [d], and the high-starting group, heard as [g]. Why does this not go in continuous steps, beginning with a very clear [b], and then intermediate consonants between [b] and [d], then to a clear [d] and intermediate perceptions between [d] and [g], and finally to very clear [g]? This question was studied in an experiment where the listener was required to discriminate between two synthetic stop consonant patterns that differed in only one or two steps in the series of the starting frequency of the second formant transition (Liberman et al., 1957). Instead of identifying the transition pattern as being [b, d], or [g], the listener was asked to discriminate between transition patterns in the following way. First he heard two different patterns, called Pattern A and Pattern B, and then he heard a third pattern, which was the same as either A or B. The listener was required to say whether the third pattern, called X, was the same as A or B. In the testing of auditory discrimination, this method is called the ABX method. It was found that listeners were very poor in discriminating between formant transition patterns that were within an identification category, that is, in a region before the jump in identification labeling took place between [b] and [d] or between [d] and [g]. For example, when A and B were rising transitions of the second formant starting from two different frequency locations, but in a low range of starting points, the listeners were unable to tell whether X (which was either the A or B pattern) was the same as A or the same as B. Similarly, when there were two different falling transitions of F2 from two different high frequency starting points, the listeners were not able to tell whether X was the same as A or B. On the other hand, when an equal difference in starting points bridged a phoneme boundary the listeners were very accurate in telling whether X was A or B. For example, when A and B differ in that a slightly rising transition and a flat transition were the two patterns, A and B, then the two different stimuli bridged the [b-d] phoneme boundary and listeners were highly accurate in telling whether X was the same as A or the same as B. Thus it appeared that the perception of stop consonant formant transitions was a categorical affair rather than a continuously discriminating response to steps on a continuum of second formant transitions.

It was found also that the perception of the voiced/voiceless contrast appeared to be categorical along a continuum of the delay of onset of the first formant (VOT) in relation to the onset of the second formant.

A similar experiment was carried out with vowel identification and vowel discrimination depending on the frequency positions of the first and second formants, to test whether vowel discrimination was categorical, i.e., whether discrimination was poor for slightly different formant patterns that would be identified as the same vowel. In contrast to the consonants, vowel discrimination did not seem to be categorical. Listeners could discriminate between small differences in formant positions equally well over the whole range of vowel second formants, for example, going from high to lower second formants [i, e], and [æ] (Fry et al., 1962).

The Haskins investigators pointed out that the difference in categorical vs. noncategorical perception between consonants and vowels might be related to a difference in the motor conditions of articulation. The consonants are produced by discrete motions that must attain certain targets, for example, closures at certain places for the stop consonants and a state of closed or open glottis for producing the voiced/unvoiced distinction. The alveolar stop consonants must attain a closure at the alveolar position. There are no stop consonants that are produced in between the labial and alveolar closure positions.

For the vowels, on the other hand, the tongue position can assume a large number of different positions in the front vowels, for example, from very close [i] to less close [i], and so on over different degrees of closeness between [i] and [e] and [ɛ] and on to the most open front vowel [æ]. Thus it would seem that the degree to which categorization of perception occurs along the acoustic dimensions of the cues depends on whether the sounds are produced categorically (consonants) or noncategorically (vowels). Perception seems to correspond to the nature of articulation rather than to the continuum of acoustic cues. The Haskins group suggested that speech perception might involve a process in which the articulations that would be necessary to produce a heard acoustic pattern are the basis for the perception. This "motor" theory of speech perception is discussed further in the next chapter.

PROSODICS PERCEPTION

The perception of the rhythmic, intonational, and stress patterns of speech is extremely important. These are the prosodic patterns that the listener uses to mark the boundaries of syllables and words in the flow of speech sound; in addition the prosodics carry grammatical and meaning differences.

The prosodic features, as we saw in Chapter 5, are produced physiologically by manipulations of the subglottal pressure, the tension on the vocal folds, and the patterns of articulatory gestures in coordination with the sound sources. The acoustic correlates of these features are the intensity, pitch, duration, and spectrum of the vowels and the durations of the consonants. How are all these acoustic cues organized or integrated by a listener into percepts of the prosodics of speech: perception of the word stress, the rhythms of phrases and sentences, and the appreciation of the expressive intents and emphases desired by the speaker? Only the perception of the linguistic prosodic features, of word and phrase stress, have been studied acoustically to any great extent. Some research on the perception of English prosodic features is summarized here. A more complete review is given by Lehiste (1970), who discusses the stress patterns of a number of languages.

In English the intensity of a vowel in a stressed syllable is greater than the intensity of the same vowel in an unstressed syllable, which suggests that the increased vocal effort of stressed syllables produces a simple intensity difference, which can serve as the cue for perceiving the stress pattern. However, the different vowels also differ systematically between each other in intensity even when spoken with equal effort. As might be expected from source-filter theory, the vowels with F1 and F2 in close proximity, such as [ɑ], and [ɔ], are much more intense than the vowels with F1 and F2 far apart, such as [i] and [ɪ]. However, Lehiste and Peterson (1959) found that the different vowels all sounded equally loud. They then compared the loudness of the vowels spoken at equal intensities but, of course, with different amounts of effort. The vowels that had to be spoken with greater effort to achieve equal intensity, e.g., [i] and [ɪ], sounded louder than the naturally "more powerful" vowels, such as [ɑ] and [ɔ], at equal intensity. Lehiste and Peterson concluded that the intensity and quality (now we might say formant proximity) of a spoken vowel are both interpreted by the listener in terms of the vocal effort that produced the vowel. They also suggested that the pitch and duration of the vowel, being correlated with vocal effort, are additional cues that contribute to the perception of word stress in terms of vocal effort.

The availability of synthetic speech from the Haskins Pattern Playback made it possible to vary the pitch, duration, intensity, and formant positions independently. This was the method used by Fry (1958), in an interesting experiment on listeners' judgments of the syllable stresses that differentiate words, e.g., sub*ject* vs. *sub*ject. He used the Pattern Playback to make synthetic versions of these and other two-syllable words in which he was able to control and set the vowel durations, intensities, and pitches at different ratios between the two syllables. It was found that the perception of the stress relation between the syllables was not as sensitive to differences in intensity as to differences in duration and pitch pattern between the syllables.

Fry carried out a further perception experiment on the relative cue power of vowel quality (i.e., formant structure) and vowel duration as cues to syllable stress in synthetic two-syllable words like *sub*ject and sub*ject* (Fry, 1964a). He concluded tentatively that duration had the greater cue power but that further study was necessary to determine how to compare perceptual differences on two such different scales as duration and F1/F2 frequencies.

Hadding-Koch and Studdert-Kennedy (1964) studied the shapes of intonation contours that would cause listeners to perceive a question vs. a statement. It will be recalled that in Lieberman's breath group theory of intonation the natural, archetypal maneuver for speaking a phrase produces a terminal fall in pitch because of the fall in subglottal pressure that would naturally precede taking a new breath (see Chapter 5). If a phrase is spoken as a question the terminal portion is marked by an increase in vocal fold tension, which prevents the fall in pitch that would otherwise occur. The increase in vocal fold tension can also be large enough to cause a terminal rise in pitch. Hadding-Koch and Studdert-Kennedy employed different shapes of pitch contours to find out how much contrast with a falling contour would cause listeners to switch from hearing a statement to hearing a question. Is only a level contour required to signal a question, or is a rise necessary, and if a rise, how much? The results showed that it depended on how high the pitch was at a peak in pitch that preceded the terminal portion of the utterance. If the peak pitch was high, then a small terminal rise was required to signal a question.

Most acoustic studies of the perception of prosodics, like those discussed previously, have dealt with word stress and phrase stress. However, the prosodic features of speech are also used by speakers to signal the beginnings and ends of the larger units of meaning: sentences, and paragraphs. Lehiste and Wang (1976) recently studied these larger units using a computer to alter the spectrum of speech while retaining the normal prosodic features of pitch intonation and durational patterns. The spectral alteration consisted of inverting the normal patterns so that the formant frequencies were inverted, thus making the speech unintelligible, but with pitch and harmonic spacing unchanged; the result sounded like unintelligible English. Listeners were able to mark correctly many of the ends of spoken sentences (the sentences had been spoken spontaneously by a speaker recounting a personal experience). Most of the marked sentence endings seemed to be signaled by a fall in pitch and a lengthening of the final phrase of the sentence; however, a fairly large number of terminal falls did not correspond to the ends of sentences, indicating that some other cues were being used by the listeners to detect the ends of sentences. The altering of speech by computer methods will make it easier to study the ways in which speakers manipulate their speech in communicating lengthy information.

The intonation patterns of speech are used by speakers to convey attitudes and emotions, in addition to the linguistic structure we have just been discussing. There has not been a great deal of acoustic study of the communication of emotions and attitudes. The expression of emotions by speech has been studied acoustically by Williams and Stevens (1972). A study of perception has shown how certain contours of intonation may convey to listeners attitudes like interest or disinterest and pleasant vs. unpleasant (Uldall, 1960). Another study showed that the intonation contour conveyed to listeners the intended emotions of speakers (Lieberman and Michaels, 1962).

FUNCTION OF PROSODIC FEATURES IN SENTENCE PERCEPTION

A group of speech scientists in Leningrad carried out an interesting study on the perception of the rhythmic structure of speech messages and they interpreted the results in terms of a theory of speech perception (Kozhevnikov and Chistovich, 1965, p. 238 ff). The translation is not easy to obtain and understand, so the study is described here in some detail. The question was: To what extent is the rhythmic structure of a message used by the listener in perceiving the units of meaning, that is, the words and sentences? The method was to analyze the errors committed under conditions of listening to speech from which much of the spectral information had been removed. If the rhythm is important in dividing the message into words, as well as for their recognition, the words and phrases perceived, even though their phonemes are not heard correctly, should coincide with the spoken phrases in number of words and in the rhythm of the sequence of stressed and unstressed syllables. Meaningful sentences of different lengths from 3 to 12 syllables were prepared. Each sentence contained from two to five words, and in most cases two or three words. For the experiments, the spoken sentences were put through a bandpass filter that passed only the frequency range from 906 to 1141 Hz, a very severe limitation that removes much of the phonemic information. The listeners were required to write down complete, meaningful phrases or sentences, in response to each sentence presented, and to guess when they were uncertain, or even when they felt they had understood very little of what was said.

The response sentences and words always had a meaning. However, the number of words corresponding to the stimulus words was low; only about 30% of the words were correct. This score was higher for short sentences (seven syllables or less) than for long sentences of more than seven syllables. In general, the response vowels and consonants were not correct, of course. However, although incorrect in their sound composition, the responses were nevertheless rather correct in number of words and number of syllables. Out of the 79 short sentences, 68 coincided with the stimulus sentences in the number of words and 57 in the number of syllables. In the long sentences the number of words was correct in 16 cases out of 22, but the response words were often found to have fewer syllables than the stimulus words. As a result, only 6 out of the 22 long sentences were correct in the number of syllables.

The responses were also scored according to type of word stress. In the short and long sentences, respectively, 90% and 84% of the word stresses were correct.

An analysis of the errors showed that the selection of response sentences made use of the information on the rhythm of the message and on the features of the individual sounds. The correct reproduction of the rhythm of the message, and also the absence of meaningless phrases, indicated that the listeners reached decisions about large meaningful lengths of speech without great delays.

How does the process of choosing response words proceed? If it proceeds sequentially, i.e., by choosing the first word, and then the second, and so on, then there should be an increase in correct perception going from the first word toward the last word because the developing meaning would limit the number of possible words for each subsequent word in the sentence. On the other hand, if the decision of the listener is reached at once for the entire sentence, the position of the word should not affect its recognition. An analysis of the data showed that the position of the word within the sentence had a marked influence on its correctness. In two-word sentences the last word was recognized more correctly. In the three-word sentences, which were 5 to 12 syllables long, the middle word of the sentence was recognized less correctly than the first word and the last word. Kozhevnikov and Chistovich speculated that the reason is that the relatively long decision time, typically found for recognition of heavily distorted words, must have prevented the flowing recognition of the words in the middle of the sentence, the sound of which started at the time when a decision had not yet been reached concerning the first word and was still being processed when the last word was arriving. They believed that these data make it necessary to assume that the listener reaches decisions concerning words without waiting for the termination of a whole sentence. This behavior would be appropriate if the size of the perceptual memory is limited and cannot hold the image of the entire sentence as a whole.

If the memory capacity were unlimited, then the intelligibility of sentences would increase with their length. An analysis was made of recognition as a function of sentence length (in terms of number of syllables); it was found that an increase of recognition with increasing length did take place, but only up through seven syllables; then recognition declined very rapidly for 8-, 9-, 10-, 11-, and 12- syllable sentences. It was concluded that about seven syllables constitute the limit of capacity of the processing memory for recognizing spoken messages.

It would appear that the words are recognized as they arrive, in the short as well as in the long messages, because correct recognition of words increases with increasing number of syllables for the short sentences. However, not all the words are recognized as they come in. It seems that, after the end of a short message that does not exceed the size of memory, it is possible to use the features retained in the memory, in conjunction with the decisions held in abeyance about the words not immediately recognized, to come to final recognition. On the other hand, if the sentence is a long one, the image of the word, that is, the information on its size, its stress pattern, etc., may be lost. In such a case, the decisions concerning the unrecognized portion of the sentence could be made only as a guess solely on the basis of linguistic probabilities without benefit of the lost features information about the word, and therefore with a greater chance of error. The results of this study indicate that the length of the stored speech information on which final meaning decisions are reached exceeds the length of a syllable, since the erroneous responses show that word selection was constrained by the rhythm of alternation of stressed and unstressed syllables, but the length stored for processing does not exceed seven syllables.

In summary, the Leningrad group described the recognition of the larger meaningful units of speech, the words and sentences, as follows. The incoming sounds of speech are recorded in short-term memory as syllables having specified distinctive features; the vowels are recorded with indications of their degree of stress. After the perception of a stressed syllable, the probable boundary of the word is located and the "dictionary" is searched for a suitable word. When the word decision is reached this marks the boundaries for the word in the sequence of syllables. This first word decision also reduces the number of words that need to be considered for subsequent word choices. The stress patterns of the words allow the determination of the number of complete words in the sentence; at the same time the place of the stress in the words is an important feature of the word for its recognition. Thus the large rhythmic units of the message, larger than syllables, are believed to have very important functions in determining word boundaries, word meaning, and sentence meaning.

In the discussion of the prosodic features of speech in Chapter 5 we saw that the durations of speech sounds were greatly influenced by their position in words, phrases, and sentences. Yet perceptually the individual sounds are not heard as short or long; rather it is phrases and sentences that seem to be either brief or extended. In fact there is an impression that the main words of an extended utterance are of about equal duration and that the time is about equal between the main stressed syllables of the rhythmic subunits. The apparent equality of intervals between stressed syllables is called *isochrony*. It occurs in highly "stress-paced" languages, such as English, Swedish, and German.

Isochrony exists to some extent in the actual production of speech. One factor favoring isochrony is the shortening of the unstressed syllables as the number of syllables in a word increases. This tends to make the time interval between the main stressed syllables have a typical duration. Still the measured time between the main stressed syllables has a wide variation, even under well-controlled conditions of rate of utterance (see Lehiste, 1977, for a review of all the evidence on isochrony in speech production).

In experimental studies of the heard isochrony effect, Lehiste (in press) found that there was a tendency for listeners to hear final intervals as shorter than the preceding intervals even when all the intervals were equal in duration. In other words, the listener seems to expect a lengthening of the final interval and, if the final interval is made equal to preceding ones, it sounds shorter.

Lehiste also studied the ways in which speakers make durational changes in words or phrases to signal different meanings. For example, in speaking the sentence "The old men and women stayed at home" a speaker can indicate by his prosodic patterns whether he means that both the men and women were old or only the men. It was found that either a long pause after *men* or a lengthening of *men* successfully caused the listeners to hear the intended meaning. In a subsequent study the same sentences, which had been recorded for the previous study, were processed by a computer program to eliminate any variations in voice pitch. Then lengthening of words, or of pauses, at possible grammatical points was carried out by artificial stretching of the speech sounds by the computer. This lengthening alone was found to produce the intended differences in meaning (studies reviewed in Lehiste, 1977).

Thus, Lehiste concluded that the listener experiences equal apparent intervals between the main stressed syllables of an utterance, and when an interval between stresses is lengthened it stands out as preceding a grammatical boundary within an utterance. At the termination of an utterance, the usual lengthening of the final syllables is actually heard as being shorter than it actually is, thus giving a perceptual equality, isochrony, of all the intervals between the main stressed syllables of an utterance.

SUMMARY

The perceptual cues for the speech features are given in Table 7. The table includes all of the cues discussed in this chapter and a few additional ones that have been established or would be expected to be obvious cues.

Table 7.   Speech features and acoustic cues

Features	Acoustic cues
Prosodic functions	
Syllable stress pattern	Vowel pitch, duration, spectrum, and intensity (in order of importance)
End of phrase or sentence	Longer duration of vowel and continuant consonants
End of statement	Falling pitch
End of question	Level or rising pitch
Word importance	Longer duration in more important words
Vocal effort	Increased intensity of F3, and higher formants, relative to F1
Vowel features	
High (constricted) vs. low (more open)	First-formant frequency, F1, low vs. high
Front tongue constriction	High second-formant frequency, F2; stronger in F2, F3, F4 amplitude
Back tongue constriction	Low second-formant frequency, F2; weaker in F3 and above
Retroflex tongue (ɝ)	Low third-formant frequency, F3
Tense vs. lax	Long vs. shorter duration
Nasalization	Raised F1 frequency and wider F1 bandwidth
Consonant features	
Glide vs. oral-occlusive, [w, j] vs. [b, d, m, n]	Long vs. brief formant transitions (F1 alone probably sufficient)

—continued

Table 7—*continued*

Features	Acoustic cues
Retroflex tongue, [r] vs. other glides and nasals	Large F3 transition to or from low frequency
Lateral	Low frequencies strong and broadband, plus moderate strength midformants
Nasal	Low frequency murmur, narrowband with weak midformants. Adjacent vowel affected by nasal coupling (F1 weakened and raised in frequency)
Stop	Silent interval, rapid, brief formant transitions
Fricative	Longer constriction interval showing weak or absent low frequency sound, relatively strong high frequency, random amplitude sound
Voiced vs. unvoiced	Stops: release-burst weak and brief vs. strong and longer; following vowel F1 onset early vs. delayed; intervocalic interval short vs. long; preceding vowel long vs. short for final stop at a boundary Fricatives: short vs. longer high frequency sound; weak vs. strong high frequency sound; duration cues same as for stops
Place of articulation	Direction of F2 transition; location and transitions of release-burst spectrum; compact-diffuse, spreading, or parallel transitions of F2 and F3; spectrum of fricative sound

MODELS OF
SPEECH PERCEPTION

CONTENTS

> ...what we hear [in speech] is not a mere acoustic pattern but a series of movements...
>
> R. H. Stetson, 1928

The results of research on the acoustic cues for speech perception have led to some interesting models (or theories) of the speech perceptual process. These models try to explain how the auditory system analyzes the speech sounds received and how this information is processed by the listener to correctly understand the message of the speaker. The input to such a model is the sound wave of an utterance and the final output should be a sequence of words understood, making up a meaningful phrase or sentence.

This chapter presents some of the models proposed and some of the experiments supporting them. For the most part these models are versions of a single model called the motor theory of speech perception. Motor theory has stimulated a great deal of important research on speech; it has also caused some lively controversies and opposition.

MOTOR THEORIES OF SPEECH PERCEPTION

Motor theory in essence says that, in perceiving speech messages, the listener interprets the received auditory patterns in terms of articulatory patterns that would produce auditory patterns like those received. In other words, motor theory hypothesizes that the speech perceptual process has a stage where the auditory patterns are interpreted by reference to speech movements, including the adjustments of the vocal folds. Perception by motor reference is not conceived to be a conscious process by the listener but rather a very rapid, computer-like "cross-check" performed automatically by the sections of the nervous system that deal with auditory, speech-motor, and linguistic functions.

This approach to explaining a perceptual process, that is, by referring the information from the senses to movements by the receiver that might produce that information, is not new. It derives from the "functional" school of psychology, a typically pragmatic, American psychology, developing around the turn of the twentieth century, that in turn arose from evolutionism (Darwinism). The functionalists insisted that all perception is organized to serve as a basis for behavioral action (Boring, 1950, pp. 505–559). Evolution would favor behaviorally oriented perception because, for survival, an efficient perceptual code would be one that embodied all the relevant behavioral aspects of the perceptual situation; then the organism would be able to act appropriately without unnecessary hesitation or further "reflection." Thus the idea of motor reference in the process of sensory perception is rooted in the early history of American experimental psychology.

Early Motor Theories

The first applications of motor reference to explain the perception of the acoustic patterns of speech came about 50 years later. One factor appears to have been the 1940s development of the sound spectrograph at the Bell Laboratories. Spectrograms of speech made it easy to see that a given vowel phoneme did not have an invariant acoustic pattern. Martin Joos, a University of Wisconsin linguist, working with the first spectrograph at Bell Laboratories, found that the formant positions of a given vowel varied considerably among speakers and different syllables. He posed the question of how the different variations of a vowel can be perceived by the listeners as the same vowel. He proposed that the listener interprets the formant pattern in a motor framework of the two vowel articulation dimensions, front-back and open-close, and that the formants of an individual speaker were fitted to these articulation dimensions by a perceptual "warping" by the listener of the motor vowel framework (Joos, 1948).

The psychologist/phonetician R. H. Stetson, who in 1928 proposed that the motor organization of the syllable was the basic unit in speech production, later described a syllabic motor model of speech acquisition by the child. This model describes how the child learns to articulate syllables that match the articulation of adult syllables. The child does this by learning to speak to be understood. Correct articulations in imitating the adult result in more instances of reward than do faulty imitations. This conditioning process ensures that the variant cues to a phoneme, heard in different syllables spoken by different persons, are perceived as the same phoneme. In other words, it is through the successful articulation of a given phoneme in different syllables that the child perceives the variant acoustic cues as one and the same phoneme because of the consistent motor patterns the child must make to produce the phoneme successfully (Stetson, 1951, pp. 144–149). This model is a functionalist theory of speech perception that was deduced from data on the articulatory movements of syllables and the variant acoustic patterns of the same phoneme in different syllables seen in the spectrograms published from the Bell Laboratories by Potter, Kopp, and Green (1947).

Stetson's motor model, like Joos's motor explanation of vowel perception, was speculative and not based on data from studies of speech perception; such data were to be developed extensively in the succeeding decades by later speech scientists.

Current Motor Theories

The Haskins group noted that a motor theory of perception might explain their findings on the cues to place of stop consonants (Cooper et al., 1952) (see Chapter 11). They asked why, in their studies of burst frequency and F2 transition, the same burst was sometimes heard as [p] and sometimes [k]. A burst at 1440 Hz was the cue for [p] when F_2 of the following vowel was higher than the burst, but it was the cue for [k] when the following F_2 was at the same frequency as the burst (see Figure 58 in Chapter 11). In the study of the F2 transition cue, the same downward F2 transition was sometimes heard as [d] and sometimes as [g] depending on the following vowel. The articulation of bilabial vs. alveolar vs. velar stop differs mainly in the place of constriction; but the movements to and from a given constriction are different depending on what position is necessary for the following vowel. Somehow the perceptual mechanism of the listener seems to "know" this and hears the appropriate different patterns of acoustic cues as the same consonant sound. Also he hears different consonants for the same downward transition in F2, as they would have to be in order to produce different following vowels. In other words, different acoustic patterns that would be produced by the same place of articulation are heard as the same consonant: the perception follows the articulation. The same burst frequency may be heard as different consonants, depending on the following vowel; that is, when the same burst-cue is presented with different vowels, perception goes by the articulations that would produce the combinations, and we hear different places of articulation of the consonants.

The perception of same consonant for different formant transitions is an example of perceptual invariance, a phenomenon characteristic of sensory perception in general. For example, in visual perception of an object the object is perceived as constant, invariant, despite changes in distance and point of view, which change the pattern in the eye. In consonant perception by ear the object perceived is the consonant articulation, despite changes in the sound pattern because of different adjacent sounds and different sizes of vocal tract.

Remember from the previous chapter that the acoustic cues to consonant perception seem to function categorically. The cues of direction of F2 transition for place of stop articulation and voice onset time (VOT) for stop voicing, when varied in equal steps, cause consonant perception and discrimination to change in jumps rather than gradually. The acoustic boundaries at which the jumps occur correspond to acoustic-articulatory conditions that are mutually exclusive, i.e., categorical by articulation. Consider, for example, the VOT perceptual boundary value of about 50 ms between voiced and unvoiced stops. The articulatory contrast of closed vocal folds for a voiced stop provides nearly immediate voice onset compared with a delay in VOT because of the open vocal folds for an unvoiced stop; these are two mutually exclusive articulatory states. Thus the perception of the voicing cue, VOT, has a category that corresponds to the articulation.

On the other hand the different vowels are not produced categorically and they are not perceived categorically.

The articulatory explanation of perceptual invariance and "categoriality" led the Haskins group to propose a motor theory of speech perception in which the acoustic signal is compared in a consistency test against motor representations of speech sounds (Liberman et al., 1967; Liberman, Delattre, and Cooper, 1952; Studdert-Kennedy, 1974, 1976).

The Haskins group, in addition, carried out experiments comparing the left and right ears in "dichotic" presentation of the acoustic cues of speech. The findings indicated that the categorical perception of speech cues is carried out in the left hemisphere of the brain, apparently by a neural mechanism that is specially organized to decode the acoustic cues of speech (Liberman, 1974; Studdert-Kennedy, 1976).

Speech researchers at MIT proposed a motor theory that was more explicit than the Haskins theory (Halle and Stevens, 1959). A block diagram of the MIT model is presented in Figure 59, which is adapted from Stevens and Halle (1967). It is called an analysis-by-synthesis model.

The model is an arrangement by which an analysis of auditory features derived from hearing a sequence of speech can be compared with the features generated through articulatory instructions to a synthesizer; then the result of the comparison controls further attempts to match the input features until a phoneme decision is reached. The speech sound input on the left is first analyzed by the auditory mechanism, A, which may pro-

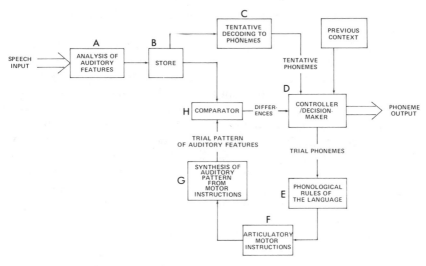

Figure 59.   Diagram of an "analysis-by-synthesis" motor theory of speech perception. (Adapted from Stevens and Halle, 1967.)

vide an analysis in terms of distinctive features. The auditory analysis is fed to a store, B, which retains the auditory features for subsequent use in the comparator, H, and in a preliminary phoneme decoder, C. This decoder converts the auditory features into a tentative sequence of phonemes, which is combined with the previous context by the controller/decision mechanism, D, to give a trial sequence of phonemes. The trial sequence is then converted by phonologic rules, E, to a set of motor articulatory instructions, F. These are fed to a synthesizer, G, which converts the instructions into a set of auditory features, a trial auditory pattern that can be compared with the original stored auditory pattern. The differences, or "error," seen by the comparator (H) are assessed by the decision mechanism; if the error is low the decision confirms and puts out the preliminary phoneme sequence as the final decision; if the error is high the differences are used to generate a new, different sequence of trial phonemes, and the synthesis process is repeated for the new phonemes. The process reiterates until a final, best decision is made. It is believed that the first trial is usually successful, because, even though the tentative phoneme sequence may contain errors, they are correctable by the controller on the basis of the preceding current context of phonemes.

The MIT model described here is represented as applied only for phoneme perception. The same process could apply at higher levels, too, i.e., for perception of syllables, words, and sentences; then the storage and synthesizer would operate in the appropriate codes or categories for the higher levels.

In the late 1950s a group of scientists at the Pavlov Institute of Physiology in Leningrad began a program of studies on speech perception and production that led them also, approximately in parallel with the Haskins and MIT groups, to adopt a motor theory of speech perception (Chistovich, 1960; Kozhevnikov and Chistovich, 1965). The Leningrad researchers seem to have favored a motor theory of speech perception because of their approach to the study of sensory perception through biophysics and cybernetics, which emphasizes the role of feedback in control systems. This approach was made feasible by the emerging capabilities of computer systems to simulate complex biological processes, thus leading to the possibility of speech understanding by computers.

The Leningrad group published a book containing summaries of their speech perception experiments and discussions of the theoretical implications of their results, as well as some important studies on the temporal organization of speech movements (Kozhevnikov and Chistovich, 1965). This reference, a preliminary translation of the book into English, is difficult to read and not readily available, so presented here is a detailed summary of those sections dealing with motor theory of perception.

The chapter on speech perception begins with the question: What are the primary units of speech perception? There are coarticulatory effects, between phonemes, that extend over spans as long as a syllable. Thus, to decide on the phonemes, a listener must coordinate information over units at least as large as a syllable. Does it follow from this that the decision unit is the syllable? Does the listener have memory images of all possible syllables of his language and does the speech perception process consist of the running, continuous selection of sequences of syllables out of the multitude of possible syllables? There may be too many syllables for this to be the case. Considering the syllables as defined by phonemes alone, there are over 4000 different syllables in English, but if the prosodic variations of the syllables are also included it is on the order of 31,000 syllables. In addition the allophonic variations of all the syllables would have to be available. This seems to be too many syllables to search among and make correct decisions at the speed of speech, which is three to seven syllables per second. Therefore, a perceptual process using syllables as the main units of perceptual decision appears to be very cumbersome and uneconomical.

The other possibility is that the main decision units correspond to phonemes. The question of whether the phoneme or the syllable is the basic unit of the decision process in perception can be tested by studying the time required, the reaction time, for recognition of consonants and vowels in consonant-vowel (CV) syllables. If the syllable is the unit of decision, then there should be no difference between the reaction time to recognize the consonant and the reaction time to recognize the vowel because both the consonant and vowel would have to occur before the syllable recognition could be made. If, on the other hand, the phoneme is the basic unit, then the time required for recognizing the consonant should be shorter than the time required to recognize the vowel because the the consonant precedes the vowel. Reaction-time listening was carried out with CV syllables beginning with alveolar stop, continuant, or fricative consonants, and the vowels [i, a], and [u]. The task of the listener was to write the consonant as soon as he possibly could on a metal plate that sensed the beginning of his writing response. His reaction time was measured by comparing the time of the start of his response with the instant of release of the consonant articulation, which was sensed by the breaking of tongue contact on an artificial palate mounted in the speaker's mouth. In a separate series of listening tests the listeners wrote the vowels in the same way and the reaction times were again measured relative to the release of the consonant. It turned out that the reaction times for writing the consonants were always faster than the reaction times for writing the vowels. This outcome supports the hypothesis that the basic decision units of speech perception are the phonemes and not the syllables.

The reaction times in writing down the vowel were found to depend on the characteristics of the preceding consonant. This fact seems to confirm the notion that the time segment to be considered in the phoneme perception process is on the order of a syllable in duration. Thus the Leningrad group concluded that, although the basic unit of perceptual decision may be the phoneme, the segment of speech necessary to be considered in order to define the phonemes is at least a consonant-vowel segment or a consonant-vowel syllable.

The Leningrad workers felt that, in view of the indications in favor of a motor theory of speech perception, they should study the perception process through the listener's use of his own speech production apparatus. For this purpose they employed the techniques of mimicry and speaking reaction time. The listener was presented a sound or a syllable and required to imitate the sound or to repeat the sound as quickly as he could, and his reaction time was measured. This mimicry task taps into the motor aspects of the perceptual process; in other words, in order to imitate accurately and quickly, the listener's auditory processing must reach a state where the input has been reduced and converted into motor commands that will produce a good imitation.

A study of vowel perception using the method of mimicking was carried out by Chistovich et al. (1966). A series of 12 synthetic stimulus vowels was prepared using combinations of F1 and F2 frequencies that formed a series based on the formants of the subject in uttering a drawn-out vowel going continuously from [i] to [ɛ] to [ɑ]. Thus the stimulus contained only vowels that the subject herself could produce. These stimulus vowels were presented to the subject in a random order. After each vowel, the task of the subject was, in two separate sessions: 1) to mimic the vowel as accurately as possible or 2) to mimic the vowel as rapidly as possible. The subject's response vowels were recorded and then analyzed to determine whether the subject's responses reproduced the F1 and F2 frequencies of the stimuli. This occurred only for those stimuli that were close to the subject's vowels [i, ɛ, ɑ]; for stimuli that were intermediate between two of these vowels, the F1 and F2 of the responses were close to the F1 and F2 of one of the adjacent vowels of the subject. This occurred both for the accurate mimicking where responses were made in about 1 sec and the rapid mimicking where the reaction times were short (about 200 ms). These results indicate that, in the first stages of rapid perception for mimicking a vowel, the sound is classified categorically according to one of the listener's own vowel phonemes.

On the other hand, if listeners are asked to compare the similarity of two vowels, they appear to be able to hear differences between two vowels that would be mimicked with the same vowel production (Chistovich, Kozhevnikov, and Galunov, 1970, pp. 34–35).

In a study of the perception of consonants the listener was required to mimic spoken consonants as rapidly as possible upon hearing a vowel-consonant-vowel utterance. The consonants were either labial or alveolar. The articulation of the listener's responses was detected by recording in time the contact of the tongue on an artificial palate (for the alveolar consonants) and by small metal contacts on the lips (for the labial consonants). In mimicking the consonant as rapidly as possible, the listener typically began his consonant response very soon after the occlusion of the stimulus consonant, so soon actually that he would be essentially unable to know completely what particular consonant was being pronounced by the speaker. The subjects often formed a stop before having sufficient information about it, that is, before the release of the consonant. Thus there were a large number of errors. In only 77% of the cases did the response start correctly. In the remainder of the cases, that is, when starting errors occurred, sometimes a double place of articulation was corrected by removing the erroneous closure. Other times a single incorrect closure was replaced by a correct one. Similar error corrections occurred for the other consonant features of nasal, voicing, and fricative.

Thus the rapid imitation of consonants seems to begin with an articulatory state reflecting a more or less random selection of the features that might have to be produced and, as more sound information is received from the stimulus, this preparatory articulatory state undergoes changes so that it finally begins to be in correspondence with the starting consonant. If the consonant had been correctly formed from the very start, the listener completed it and proceeded to the vowel with the most brief, primitive, or reflex-like, reaction times of only 100 ms from the release of the stimulus consonant to the release of the response consonant. On the other hand, if the consonant had been started incorrectly, the response release was delayed. There was evidence that, during these correction delays, the state that the articulatory organs had reached was taken into account, as well as the received acoustic signal, to finally produce a corrected consonant.

Chistovich later speculated that the occurrence of such fast reflex-like reaction times, in the cases of initially correctly formed response consonants, reflected a process of consonant perception in which the first portions of the received consonant cues are stored in motor-command terms specific to a given consonant; then the following cues, after the release of the stimulus consonant, which are also processed in motor-command terms, need only to confirm and execute the first commands to produce a correct response only 100 ms after the release of the stimulus consonant (Chistovich, personal communication).

Some of the syllables used as stimuli for rapid mimicking in the Leningrad studies were the same syllables as those used in the previous study of rapid consonant identification by writing the consonant. When the reaction time is taken from the end point of the stimulus consonant to the end point of the response consonant, the reaction times are found to be nearly identical for both speaking and writing. In other words the time to the listeners' release of spoken response consonants is the same as the time to the start of writing the consonant. The fricatives [s], [z] gave the fastest reaction time, about 100 ms. The consonants [l], [n], and [d] gave middling reaction times of about 170 ms, and [t] gave the longest reaction time, about 210 ms. This is considered to support the hypothesis that changes in articulation during rapid imitation actually reflect changes in the process that makes the perceptual decisions about the consonant phonemes. The response phoneme corresponds to the articulatory description in the end state of the perceptual process, which is then simply executed by a command "release the consonant."

What is the set of inner symbols in the phoneme perception process that is used for the description of the articulatory state? The phonemes finally arrived at are believed to be specified according to their values of the distinctive features (called differential features in Kozhevnikov and Chistovich, 1965). The distinctive feature system is an articulatory one, using features of voiced-voiceless, stop-fricative, and so on, such as we have used in this book. The statement of the values of all the distinctive features for a phoneme is equivalent to a complete description of the phoneme; when one of the features is not specified, say because of noise or poor hearing, the remaining specified features describe groups of phonemes that differ in the unspecified distinctive feature.

It is argued by the Leningrad group that the information that is transformed from auditory sensation to the phonemic code must be in terms of distinctive features because selection among all the phonemes, about 40, would require more time than is available during continuous running speech perception. Selection among distinctive features involves only about five features.

Furthermore, the information on the phonemes contained within a given section of the flow of speech, for instance a section corresponding to a syllable, is in many instances not sufficient for unambiguous selection of the phonemes. Since the remaining ambiguity can be eliminated upon subsequent recognition of words and sentences, it is evident that it would not be logical to make phonemic decisions currently during the flow of speech at every possible instant. This would unavoidably result in phoneme errors, which would only have to be corrected subsequently. It would be much more efficient to rely on subsequent resolution of the phoneme ambiguity.

Syllabic Motor Theories

In a paper from the Leningrad group (Galunov and Chistovich, 1966) a general theory of speech perception based on motor reference was developed and examined in relation to a number of speech perception studies, both Soviet and American. As Galunov and Chistovich said: "It seems to us that such an evaluation is much to be desired and bears a certain urgency, for otherwise there is the possibility that the explanatory value of the theory could...be overestimated" (p. 357). In the theory proposed there are several stages of the perceptual process that lead to a phoneme representation of speech. The first stage is the conversion of the acoustic signals into a set of auditory sensations. This conversion would apply to any sounds entering the auditory system.

The next stage, leading toward speech perception for speech sound inputs, is a stage that converts the auditory sensations into speech elements, either phonemes or syllables. The auditory information is converted, for speech representation, into motor articulatory patterns that have dimensions of articulation control. That is to say, the results of this conversion are given in terms of a motor program that would, if carried out, cause articulations that would produce the auditory patterns of the input (within certain criterial limits). Thus the phonemes of speech are represented in terms of instruction for distinctive movements that would produce them. In addition, other important speech parameters are represented, such as loudness, voice pitch, intonation contours, and rhythmic patterns. Some of these are represented in discrete categorical form, in terms of the presence or absence of articulatory features, and others may be stored in continuous forms.

It is also proposed that the syllable is the basic unit of motor representation. The perception of given phonemes is treated as dependent on the states of the motor control programs that would produce syllables containing those phonemes.

These two stages of speech perception, the acoustic-to-auditory, and the auditory-to-phonetic (motor commands for syllables), provide the input to further stages, which transform the syllables to words and the words to a final meaning. The syllable information from the auditory and phonetic stages contains both phonemic information and prosodic information, and both of these are necessary to achieve the final recognition of the meaning. Before discussing some prosodic studies let us examine a somewhat different syllabic motor theory of speech perception.

Studdert-Kennedy (1976) at Haskins Laboratories recently hypothesized that differences in perceptual processing between consonants and vowels reflect the basic structure of the "acoustic syllable." "The consonant is transient, low in energy, and spectrally diffuse; the vowel is [long], relatively stable [nontransient], high in energy, and spectrally compact. Together they form the syllable, each fulfilling within it some necessary function" (p. 270). The communicative functions of consonant and vowel differ in ways that are adapted to their acoustic differences. The vowels are quite long in duration but this is not necessary for their identification. Their longer length, compared with consonants, permits the speaker to display other useful information, such as fundamental frequency contours and patterns of duration and intensity, i.e., the prosodic features. In the flow of speech, consonants alternate with vowels providing segments of acoustic contrast between the vowels, and increasing the phonetic range of the language. The "consonant attack," i.e., the burst and transitions, is brief and so increases the rate of information, making up for the slowness imposed by the long length of the vowels which, however, is necessary to transmit the prosodic features. Also, even though the consonant cues are briefer, time is needed to process them to complete phonetic identity and this is provided by the longer duration of vowels. "Vowels are the rests between consonants. . . Rapid consonantal gestures cannot carry the melody and dynamics of the voice" (Studdert-Kennedy, 1976, p. 270). The phonemic and prosodic loads are therefore unequally divided between consonant and vowel: the consonant carries most of the phonemic load, the vowel the prosodic load. (It should be noted, however, that the durations of some consonants show prosodic variations that may be communicatively significant, as implied by the data of Umeda and Klatt, discussed in Chapter 5.) "There emerges the acoustic syllable, a symbiosis of consonant and vowel, a structure shaped by the articulatory and auditory capacities of its user, fitted to, defining, and making possible linguistic and para-linguistic communication" (Studdert-Kennedy, 1976, p. 270).

Studdert-Kennedy proposed a motor theory of speech acquisition in the infant that postulates the existence of inherited articulatory templates and auditory templates, which are both involved in the learning of speech communication. The theory might be called a speech-development form of the Haskins Laboratories' motor theory of articulatory reference for speech perception. Studdert-Kennedy hypothesized that

> the infant is born with both auditory and articulatory templates. Each template embodies capacities that may be [used] in the particular language to which the infant is exposed. For effective function in language acquisition the auditory template must be tuned to specific acoustic properties of speech in the language of the child's environment. The articulatory template, on the other hand, is more abstract, including a range of gestural control, potentially isomorphic with the segmented feature matrix of the language by which it is modified. . . It seems likely that both infant and adult articulatory templates are control systems for a range of functionally equivalent vocal tract shapes rather than for specific patterns of muscular action. In fact, it is precisely to exploration of its own vocal tract and to discovery of its own patterns of muscular action that the infant's motor learning must be directed. . . The infant discovers phonetic "meaning" (and linguistic function) by discovering auditory-articulatory correspondences, that is, by discovering the commands required by its own vocal tract to match the output of its auditory template. [Because] the articulatory template is relatively abstract, the infant will begin to discover these correspondences before it has acquired the detailed motor skills of articulation; perceptual skill will precede motor skill. . . In due course the final system serves to segment the acoustic signal and perhaps, as analysis-by-synthesis models propose, to resolve the acoustic variance of phoneme or syllables. But its prior and more fundamental function is to establish the natural categories of speech. To perceive these categories is to trace the sound patterns of speech to their articulatory source and recover the motor commands from which they arose. The phonetic percept is then the correlate of these commands (Studdert-Kennedy, 1976, pp. 281–282).

The two current syllabic motor models of speech perception, from the Leningrad group and Haskins Laboratories, are modern versions of

Stetson's (1951) speculative model, now backed up by a large body of evidence from speech research in acoustics, physiology, and psychology. An important new aspect of the Haskins model is the auditory templates, which are assumed to be present at birth.

AUDITORY FEATURE DETECTORS AND SPEECH PERCEPTION

The existence of "auditory templates," as proposed in Studdert-Kennedy's theory, is supported by evidence from studies of infant perception of speech cues. First it was found that infants as young as 1 month reacted as if they discriminated the acoustic cues to voicing and place of articulation of stop consonants in ways very similar to adults. In particular, the infants discriminated between patterns where the pattern difference spanned an adult phoneme boundary, but did not seem to discriminate the same amount of difference when it did not span an adult phoneme boundary. For example, the 40-ms difference between a VOT of 20 ms and a VOT of 60 ms, which would cause an adult to hear a voiced vs. unvoiced stop, was discriminated by the infants; however, a 40-ms difference, between a VOT of 60 ms and a VOT of 100 ms, both of which would be heard by adults as unvoiced, was not discriminated by the infants. Thus it would appear that the infant is equipped with built-in "feature detectors" that detect an important difference for discriminating the voicing of stop consonants. The articulatory feature of place was studied in a similar way with the same results: differences in F2 transition that would cause an adult to hear the place difference [b] vs. [d] were also discriminated by infants, but equally different F2 transitions that would be heard as [b] by adults were not discriminated by infants (Eimas, 1974, 1975; Eimas et al., 1971). It would appear that the infant is equipped with built-in place detectors and voicing detectors which can be used to perceive consonants.

The second line of evidence for the existence of inherent auditory feature detectors for speech came from experiments to see whether the infant's feature detectors showed the same adaptation effect found with adults. The results were positive (Cooper, 1975; Eimas and Corbit, 1973).

The fact that speech feature adaptation occurs in infants implies that the feature detectors are located in the lower centers of the auditory system, not at higher levels, where learning processes would be necessary to form detector networks. Thus feature-detector processes may be carried out by the ear and the immediately subsequent auditory centers, in the early stages of speech perception, before the conversion into syllables and phonemes.

Recently the Leningrad group studied the auditory detection and temporal marking of syllables by listeners and proposed that the early auditory processes consist of the detection of the discontinuities in the temporal stream of the spectrum patterns of the incoming speech signal (Chistovich et al., 1975; Chistovich, Skeikin, and Lublinskaya, 1979). The shape of the vowel spectrum is analyzed by the auditory system and then discontinuities in the shape are detected. For example, amplitude discontinuities in the onset spectra in the F1–F2 region might be detected by an "unvoiced" feature detector. The information provided by the discontinuity detectors is, of course, in discrete categorical classes, and this would explain the occurrence of categorization in speech discrimination. Thus categorization arises in the earliest stage of the perceptual process, because the acoustic information supplied to the next stage (where syllabic motor commands will be formed) is in terms of types of acoustic discontinuities (Chistovich, personal communication).

Categorization of consonant perception may reflect auditory and speech processes that conform with one another: by their nature consonant articulations produce discontinuities in the sound pattern and the auditory system is designed to detect such discontinuities. Studdert-Kennedy et al. (1970), as part of a rebuttal to criticisms of motor theory, concluded that the evidence of categorization of perceptual response to consonant cues was not necessarily solely because of motor discontinuities.

CRITICISMS OF MOTOR THEORY

A number of speech researchers have criticized motor theories of speech perception. First, the acoustically oriented speech scientist knows that the limited physical possibilities and constraints on the vocal mechanism ensure that only certain pattern types are produced and thus he might expect that these patterns could easily be learned on the auditory basis of only a limited number of pattern types. Second, some auditory psychologists believe that the categorization of consonant perception may be due to the basic nature of the auditory system, not to the nature of consonant production. These arguments are reviewed as presented by some representative members of the "opposition" to motor theory.

How necessary is it for the child, in learning the language, to employ motor representation as a way of sorting out and identifying the phonemes? This might be the only feasible way if the phonemes were merely some unorganized source of stimulation in the child's world. However, as we have seen in our study of the acoustic features of the vowels and consonants, the acoustic structure of the features are consistently patterned because they are generated by consistent combinations of states and movements of the articulators. For example, the articulation of the nasal consonants always produces a strong low frequency murmur because of the closed oral tract, the open velar port, and the ongoing phonation of the vocal folds. The articulation of the stops produces gaps and discontinuities in the sound stream that have a limited range of durations because of the mechanical constraints in producing complete obstruction and reopening of the vocal tract. The voicing state of the vocal folds is either closed for voiced or open for unvoiced and this produces consistent differences in sound pattern. Stevens (1972) has reviewed the acoustic production of these consistent patterns and pointed out that they exist even to the extent of "favored" regions of consonant articulation where differences in position of constriction produce little or no difference in the formant pattern; it is as if language seeks out regions of relatively invariant, "quantal" patterns for use in the communication code.

Thus learning to identify the phonemes might simply involve learning to identify those consistent acoustic patterns that occur along with the situations and objects involved in communication. Since the only acoustic consistencies are due to articulatory consistencies, the perceptual responses naturally must reflect the articulatory sources, but no articulatory representation is necessary to the perceptual process nor to its acquisition by the child.

Fant first voiced objections to a motor theory of phoneme perception in 1963. He pointed out that, theoretically, distinctive articulatory features exist in speech production and in the speech acoustic wave, and that the perceptual features could be based solely on "being exposed to language in the first place and by reference to our own speech only in the second place" (Fant, 1967). In discussing the Halle-Stevens version of motor theory, where an analysis-by-motor synthesis model is proposed, Fant speculated that such a process was not suitable for phoneme perception, but might be useful in explaining characteristics of verbal message perception, where a running prediction is made of what words are to come, thus limiting the number of phonemic combinations that must be synthesized for comparison with the incoming auditory information. "My guess is that we have means of direct sensory decoding of speech and that prediction and correction via impulses from the motor system mainly add accuracy in making up for communication deficiencies [as under noisy conditions]...this prediction is probably indispensable for [perceiving speech at normal rates]...it ensures that the listener hears what he [can expect] to hear. But this is not the same as stating that one hears only what one can say" (Fant, 1967, p. 115).

The consistent patterning of speech sounds in time provides corresponding temporal consistencies for perceiving phonemic distinctions.

For example the fricative feature always involves a spectral discontinuity in time as the change takes place between the strong high frequency energy of the frication sound and the low frequency energy of an adjacent vowel or the silence of a stop. Also nasals and laterals produce spectral contrasts in time between louder and softer sound, and shifts in the spectral balance within the F1 and F3 region. Human sensory functions "are especially sensitive to variations of stimuli in place and time. We should pay more attention to this principle [in dealing] with basic dimensions of perceiving sound patterns to approach a dynamical theory of speech perception" (Fant, 1967, p. 119).

Fourcin (1972) suggested that the learned ability to produce speech correctly may actually be dependent on general auditory processes that can infer from received sound the forms of signal sources that produced the sound. He argued that the learner's acquisition of speech communication must be a process where the production processes of utterances are inferred by the perceiver, but that once the auditory processes for speech perception are learned there is no need for the details of production to be involved in perception.

The most extensive early criticisms of the idea that the categorization of consonant perception reflected the operation of a special motor reference were made by Lane, who wrote an excellent review of the Haskins Laboratories' studies on the categorization of discrimination of consonant cues and their interpretations of these findings (Lane, 1965). In one of these studies it was found that stimuli having VOT patterns of formant onset, causing them to be identified as [do] and [to], sounded merely like complex tone patterns when inverted in frequency so that the low formant onset preceded the onset of the high formant (from the [to] stimulus); these inverted patterns were heard as nonspeech sounds; they were not discriminable even though they had the same temporal patterns as in [do] and [to] (Liberman et al., 1961). The conclusion was that the normal VOT difference was perceived by a special motor reference speech decoder that was sensitized to this difference by previous motor experience in producing the voiced/unvoiced distinction in stop consonants.

Lane and his co-workers asked whether or not the categorization of the speech stimuli was in fact because they were heard as speech in contrast to the nonspeech stimuli. If one were trained to identify the inverted nonspeech stimuli, would their discrimination become more sensitive? Training was carried out, paying the listeners for each correct response, until some of the listeners could identify the two inverted nonspeech stimuli with a high degree of accuracy. These subjects were then given ABX discrimination tests covering the whole range of onset delays of the high formant. They showed better than chance discrimination at all points and sharpened discrimination between pairs of stimuli where one was the stimulus used in training (Lane, 1965, pp. 298–299). Thus it seemed to Lane that the categorization and associated sharp discrimination of speech cues was not necessarily due to the operation of a special motor reference process, because the same results can be obtained, after proper auditory training, for stimulus differences that are not produceable by speaking. A further experiment demonstrated that sharpened discrimination could also be produced by training in a visual discrimination task, and that therefore the effects were not peculiar to audition (Lane, 1965, p. 299). For Haskins Laboratories' rebuttal to Lane see Studdert-Kennedy et al. (1970).

Critics of motor theory also noted that the nature of the acoustic cues of consonants vs. those for vowels might explain the effect of categorization of consonant perception and the noncategorization of vowel perception. For the stop consonants, at least, the cues are rapid changes in the spectrum at the release of the consonant and at the onset of the vowel (the formant transitions). These events take place in 30 to 50 ms. On the other hand many of the vowels are identified on the basis of more steady frequency patterns. Thus we have very brief spectral changes for consonants and longer, slower changing spectral patterns for vowels, and this difference alone might account for consonants being perceived categorically but vowels on a continuum. Some experiments were carried out to study this possibility by Fujisaki and Kawashima (1969, 1970) and Pisoni (1975). In these studies it was found that vowel stimuli having very short duration are perceived more categorically than the same stimuli with longer duration.

Categorical perception of nonspeech sounds was demonstrated by Pisoni (1977). He used stimuli consisting of two sinusoidal tones, one of which was turned on with a delay relative to the other. A series of these tone pairs, with progressively greater delay, was perceived categorically. Discrimination was better between stimuli taken from different categories than between stimuli with the same difference in delay but taken from the same category. In other words, it would appear that, when suitably complex nonspeech acoustic stimuli are employed, perception tends naturally to organize itself categorically. Complex stimuli may be designed as a series and arranged on some physical continuum, as for example the relative onset time of the pure tones in Pisoni's experiment, but when these are heard as a series there tend to be natural psychophysical boundaries, points at which the perception abruptly shifts from one impression to another. This natural perceptual tendency generates two or more different regions along the continuum such that in regions between boundaries discrimination sensitivity is low or poor, but sensitivity across the boundaries is high because of the natural perceptual organization tendency.

Another line of evidence on the categorical perception of complex sounds comes from experiments where animals (chinchillas) were trained to discriminate the consonants [d] and [t] spoken with different vowels (Kuhl and Miller, 1975). After these animals had been trained, they were tested with synthetic speech sounds that varied in voice onset time (VOT). The previous experience enabled the animals to quickly learn to discriminate the synthetic voiced [d] from the synthetic unvoiced [t] on the basis of the voice onset cue alone. In addition, the identification as voiced or unvoiced by the chinchilla seemed to be categorical as a function of voice onset time, in that the identification showed a sharp crossover from voiced to unvoiced going from short to long voice onset times, at about the same voice onset time as found for humans listening to the same synthetic stimuli. Thus some evidence from animal discrimination suggests that the auditory systems of an animal can show categorical responses to speech cues even though the animal has no possibility to produce the cues.

It should also be pointed out that the category boundaries of speech features are probably not inherently fixed because the boundaries and sensitivity across or between boundaries are affected by linguistic experience. It is possible that there are more psychoacoustically natural perceptual categories than are actually employed in a given language, and with experience in learning the language only those perceptual categories remain discriminable that signal phoneme categories of the language to which the learner is exposed in early life. The study of the very complex interactions of natural perceptual categories and language experience is only in its beginning stages (see the analysis by Aslin and Pisoni, 1978).

STATUS OF MOTOR THEORY

Presently motor theories of speech perception are very vigorous because they stimulate important experiments that promise many further discoveries about speech. Two areas of knowledge about speech perception are poorly developed at present: the physiology of speech perception and the motor organization of speech production. Motor theory forces a focus on these two problems. At this stage the theory seems to be appealing rather than compelling, but it leads toward a complete knowledge of how the ear, brain, and motor system for speech can produce the highly efficient and flexible system that is speech communication (Liberman, 1974; Liberman and Studdert-Kennedy, 1977).

APPENDIX A
LABORATORY EXERCISES

To thoroughly learn acoustic phonetics students should analyze the sounds of speech themselves; they should measure the spectral and temporal features corresponding to the important phonetic features. The laboratory exercises that follow are designed for this purpose. They should be used in conjunction with the text; each exercise is assigned to a text chapter.

The exercises are not completely self-explanatory. Successful use requires supervised interpretation by an instructor who has experience in speech analysis and who has tried each exercise and modified it if necessary.

The major equipment needed is a sound spectrograph designed for speech analysis. Two suitable spectrographs are available on the market that record the analysis by repeatedly scanning a recorded utterance: the Kay Elemetrics Sona-Graph and the Voice Identification Inc., VII 700. These spectrographs produce spectrograms quickly, so that each student can have a spectrogram to measure during the lab period. If the older, slower version of the Kay Sona-Graph is used, a Sona-Graph should be provided for every two students. The author has used these older models, obtained from government surplus and reconditioned by the electronics staff; this provides the least initial expense for instrumentation. The quality of spectrograms that can be produced by Kay instruments is excellent. The VII 700 spectrograph is more expensive, also of very high quality, and fast enough to use for a group of about 10 students.

A new video spectrograph, the SSD, of Spectraphonics, Inc., is faster than any other on the market; it has the advantages that two independent records can be made and instantly displayed on a video monitor; the display is large enough to be used by the instructor before a group as large as 20 students, to point out salient spectral features for measurement by the student; the measurements can be carried out on copies made by a hard-copy attachment. The resolution is not as sharp as with the Kay or Voiceprint instruments, but it may be adequate for instructional purposes.

LAB 1. INTRODUCTION TO THE SOUND SPECTROGRAPH
(Text Chapter 2)

The purposes of this lab are to learn how to make spectrograms, to calibrate the two dimensions of the spectrogram (time and frequency), and to get a general idea of what a speech spectrogram presents. As a background, before lab, the student should briefly review Chapter 2 to be familiar with how the spectrograph works.

Making a Spectrogram

The instructor will demonstrate how to set and change the controls of the spectrograph, to first record speech and then reproduce the analysis. Use the 4-kHz frequency range and broadband filter, and the utterance *The spectrum of speech in time* spoken very distinctly by a male talker.

Each student should then go through the same procedures as demonstrated. If the spectrogram is not clear, as judged by the instructor, the controls should be readjusted and another spectrogram made. Usually each spectrograph requires somewhat different settings compared with others. The best settings should be noted down for each spectrograph. In general a light spectrogram shows more than a dark one.

Calibrations

The instructor will provide a standard signal generator that you can use to record a time calibration and a frequency calibration (on separate spectrograms).

Set the signal generator at 100 Hz for a time calibration and make a spectrogram. The spectrogram should show finely spaced vertical striations; these are spaced 10 ms apart in time. Make a marked time scale, 500 ms long, on the edge of a card or small sheet of paper. Within the scale mark every 20 ms and every 100 ms.

Set the signal generator at 500 Hz, the spectrograph on narrowband filter, and make a spectrogram for a frequency calibration. This will be a spectrogram showing parallel bands at 0 Hz and each multiple of 500 Hz, i.e., 500, 1000, 1500, 2000, 2500, 3000, 3500, and 4000 Hz. The odd multiples may appear to be darker. Make a frequency scale on another edge of your calibration card; first mark the positions of zero, 500 Hz, etc., opposite the centers of the parallel bands on the spectrogram. Then interpolate marks every 100 Hz.

The Speech Spectrogram

Try to locate the center point in time of each vowel in the speech spectrogram. Then calculate the syllable rate. There is always one vowel per syllable, so the time between syllables is indicated by the time between vowel centers.

What, approximately, is the average time in ms between vowel centers? Based on this, what is the average syllable rate? Remember:

$$\text{Syllable rate} = \frac{1000}{\text{Average time between vowel centers}}$$

Notice the gross changes between higher and lower frequency sounds. For example, the [s] and [ʃ] sounds do not have strong energy in the same frequency ranges as the vowels. What are these frequency ranges, approximately, as indicated in your spectrogram?

Notes to Instructor

This lab is written as if there are no more than two students per spectrograph and the spectrograph does not have internal calibration signals. All spectrograms should be made with the high frequencies emphasized (setting "HS" for initial recording on the older Sona-Graphs). The calibration signal generator should provide a sawtooth waveform. If this is not available a sine wave generator may be used with a high input level to the spectrograph, high enough to severely overload the input stages, causing them to generate all the harmonics of the frequency of the input signal; then usually the odd harmonics are stronger and the even harmonics may have to be interpolated in the calibration spectrogram. Thus, for the frequency calibration, the marked bands are strong for 0, 500, 1500, 2500, and 3500 Hz.

The position of the vertical range marked on the paper by the spectrograph should be adjusted (via a screw designated "zero adjust" on some models) so that all of the noise base band is marked; the center of this band is zero frequency.

LAB 2. LENGTH RULE FOR TUBE RESONANCES (Text Chapter 3)

The purpose of this experiment is to demonstrate by measurement the dependence of the frequency of the main resonance of a tube on its length. The main tube resonance is due to repeated reflections of the sound disturbances between the ends of the tube. In speech it is the reflections of the vocal pulses between the ends of the pharyngeal-oral tube that produces the main voice resonance (the first formant).

If we use a tube that is very long, the reflections are far enough apart in time to be seen on a spectrogram as separate pulses. Thus in this experiment we first use long tubes so we can measure the time between reflections and calculate from this the main resonant frequency. We then turn to short, vocal-tract size tubes and measure their resonant frequencies on the spectrograph frequency scale.

The main resonance of a tube in response to an air pulse is caused by the reflection of the pulse at the ends of the tube and the consequent reversal of the travel of the pulse wave. The frequency of the resonance is determined by two factors: 1) the length of the tube and 2) the types of reflection at the ends. The longer the tube, the longer the time for the pulse to travel between the ends, and thus the lower the frequency of appearance of pulses at the open end. The vocal tract is a tube that is closed at the glottis end and open at the lip end. The reflection from the open end is the inverse in orientation of the original pulse arriving from the closed end; this "inverse pulse" then travels back down the tube, is reflected at the closed end, travels back out, is reinverted at the open end, makes another round trip of the tube, and reappears at the open end with the same orientation as the original pulse. Thus *two round trips are required for a complete cycle of repetition* of the appearance of the original pulse orientation. Therefore the main resonant frequency of a tube that is closed at one end and open at the other is dependent on the necessity of four traverses of the tube per cycle, and the frequency is equal to 1 second divided by four times the traverse time.

Measure the time between reflections of a sound pulse in long tubes. Pulse the large tubes at one end by hitting the open end with the palm of the hand. After the hand hits, keep it against the end to close off that end while leaving the other end open near the microphone of the spectrograph. A good resonance of the pulsed tube is fairly loud and long, lasting about 1 second; it sounds like a brief low organ tone or a "boing." If only a short, dead thud is heard the hit was not solid enough. Record and make a spectrogram of two solid hits.

What is the time between reflections of a sound pulse in the following tubes, closed at one end?

a.   A 20-foot tube
b.   A 10-foot tube

(Two 10-foot sections of 2 inches in diameter Amoco Underground Electrical Duct Type II can be used with a matching sleeve for connecting the two 10-foot sections to make the 20-foot tube.)

Sound propagates at 344.4 meters per second or 1130 feet per second, taking approximately 0.9 ms to travel 1 foot. Are the pulse reflections on the spectrograms the correct distance apart in time, according to the two different lengths of tube and the time required to travel 1 foot? Remember that, after the pulse first reaches the open end, where the microphone is located, it must travel down the tube and back again before another pulse arrives at the open end.

Also there are two intervals between pulses for each four traverses of the tube length. What are the resonant frequencies corresponding to four traverses of each tube?

Measure the main resonant frequencies of model vocal tract tubes.
Two short plastic tubes are provided, which are model vocal tract tubes:

1.   An 18-cm tube; model of adult male vocal tract
2.   A 9-cm tube; model of an infant length vocal tract

Using the model vocal tract tubes, record and measure the sound resulting from pulsing the tubes. Pulse the tube by making a "Bronx cheer" between pursed lips held tightly pressed to one end of the tube. Record the sound from the open end of the tube and make spectrograms.

Assume that the 18-cm tube is 7 inches long. What would be the time between appearances of reflections at the open end? (This cannot be measured on the spectrogram because the pulses are too close together on the spectrogram.)

Every other reflection is inverted. What is the time period between the inverted reflections and what is the corresponding frequency? How is this frequency represented in the spectrogram?

Notes to Instructor

The tricky thing in this exercise is that the inverted polarity pulses and the noninverted pulses appear in the spectrogram in the same upward-pointing orientation. On close examination it will be seen that the "original orientation," noninverted pulses are marked differently from the inverted. The first pulse recorded is the "original" (only its reflection is inverted, not the pulse radiated to the microphone). The interval between any two pulses is the time for one round trip down the tube toward the closed end and back out to the microphone.

The 18-cm and 9-cm tubes should be rigid, about 1 inch inside diameter, and smooth walled. The author has found Lucite tubes of about $1/8$-inch thickness to be satisfactory.

LAB 3. TUBE CONSTRICTION/FORMANT RULES (Text Chapter 3)

The purpose is to see how different constrictions affect the location of formant frequencies. A flexible tube, 18 cm long and about 1 inch in diameter, is provided. The tube is excited with air pulses by blowing through pursed lips applied to one end, which is held tightly against the lips, as in the previous experiment. Record the sound output on the spectrograph from pulsing the tube under four different conditions of constriction:

1.   Varying, for a single spectrogram, the amount of an "alveolar" constriction by squeezing the tube between thumb and forefinger at a

point 13 cm from the pulsed (closed) end of the tube. Measure the frequencies of F1, F2, and F3 for several amounts of constriction.
2. Varying amounts of back constriction at 6 cm from the closed end. Repeat the formant measurements.
3. Rounding plus back constriction; repeat (2) with "front" constriction at the open end of the tube. Repeat the formant measurements.
4. Constriction of the "pharynx" area of the tube (constrict the tube over the portion near the closed end over a distance of about 3 cm toward the open end). Measure the frequencies of F1, F2, and F3.

Notes to Instructor

The tubing used for this exercise should be semi-rigid but not too difficult to squeeze to a narrow constriction. If the tubing is too thin and flexible the tube formants can be damped by the loss of sound energy through the tube walls, and zeros in the tube response can cause the formant frequencies to appear to be shifted. Heavy rubber tubing from a chemistry lab works well if it is about 1/8-inch in wall thickness. The tubes should be marked off in cm from the "closed end."

LAB 4. VOICE PITCH (FUNDAMENTAL FREQUENCY), HARMONICS, AND FORMANTS (Text Chapter 4)

The purpose is to learn how to measure pitch and to see how it is independent of formants.
Select and record a vowel using a male talker who pronounces it with slow changes in pitch, up and down. The vowel [æ] is especially good for this. Make both broadband and narrowband spectrograms.

Independence of Voice Pitch and Formants

The broadband spectrograms show the frequency positions of the formants, which should be relatively steady frequencies if the vowel shape was held constant by the talker while he changed his pitch. Measure the approximate formant frequencies.
The narrowband spectrogram shows each individual harmonic of the vowel sound. The harmonics are multiples of the fundamental frequency and therefore will be seen to move up or down in frequency as the voice pitch changes up or down. The harmonics are strong or weak depending on their frequency relations to the steady formant frequencies of the vowel. When a harmonic is near a formant frequency it is strong (darker on the spectrogram) and when it is not near a formant it is weak or not visible on the spectrogram. Note on the spectrograms that the pitch of the voice, i.e., the fundamental frequency, is independent of the formants.

As the voice pitch changes, gliding up or down, the formants remain at the same frequencies.

Measurement of Pitch

The voice pitch (fundamental frequency) can be measured in two different ways: 1) by counting the number of voicing pulses in a given time period on the broadband spectrogram and 2) by measuring the frequency spacing of harmonic intervals on a narrowband spectrogram.

Pitch by Number of Voice Pulses Per Unit of Time

During vowels the broadband spectrogram shows vertical striations that correspond to the individual pulses of airflow from the glottis as they excite the resonances of the vocal tract. The voice pitch or fundamental frequency is equal to the pulse rate of the airflow pulses. You can measure the pitch by finding the number of striations (pulses) per unit of time. A convenient subunit to use is 200 ms; 200 ms is $^1/_5$ second; you can measure the pitch by counting the number of striations in 200 ms and multiplying this number by 5. Measure the pitch at points of high and low pitch in the broadband spectrogram.

Pitch by Frequency Spacing of Harmonic Intervals

You can also measure the pitch by using the principle that the harmonics are multiples of the fundamental frequency and thus are spaced at frequency intervals equal to the fundamental frequency. At any time point on the narrowband spectrogram, the pitch can be determined by measuring the frequency range spanned by a given number of intervals between harmonics and dividing by the number of intervals. This is a more accurate method. Make the measurements at a point midway in the 200-ms time intervals used previously. Some harmonics may be too weak to see but must be counted anyway. Taking the span of 10 successive harmonic intervals is a convenient way to measure the fundamental frequency; the fundamental frequency is then the frequency range spanned by 11 harmonics (10 harmonic intervals) divided by 10.

Note to Instructor

No more problems after this one.

LAB 5. SPECTRA OF FRONT VOWELS (Text Chapter 4)

The purpose is to study the formant patterns of the front vowels.

A. Record and analyze the isolated vowels [i, ɪ, e, ɛ, æ]. Record and analyze [i] with a slow pitch change of about one octave.

B.   Measure the formant frequencies and amplitudes of F1 and F2. Note
     that the F1 and F2 frequencies follow a certain progression from the
     more constricted [i] to the least constricted [æ].
C.   Make a narrowband spectrogram of the [i] having the pitch change.
     Note that the pitch changes over a large range but the formant fre-
     quencies do not change.

LAB 6. SPECTRA OF BACK VOWELS AND DIPHTHONGS (Text Chapter 4)

The purpose of this lab is to study the formant patterns of the back vowels
and diphthongs.

Make broadband spectrograms of the back vowels [ɑ, ɔ, ʊ, o, u] and
the diphthongs [ɪu, eɪ, aɪ, ɔɪ, ɑu].

Measure the F1 and F2 frequencies and note how they change with
different locations and degrees of tongue constriction.

The large contribution of lip-rounding to formant lowering can be
studied by recording a spectrogram beginning with [o] and smiling while
holding the same tongue position.

LAB 7. PROSODIC FEATURES (Text Chapter 5)

The prosodic features of a sentence are embodied in variations in pitch,
duration, and spectral balance. The purpose of this lab is to demonstrate
all three of these variations.

A.   Of first concern are the pitch contours that typically differentiate the
     grammatical function of a statement vs. that of a question. Record
     on the spectrograph the statement *That's a buy* and the question *Is
     that a buy?* Make a narrowband spectrogram.

     We also use the prosodic features to make emphatic statements
     with the same inverted order of subject and verb employed for ques-
     tions. For example, we can say "Is that a buy!", a statement express-
     ing enthusiastic emphasis. The emphasis can be put on any word we
     wish to especially impress on the listener.

     Record and study these effects, putting the emphasis on *that* in
     one statement and on *buy* in another. Make both narrow- and broad-
     band spectrograms of the two statements:

                          "Is *that* a buy!"
                          "Is that a *buy!*"

     Trace the pitch contours of all the sentences along either the 5th
     or 10th harmonic of the voiced sounds.

Measure the pitch at the beginning, middle, and end of each vowel. The pitch at any point is easily obtained by measuring the frequency level of a harmonic and then dividing this frequency by the harmonic number. For example, if the fifth harmonic is at 550 Hz, then the pitch is $550/5 = 110$ Hz. Make sure you have identified the harmonic number correctly; this can be difficult when the pitch is low and the harmonics are closely packed together in the spectrogram.

How do the statements and question differ in overall trend of pitch from beginning to end?

How does the pitch vary with emphasis, between words and within words?

B. Measure the duration of each syllable. How does duration vary with emphasis?

C. See whether there is a change in spectrum balance by comparing intensities of F2, F3, F4, relative to that of F1, depending on emphasis.

LAB 8. FORMANT TRANSITIONS—DIPHTHONGS vs. GLIDE CONSONANTS vs. STOP CONSONANTS (Text Chapter 6)

The purpose is to measure the formant transitions, including the rate and amount of transition, for glide consonants vs. diphthongs vs. stop consonants.

Make broadband spectrograms of the following phrases:

"That's a wow."
"That's a bow [baʊ]."

"Paint a yacht."
"Paint a dot."

Measure the F1 transitions, comparing durations of transition between diphthongs, glides, and stop consonants; observe transitions in F2.

The rate of change in articulation governs the duration of F1 transition. Change in articulation occurs fastest for stops, slower for glides, and slowest for diphthongs.

In looking at the formation of [w], in "That's a wow," we can see that, as the lips start to round, the formants are all lowered, and in the transition to the vowel following the [w] the formants go up again as the mouth opens.

For [b] in "That's a bow [baʊ]" there is a period of complete closure followed by a burst and a rapid F1 transition as compared to the glide and diphthong.

In "Paint a yacht" vs. "Paint a dot," again we see that the F1 transition for glides is longer than the transition for stop consonants.

The difference between the alveolars [d] and [j] and the labials [b] and [w] is in the F2 transitions. Constriction at an alveolar position causes F2 to rise in frequency whereas constriction or rounding at the lips causes F2 to decrease in frequency.

The F1 patterns are nearly the same for both alveolars and labials. F1 is lowered in frequency during the transition from vowel to consonant and rises in frequency during the transition from consonant to vowel.

LAB 9. NASALS AND GLIDES (Text Chapter 7)

The purpose is to study the acoustic features of nasals and glides and compare them with other consonant groups.

Record the following phrases on four or five spectrograms: 1) a nod, anon, a Dodd; 2) a mob, a bob, a bomb; 3) a bang on, a bag on, a ban on; 4) a yacht, a lot, a watt, a rot.

Study the spectrograms for the following characteristics:

a.   Similarity of nasals and stops in a given spectrogram (same place of articulation) of the F2 formant transitions
b.   Spectra of the nasal murmurs during constriction
c.   Note effects of any zeros in vowels adjacent to nasals
d.   Differences among glides
e.   Differences between glides and nasals in speed of F1 transition and spectra during the constrictions

LAB 10. FRICATIVE/STOP DISTINCTION (Text Chapter 7)

The purpose is to study the sound patterns of stops and fricatives.

Record the following phrases in four spectrograms: 1) a top, a sop, a shop; 2) a dog, a zog, a ʒog [əʒɔg]; 3) a pop, a fop, a θop [əθap]; 4) a bog, a vog [əvɑg], a ðog [əðɑg].

Compare the following characteristics: fricative/stop formant transitions, fricative/stop constriction durations, unvoiced fricative spectra among [s, ʃ, f, θ], and male vs. female [ʃ].

Answer the following questions, based on the spectrograms:

What are the main differences between stops and fricatives?
How do the unvoiced fricatives differ among each other in constriction spectrum and in formant transitions?

How does voicing affect these differences?

How are male and female size differences reflected in the friction spectrum?

LAB 11. VOICED/UNVOICED DISTINCTION (Text Chapter 8)

The purpose is to study differences between voiced and unvoiced consonants by comparing spectrograms of both.

Make a spectrogram of the phrases "a buy" and "a pie." For the voiced bilabial stop [b] there is a period of weak sound during the complete occlusion of the lips. This is followed by a release burst of sound before the following vowel begins. Vocal fold pulsing continues for most of the closure period and the burst at the release is short and weak. On the spectrogram this appears as a transient "spike" followed by the immediate resumption of the vocal fold pulsing for the vowel. (Make a very dark spectrogram to see the transient best.) Why is the voicing during the [b] closure weak or absent in part?

For the unvoiced [p] there is no vocal fold pulsing during the closure and the burst on release is strong and of longer duration. On the spectrogram this appears as a strong transient burst followed by further turbulent sound, called aspiration, before the vowel begins. Describe the spectrum of the aspiration.

Because the release burst is longer for the unvoiced consonant the resulting voiced phase of the syllable is shorter for the unvoiced consonant than it is for the voiced consonant.

The vowel preceding the voiced stop is longer than the vowel preceding the unvoiced stop, perhaps because the closing movement for voiced stops is a little slower. Is a difference in rate of movement seen in the formant transitions, especially in F1?

Make a spectrogram of the phrases "a die" and "a tie." All of the preceding comments about the voiced-unvoiced labial stop distinction also apply here to the alveolar stops. There is one main difference between the alveolar stops and the labial stops, because the consonant closures are made at different locations in the vocal tract. This difference appears in the frequency transitions of F2. For the labial stops, F2 is lowered in frequency by the labial constriction. For the alveolar stops F2 is raised by the constriction. Often the unvoiced F2 transition occurs only in the release burst. (See Chapter 9 on place effects.)

Make a spectrogram of the phrases *a V* and *a fee* (be sure to use the high frequency emphasis "HS"). The essential difference between the fricatives and the stops studied previously is that the stops make a complete closure of the oral tract whereas the fricatives are produced with a narrow constriction. The duration of this constriction period is usually longer than the closure period of a stop. During the constriction a high frequency friction sound is seen, provided there is sufficient playback level when making the spectrogram.

The release of the fricatives is not as sharply defined as it is for the stops because there is no release burst for fricatives.

Voicing pulses are usually seen during the constriction of voiced fricatives, but partial or complete de-voicing can occur just as for voiced stops. The glottal pulsing provides the air flowing into the mouth and this causes a corresponding pulsing in the friction sound in the high frequencies. Is there an intensity difference between the voiced and unvoiced friction sound in the high frequencies? Why?

Is the vowel preceding the voiced fricative consonant longer than the one preceding the unvoiced fricative, as it was for stops?

Make a spectrogram of the sentence *He sued the zoo*. For the unvoiced [s] we see a more intense high frequency friction sound than for [z]. This is a typical difference between unvoiced and voiced fricatives. For unvoiced consonants the glottis is held wide open, allowing a high flow into the vocal tract and a high flow through the constriction. For the voiced fricatives the glottis is continuously closing and opening; it is constricted a great deal of the time, thus reducing the airflow through the upper constriction, causing less turbulence and a lower intensity of high frequency friction.

LAB 12. COARTICULATION EFFECTS (Text Chapter 10)

Make spectrograms to observe and analyze the following coarticulation effects: 1) effect of following vowel on preceding consonant and 2) effect of following vowel on two consonants.

The following words and utterances may be grouped in three spectrograms: 1) seat [sit], sought [sɔt], suit [sut]; 2) sweep [swip], swap [swɑp], swoop [swup].

Take care that the words and sounds are spoken rapidly with natural fluency because a very careful or stilted style reduces normal coarticulatory effects.

How does the spectrum of [s] depend on the following vowel? How is the compound consonant [sw] affected by the following vowel?

APPENDIX B
CLASSIFIED BIBLIOGRAPHY
FOR FURTHER READING

Most of the readings cited in the text on various topics are original research literature. They are suitable for the advanced student but sometimes do not take a broad view of the topics discussed. The following literature can be consulted for further general study of speech and its acoustic communication, or for more depth on a variety of related topics collected in one publication.

SPEECH ACOUSTICS AND COMMUNICATION

Denes, P., and E. Pinson. 1973. The Speech Chain: The Physics and Biology of Spoken Language. Anchor Press/Doubleday, New York. This book is written on a very elementary level, making it easy to quickly survey the acoustics of speech communication and some of its applications.

Fant, G. 1960. Acoustic Theory of Speech Production. Mouton & Co., The Hague. The classic treatise on the acoustic analysis and synthesis of speech production. It covers all major sound classes and features.

Fant, G. 1973. Speech Sounds and Features. The MIT Press, Cambridge, Mass. This book presents further studies and extensions of Fant's analysis of speech sounds, production, and their relation to the theory of distinctive features.

Flanagan, J. L. 1972. Speech Analysis Synthesis and Perception. 2nd Ed. Springer-Verlag, New York. The most complete technical book summarizing all aspects and ramifications of speech communication from the acoustic point of view.

Flanagan, J. L., and L. R. Rabiner. 1973. Speech Synthesis. Dowden, Hutchinson, & Ross, Stroudsburg, Pa. A reprint collection of 46 important research papers on speech analysis, perception, and synthesis of speech, leading up to our current technology of computer speech from printed text.

Fry, D. B. 1979. The Physics of Speech. Cambridge University Press, Cambridge, London. An introduction to the physics of sound, the acoustic composition of the major speech sounds, and acoustic cues in speech perception. The level is somewhere between that of the Denes and Pinson Speech Chain and that of the present book.

Lehiste, I. (ed.). 1967. Readings in Acoustic Phonetics. The MIT Press, Cambridge, Mass. A collection of important studies on acoustic theory of speech, speech sound patterns, synthesis of speech, and speech perception.

IMPAIRED SPEECH COMMUNICATION
AND AIDS FOR THE HANDICAPPED

Calvert, D., and R. Silverman. 1975. Speech and Deafness. Alexander Graham Bell Association, Volta Place, Washington, D.C. A basic textbook on teaching speech communication to deaf children, based on acoustics and articulatory information.

Fant, G. (ed.). 1972. International Symposium on Speech Communication Ability and Profound Deafness. Alexander Graham Bell Association, Volta Place, Washington, D.C. Contains many original research papers on the acoustic-phonetics approach to describing hearing impairment.

Frisina, R. (ed.). 1976. A Bicentennial Monograph on Hearing Impairment: Trends in the USA. Alexander Graham Bell Association, Volta Place, Washington, D.C. A wide-ranging collection of papers by experts in audiology, speech, and the education of the deaf, with considerable emphasis on speech communication.

Kavanaugh, J., and W. Strange (eds.). 1978. Speech and Language in the Laboratory, School, and Clinic. The MIT Press, Cambridge, Mass. Papers and discussions by prominent scientists on theory and applications of research to improve practices in hearing and speech clinics and special education classes.

Levitt, H., J. M. Pickett, and R. Houde (eds.). 1979. Sensory Aids for the Hearing-Impaired. Institute of Electrical and Electronics Engineers, New York. (Order from IEEE Service Center, 445 Hoes Lane, Piscataway, N.J. 08854.) This is a reprint collection of over 60 important research papers and theoretical discussions on speech acoustics related to the following subjects: hearing aids, residual hearing and frequency lowering, visual and tactile speech for the deaf, and electrical hearing. The reader is oriented to each major area by extensive critical comments written by the editors.

Ling, D. 1976. Speech and the Hearing-Impaired Child: Theory and Practice. Alexander Graham Bell Association, Volta Place, Washington, D.C. A book reviewing the speech production problem of deaf children from a phonetic point of view and prescribing a systematic series of speech training procedures.

Stark, R. E. (ed.). 1974. Sensory Capabilities of Hearing-Impaired Children. University Park Press, Baltimore. Contains papers and extended discussions by communication scientists, clinical and educational researchers, on the speech communication problem of deaf children.

Tower, D. R. (ed.). 1975. The Nervous System, Vol. 3, Human Communication and Its Disorders. Raven Press, New York. A large compendium of state-of-the-science papers providing succinct summaries of many topics related to impaired and normal speech communication.

Winitz, H. 1975. From Syllable to Conversation. University Park Press, Baltimore. A distinctive features approach to the training of deficient articulation.

SPEECH PERCEPTION

Carterette, E. C., and M. P. Friedman. (eds.). 1976. Handbook of Perception, Vol. VII, Language and Speech. Academic Press, New York. This volume covers a wide range of important topics. The chapters on the organization of speech production and speech feature detectors in perception are especially good.

Cohen, A., and S. G. Nooteboom. 1975. Structure and Process in Speech Perception. Springer-Verlag, New York. A collection of papers for a 1975 symposium by many of the major researchers in speech perception. For the advanced student, an excellent introduction to the wide variety of experimental approaches, issues, and techniques.

Fant, G., and M. Tatham (eds.). 1975. Auditory Analysis and Perception of Speech. Academic Press, New York. A collection of recent papers on the auditory system and related acoustic theories of speech perception, including some work in the Soviet Union. For the advanced student.

Fischer-Jørgensen, E., J. Rischel, and N. Thorsen (eds.). 1979. Proceedings of the Ninth International Congress of Phonetic Sciences, Copenhagen, Vols, I, II, III. Institute of Phonetics, University of Copenhagen, 96 Njalsgade, 2300 Copenhagen S, Denmark. An excellent source for the advanced student of recent state-of-the-science reports on the phonetic sciences, including speech perception and phonologic theory. Volume I contains status reports on speech production by MacNeilage, Ladefoged, and Sawashima and on speech perception by Studdert-Kennedy, Chistovich, and Fujisaki (these are also scheduled to be published in Language and Speech, 1980). Volume I also contains abstracts of special lectures for about 250 contributed papers. Volume II contains summaries of papers presented in Congress symposia on specific topics, such as speech-motor control, perception, prosodics, speech acquisition by children, and socio-phonetics. Volume III, to be published after the Congress, will contain more complete versions of some of the lectures of the Congress and discussion sessions.

Massaro, D. (ed.). 1975. Understanding Language. Academic Press, New York. An advanced text on speech perception and reading, written by experimental psychologists. The chapter on theories of speech perception is very complete, although it does not cover the work in the Soviet Union.

Restle, F., R. M. Shiffrin, N. J. Castellan, H. R. Lindman, and D. B. Pisoni (eds.). 1975. Cognitive Theory, Vol. 1. Erlbaum Associates, Hillsdale, N.J. Part I, entitled Contemporary Issues in Speech Perception, contains good review articles on the nature of phonetic categories, speech feature detectors, and others.

GENERAL SPEECH SCIENCE AND EXPERIMENTAL PHONETICS

Kent, R. J. 1976. Models of speech production. In N. Lass (ed.), Contemporary Issues in Experimental Phonetics, pp. 79–104. Academic Press, New York. An excellent review for the advanced student, giving a clear exposition of the issues and current models in the study of the organization of speech production.

Lass, N. (ed.). 1976. Contemporary Issues in Experimental Phonetics. Academic Press, New York. An excellent collection of advanced discussions and reviews; covers methods of research, speech production, speech acoustics, and perception.

Lehiste, L. 1970. Suprasegmentals. The MIT Press, Cambridge, Mass. A thorough review of research on the acoustics, production, and perception of prosodic features.

Lieberman, P. 1967. Intonation, Perception, and Language. The MIT Press, Cambridge, Mass. An extended experimental study and discussion, presenting the original version of the breath group theory of intonation and stress, and its linguistic implications.

Lieberman, P. 1977. Speech Physiology and Acoustic Phonetics. Macmillan Publishing Co., New York. An introductory textbook, somewhat like the present one but with more emphasis on physiology and less on acoustic features. Good summary chapters on speech synthesis, perception, and phonetic theories.

Lindblom, B., and S. Öhman (eds.). 1979. Frontiers of Speech Communication Research. Academic Press, London. A collection of current research papers, suitable for the advanced student, covering a wide range of acoustic, physiologic, and perceptual topics in speech communication science.

Malmberg, B. (ed.). 1970. Manual of Phonetics. North-Holland, Amsterdam. Not really a manual for doing phonetic research but contains good chapters by Fant, by Fry, and by Jakobson/Halle (on distinctive feature theory).

Minifie, F., T. Hixon, and F. Williams. 1973. Normal Aspects of Speech, Hearing, and Language. Prentice-Hall, Englewood Cliffs, N.J. A good introductory text to the broad field of the speech and hearing sciences.

Zemlin, W. 1968. Speech and Hearing Science: Anatomy and Physiology. Prentice-Hall, Englewood Cliffs, N.J. An advanced textbook, especially good in its anatomical description of the speech and hearing mechanisms.

MOTOR AND NEURAL ORGANIZATION OF SPEECH

Gilbert, J. (ed.). 1972. Speech and Cortical Functioning. Academic Press, New York. Not a complete coverage of its topic but contains excellent advanced papers by researchers in this area of study.

Houde, R. 1968. A Study of Tongue Body Motion During Selected Speech Sounds. SCRL Monograph No. 2, Speech Communications Research Laboratory, Santa Barbara, Cal. Also designated as AF-AFOSR-1252-67 of the Air Force Office of Scientific Research. A research study of tongue movements for vowels spoken in syllables with different consonants. In this report, and in Perkell's (1969), the student will find curves of speech movements, together with spectrograms of the resulting utterances, available for detailed study.

MacNeilage, P. 1970. Motor control of serial ordering of speech. Psychol. Rev. 77:182–196. A theoretical paper by one of the prominent researchers on the motor control processes of speech.

Perkell, J. 1969. Physiology of Speech Production: Results and Implications of a Quantitative Cineradiographic Study. The MIT Press, Cambridge, Mass. A research study of the movements of the articulators in producing consonants and vowels.

Perkell, J. Phonetic features and the physiology of speech production. In B. Butterworth (ed.), Language Production. Academic Press, New York. In press. A very recent review of theories of the motor organization of speech production.

Sawashima, M., and F. S. Cooper (eds.). 1977. Dynamic Aspects of Speech Production. University of Tokyo Press, Tokyo. Symposium papers by current workers on the movements of speech.

Stelmach, G. E. (ed.). 1976. Motor Control: Issues and Trends. Academic Press, New York. For advanced reading by the scientific student of neuromuscular organization of motor performance of all types, including speech.

ACOUSTIC LINGUISTICS[1]

Chomsky, N., and M. Halle. 1968. The Sound Pattern of English. Harper & Row Publishers, New York. For the advanced student, a complete exposition of distinctive feature theory applied to English.

Delattre, P. 1965. Comparing the Phonetic Features of English, French, German, and Spanish. Chilton Books, Philadelphia. A detailed description of the acoustic pattern differences of four major languages.

Halle, M. 1959. The Sound Pattern of Russian. Mouton & Co., The Hague. A distinctive feature analysis of Russian with spectrograms and tables of acoustic characteristics. Also contains a historical chapter on acoustic analysis of speech.

Hammerich, L. L., R. Jakobson, and E. Zwirner (eds.). 1971. Form and Substance. Akademisk Forlag, Copenhagen. Research and theoretical papers on phonology, speech acoustics, and perception.

Jakobson, R., G. Fant, and M. Halle. 1969. Preliminaries to Speech Analysis, The Distinctive Features and their Correlates. The MIT Press, Cambridge, Mass. The original description of distinctive features, first published as an MIT research report in 1951.

Kavanaugh, J., and J. Cutting. 1975. The Role of Speech in Language. The MIT Press, Cambridge, Mass. This book is hard to classify because it contains interdisciplinary research and discussions of why such a complex coding, in phonology and grammer, is necessary to go from meaning to speech sound. Discussions of sign language codes are also included, to compare with the speech code.

GENERAL PHONETICS

Ladefoged, P. 1975. A Course in Phonetics. Harcourt Brace Jovanovich, New York. An excellent introductory text that is linguistically oriented; includes some coverage of acoustics and speech physiology. An authoritative approach by a distinguished experimental linguist.

Singh, S., and K. S. Singh. 1976. Phonetics: Principles and Practices. University Park Press, Baltimore. This introductory text is interesting for its motion pictures of the front facial view of articulations and correlated soundtracks and spectrograms, for numerous vowels and consonants.

---

[1]Works that are primarily linguistic but with considerable emphasis on speech acoustic patterns.

BIOLOGY OF SPEECH

Lenneberg, E. 1967. Biological Foundations of Language. John Wiley & Sons, New York. An advanced presentation of the many fascinating aspects of this subject by a recognized authority.

Lieberman, P. 1975. On the Origins of Language, An Introduction to the Evolution of Human Speech. Macmillan Publishing Co., New York. Brings together evidence from the acoustic theory of speech, the brain size and vocal tract shapes of early man from fossil skull measurements, and the development of tool-making behavior, to argue that highly articulate speech was necessary for the evolution of our present human languages and related human culture.

Menyuk, P. 1977. Language and Maturation. The MIT Press, Cambridge, Mass. An introductory science text on the fascinating field of child language development, from first speech sound production and perception to complete knowledge of grammar.

HUMAN COMMUNICATION THEORY

Cherry, C. 1966. On Human Communication. 2nd Ed. The MIT Press, Cambridge, Mass. An introductory book, but an encyclopedic one, on communication science covering mathematical theory, the nature of languages, speech analysis, information theories, linguistics, perception, and cognition.

REFERENCES

Alekin, R. O., Y. A. Klaas, and L. A. Chistovich. 1962. Human reaction time in the copying of aurally perceived vowels. Sov. Phys. Acoust. 8:17–22.

Aslin, R. N., and D. B. Pisoni. 1978. Some developmental processes in speech perception. Psychology Department, Indiana University, Bloomington, IN 47401. (Reprint of paper for the National Institute of Child Health and Human Development Conference "Child Phonology: Perception, Production, Deviation," Bethesda, Md.)

Atkinson, J. 1978. Correlation analysis of the physiological factors controlling fundamental voice frequency. J. Acoust. Soc. Am. 63(1):211–222.

Benade, A. H. 1960. Horns, Strings, and Harmony. Doubleday & Co., New York.

Blumstein, S. E., K. N. Stevens and G. N. Nigro. 1977. Property detectors for bursts and transitions in speech perception. J. Acoust. Soc. Am. 61:1301–1313.

Boring, E. G. 1942. Sensation and Perception in the History of Experimental Psychology. Appleton-Century-Crofts, New York.

Boring, E. G. 1950. A History of Experimental Psychology. 2nd Ed. Appleton-Century-Crofts, New York.

Bruce, R. V. 1973. Bell. Little, Brown & Co., Boston.

Carlson, R., G. Fant, and B. Granström. 1975. Two-formant models, pitch, and vowel perception. In G. Fant and M. Tatham (eds.), Auditory Analysis and Perception of Speech, pp. 55–82. Academic Press, New York.

Carré, R., R. Descout, and M. Wajskop (eds.). 1977. Modèles Articulatoire et Phonétique. [Articulatory Modeling and Phonetics.] Proceedings of the Symposium at Grenoble, July 10–12. Groupe de la Communication Parlée du Groupement des Acousticiens de Langue Française (GALF). (May be ordered from Institut de Phonétique de l'Université de Bruxelles -C. P. 110-50, av. F. Roosevelt, B-1050 Brussels, Belgium.)

Carterette, E. C., and M. H. Jones. 1974. Informal Speech. University of California Press, Berkeley and Los Angeles.

Chiba, T., and M. Kajiyama. 1941. The Vowel, Its Nature and Structure. Tokyo-Kaiseikan, Tokyo.

Chistovich, L. A. 1960. Classification of rapidly repeated speech sounds. Sov. Phys. Acoust. 6:393.

Chistovich, L. A. 1968. A change in the basic frequency of the voice as a distinguishing attribute of consonants. Akustich. zhurn. 14:449–456. (Citation based on translation of Chistovich, L. A. 1969. Variation of the fundamental voice pitch as a discriminatory cue for consonants. Sov. Phys. Acoust. 14:372–378.)

Chistovich, L. A., G. Fant, A. Serpa-Leitao, and P. Tjernlund. 1966. Mimicking of synthetic vowels. Speech Transmission Laboratory Reports, STL, QPSR 2, Stockholm, Royal Institute of Technology.

Chistovich, L. A., N. A. Fyodorova, D. M. Lissenko, and M. G. Zhukova. 1975. Auditory segmentation of acoustic flow and its possible role in speech processing. In G. Fant and M. Tatham (eds.), Auditory Analysis and Perception of Speech, pp. 221–232. Academic Press, New York.

Chistovich, L., V. Kozhevnikov, and V. Galunov. 1970. Theory and Methods of Research on Perception of Speech Signals. [Voprosy Teorii i metodov issledovanaya vospriyatiya rechevykh signalov.] JPRS-50423, Department of Commerce, Washington, D.C.

Chistovich, L. A., R. L. Sheikin, and V. V. Lublinskaya. 1979. In B. Lindblom and S. Öhman (eds.), Frontiers of Speech Communication Research, pp. 143–158. Academic Press, New York.

Chomsky, N., and M. Halle. 1968. The Sound Pattern of English. Harper & Row Publishers, New York.

Collier, R., L. Lisker, H. Hirose, and T. Ushijima. Voicing in intervocalic stops and fricatives in Dutch. J. Phonet. In press.

Cooper, F. S. 1950. Spectrum analysis. J. Acoust. Soc. Am. 22:761–762.

Cooper, F. S., P. C. Delattre, A. M. Liberman, J. M. Borst, and L. J. Gerstman. 1952. Some experiments on the perception of synthetic speech sounds. J. Acoust. Soc. Am. 24:597–606.

Cooper, W. E. 1975. Selective adaptation to speech. In F. Restle, R. M. Shiffrin, N. J. Castellan, H. R. Lindman, and D. B. Pisoni (eds.), Cognitive Theory, Vol. 1, pp. 23–54. Erlbaum Associates, Potomac, Md.

Delattre, P., A. M. Liberman, F. S. Cooper, and L. J. Gerstman. 1952. An experimental study of the acoustic determinants of vowel color; observations on one- and two-formant vowels synthesized from spectrographic patterns. Word 8:195–210.

Denes, P. 1963. On the statistics of spoken English. J. Acoust. Soc. Am. 35: 892–904.

Dorman, M., M. Studdert-Kennedy, and L. Raphael. 1977. The invariance problem in initial voiced stop consonants: Release bursts and formant transitions as functionally equivalent context-dependent cues. Percept. Psychophys. 22:109–122.

Draper, M. H., P. Ladefoged, and D. Whitteridge. 1959. Respiratory muscles in speech. J. Speech Hear. Res. 2:16–27.

Dudley, H. 1936. Synthesized speech. Bell Lab. Rec. 15:98–102.

Dunn, H. K. 1950. The calculation of vowel resonances and an electrical vocal tract. J. Acoust. Soc. Am. 22:740–753.

Eimas, P. D. 1974. Auditory and linguistic processing of cues for place of articulation by infants. Percept. Psychophys. 16:513–521.

Eimas, P. D. 1975. Auditory and phonetic coding of the cues for speech: Discrimination of the r-l distinction by young infants. Percept. Psychophys. 18:341–347.

Eimas, P. D., and J. D. Corbit. 1973. Selective adaptation of linguistic feature detectors. Cogn. Psychol. 4:99–109.

Eimas, P. D., E. R. Siqueland, P. Jusczyk, and J. Vigorito. 1971. Speech perception in infants. Science 171:303–306.

Fant, G. 1959. Acoustic description and classification of phonetic units. Ericsson Technics No. 1. (Reprinted in Fant, 1973.)

Fant, G. 1960. Acoustic Theory of Speech Production. Mouton & Co., The Hague.

Fant, G. 1961. The acoustics of speech. In L. Cremer (ed.), Proceedings of the 3rd International Congress on Acoustics. Elsevier, Amsterdam. (Reprinted in Fant, 1973.)

Fant, G. 1967. Auditory patterns of speech. In W. Wathen-Dunn (ed.), Models for the Perception of Speech and Visual Form, pp. 111–125. The MIT Press, Cambridge, Mass.

Fant, G. 1968. Analysis and synthesis of speech processes. In B. Malmberg (ed.), Manual of Phonetics, pp. 173–277. North-Holland, Amsterdam.

Fant, G. 1973. Speech Sounds and Features. The MIT Press, Cambridge, Mass.

Farnsworth, D. W. 1940. High-speed motion pictures of the human vocal cords. Bell Lab. Rec. 18:203–208.

Flanagan, J. L. 1958. Some properties of the glottal sound source. J. Speech Hear. Res. 1:99–116.

Flanagan, J. L. 1972. Speech Analysis, Synthesis and Perception. 2nd Ed. Springer-Verlag, New York.

Flanagan, J. L., and L. Landgraf. 1968. Self oscillating source for vocal tract synthesizers. IEEE Trans. Audio Electroacoust. AU-16, No. 1.

Flanagan, J., L. Rabiner, D. Christopher, D. Boch, and T. Shipp. 1976. Digital analysis of laryngeal control in speech production. J. Acoust. Soc. Am. 60:446–455.

Fourcin, A. 1972. Perceptual mechanisms at the first level of speech processing. In A. Rigault and R. Charbonneau (eds.), Proceedings of the VIIth International Congress of Phonetic Sciences, pp. 48–62. Mouton & Co., The Hague.

Fromkin, V. 1972. On the reality of linguistic constructs. In A. Rigault and R. Charbonneau (eds.), Proceedings of the VIIth International Congress of Phonetic Sciences, Montreal, pp. 1107–1110. Mouton & Co., The Hague.

Fry, D. B. 1958. Experiments in the perception of stress. Lang. Speech 1:126–152.

Fry, D. B. 1964a. The function of the syllable. Z. Phon. Sprachwiss. Kommunikationsforsch 17:215–221.

Fry, D. B. 1964b. The dependence of stress judgements on vowel formant structure. In E. Zwirner and W. Bethge (eds.), Proceedings of the 5th International Congress of Phonetic Sciences, pp. 306–311. S. Karger, Basel.

Fry, D. B., A. S. Abramson, P. D. Eimas, and A. M. Liberman. 1962. The identification and discrimination of synthetic vowels. Lang. Speech 5:171–189.

Fujimura, O. 1961. Bilabial stop and nasal consonants: A motion picture study and its implications. J. Speech Hear. Res. 4:233–247.

Fujimura, O. 1962. Analysis of nasal consonants. J. Acoust. Soc. Am. 34: 1865–1875.

Fujimura, O. 1972. Acoustics of speech. In J. Gilbert (ed.), Speech and Cortical Functioning, Chapter 3. Academic Press, New York. (On various voicing features see especially pp. 131–137.)

Fujisaki, H., and T. Kawashima. 1968. The roles of pitch and higher formants in the perception of vowels. IEEE Trans. Audio Electroacoust. AU-16:73–77.

Fujisaki, H., and T. Kawashima. 1969. On the Modes and Mechanisms of Speech Perception, pp. 67–73. Annual Report of the Engineering Research Institute, Faculty of Engineering, University of Tokyo.

Fujisaki, H., and T. Kawashima. 1970. Some Experiments on Speech Perception and a Model for the Perceptual Mechanism, pp. 207–214. Annual Report of the Engineering Research Institute, Faculty of Engineering, University of Tokyo.

Galunov, V. I., and L. A. Chistovich. 1966. Relationship of motor theory to the general problem of speech recognition (review). Sov. Phys. Acoust. 11:357–365.

Gay, T. 1968. Effect of speaking rate on diphthong formant movements. J. Acoust. Soc. Am. 44:1570–1573.

Gay, T. 1970. A perceptual study of American English diphthongs. Lang. Speech 13:65–88.

Gay, T. 1977. Articulatory movements in VCV sequences. Status Report on Speech Research SR-49, pp. 121–147. Haskins Laboratories, Yale University, New Haven, Conn.

Gay, T. 1978. Effect of speaking rate on vowel formant movements. J. Acoust. Soc. Am. 63 (1):223–230.

Hadding-Koch, K., and M. Studdert-Kennedy. 1964. An experimental study of some intonation contours. Phonetica 11:175–185.

Halle, M. 1959. The Sound Pattern of Russian. Mouton & Co., The Hague.

Halle, M., and K. Stevens. 1959. Analysis by Synthesis. In W. Wathen-Dunn and L. E. Woods (eds.), Proceedings of Seminar on Speech Compression and Processing, Vol. 2, paper D7. Air Force Cambridge Research Center Report AFCRC-TR-59-198, Hanscom Field, Bedford, Mass.

Harris, K. S. 1958. Cues for discrimination of American English fricatives in spoken syllables. Lang. Speech 1:1–7.

Harris, K. S. 1977. The study of articulatory organization: Some negative progress. Haskins Laboratories Status Report on Speech Research, SR-50, Haskins Laboratories, Yale University, New Haven, Conn.

Heinz, J. M., and K. N. Stevens. 1961. On the properties of voiceless fricative consonants. J. Acoust. Soc. Am. 33:589–596.

Helmholtz, H. 1859. Ueber die Klangfarbe der Vocale. Ann. Phys. Chem. 108: 280–290. (See also Boring, 1942, pp. 371–372, 395.)

Hermann, L. 1894. Nachtrag zur Untersuchung der Vocalcurven. Arch. ges. Physiol. 58:264–279. (See also Boring, 1942, pp. 372–373, 395.)

Hirano, M., and J. Ohala. 1969. Use of hooked-wire electrodes for electromyography of the intrinsic laryngeal muscles. J. Speech Hear. Res. 12:362–373.

Hirose, H., and T. Gay. 1972. The activity of the intrinsic laryngeal muscles in voicing control: An electromyographic study. Phonetica 25:140–164.

Houde, R. A. 1968. A Study of Tongue Body Motion During Selected Speech Sounds. SCRL Monograph No. 2. Speech Communication Research Laboratory, Inc., Santa Barbara, Cal.

House, A. S. 1957. Analog studies of nasal consonants. J. Speech Hear. Disord. 22:190–204.

House, A. S., and K. N. Stevens. 1956. Analog studies of the nasalization of vowels. J. Speech Hear. Disord. 21:218–232.

Ishizaka, K., and J. Flanagan. 1972. Synthesis of voiced sounds from a two-mass model of the vocal cords. Bell Syst. Tech. J. 51:1233–1268.

Jakobson, R., G. Fant, and M. Halle. 1967. Preliminaries to Speech Analysis: The Distinctive Features and Their Correlates. The MIT Press, Cambridge, Mass. (Originally published in 1952 as Acoustics Laboratory Technical Report 13.)

John, J. E., and J. Howarth. 1965. The effect of time distortions on the intelligibility of deaf children's speech. Lang. Speech 8:127–134.

Joos, M. 1948. Acoustic phonetics. Language 24 (suppl. 2). (Also published in 1948 as Language Monograph No. 23. Linguistic Society of America, Waverly Press, Baltimore.)

Kent, R. D., and K. L. Moll. 1969. Vocal tract characteristics of the stop cognates. J. Acoust. Soc. Am. 46:1549–1555.

Klatt, D. 1973. Interaction between two factors that influence vowel duration. J. Acoust. Soc. Am. 54:1102–1104.

Klatt, D. 1975. Vowel lengthening is syntactically determined in a connected discourse. J. Phonet. 3:129–140.

Klatt, D. 1976. Linguistic uses of segmental duration in English: Acoustic and perceptual evidence. J. Acoust. Soc. Am. 59:1208–1221.

Kozhevnikov, V. A., and L. A. Chistovich. 1965. Speech: Articulation and Perception. [Rech: Artikulyatsiya i Vospriyatiye, Moscow-Leningrad.] Translated by the Joint Publications Research Service. Clearinghouse for Federal Scientific and Technical Information, U.S. Department of Commerce, Washington, D.C. 20043. (Publication nos. JPRS: 30, 543; TT: 65-31233.)

Kuhl, P. K., and J. D. Miller. 1975. Speech perception by the chinchilla: Voiced-voiceless distinction in alveolar plosive consonants. Science 190:69–72.

Ladefoged, P. 1963. Some physiological parameters in speech. Lang. Speech 6:109–119.

Ladefoged, P. 1967. Three Areas of Experimental Phonetics. Oxford University Press, London.

Lane, H. 1965. The motor theory of speech perception: A critical review. Psychol. Rev. 72:275–309.

Lehiste, I. 1970. Suprasegmentals. The MIT Press, Cambridge, Mass.

Lehiste, I. The perception of duration within sequences of four intervals. J. Phonet. In press.

Lehiste, I. 1977. Isochrony reconsidered. J. Phonet. 5:253–263.

Lehiste, I., and G. Peterson. 1959. Vowel amplitude and phonemic stress in American English. J. Acoust. Soc. Am. 31:428–435.

Lehiste, I., and W. Wang. 1976. Perception of sentence boundaries with and without semantic information. Atken der dritten Internationalen Phonologie-Tagung, Vienna, 1976, W. U. Dresser and O. E. Pfeiffer, Eds., 277-283, 1977 Innsbrucker Beiträge zur Sprachwissenshaft, Institut für Sprachwissenshaft der Universität Innsbruck, A-6020 Innsbruck, Innrain 30.

Lenneberg, E. 1967. Biological Foundations of Language, John Wiley & Sons, New York.

Liberman, A. M. 1974. The specialization of the language hemisphere. In. F. O. Schmitt and F. G. Worden (eds.), The Neurosciences: Third Study Program, pp. 43–56. The MIT Press, Cambridge, Mass.

Liberman, A. M., F. S. Cooper, D. P. Shankweiler, and M. Studdert-Kennedy. 1967. Perception of the speech code. Psychol. Rev. 74:431–461.

Liberman, A. M., P. Delattre, and F. S. Cooper. 1952. The role of selected stimulus variables in the perception of the unvoiced stop consonants. Am. J. Psychol. 65:497–516.

Liberman, A. M., P. C. Delattre, and F. S. Cooper. 1958. Some cues for the distinction between voiced and voiceless stops in initial position. Lang. Speech 1:153–167.

Liberman, A. M., P. C. Delattre, F. S. Cooper, and L. J. Gerstman. 1954. The role of consonant-vowel transitions in the perception of the stop and nasal consonants. Psychol. Monogr. 8(8):1–13.

Liberman, A. M., P. C. Delattre, L. J. Gerstman, and F. S. Cooper. 1956. Tempo of frequency change as a cue for distinguishing classes of speech sounds. J. Exp. Psychol. 52:127–137.

Liberman, A. M., K. S. Harris, H. S. Hoffman, and B. C. Griffith. 1957. The discrimination of speech sounds within and across phoneme boundaries. J. Exp. Psychol. 54:358–368.

Liberman, A. M., K. S. Harris, J. A. Kinney, and H. Lane. 1961. The discrimination of relative onset-time of components of certain speech and nonspeech patterns. J. Exp. Psychol. 61:379–388.

Liberman, A. M., and M. Studdert-Kennedy. 1977. Phonetic perception. In R. Held, H. Leibowitz, and H. L. Teuber (eds.), Handbook of Sensory Physiology, Vol. VIII, Perception. Springer-Verlag, Heidelberg.

Lieberman, P. 1967. Intonation, Perception and Language. The MIT Press, Cambridge, Mass.

Lieberman, P., and S. B. Michaels. 1962. Some aspects of fundamental frequency and envelope amplitude as related to the emotional content of speech. J. Acoust. Soc. Am. 34:922–927.

Lieberman, P., M. Sawashima, K. Harris, and T. Gay. 1970. The articulatory implementation of the breath-group and prominence: Cricothyroid muscular activity in intonation. Language 46:312–327.

Lindblom, B. 1963. Spectrographic study of vowel reduction. J. Acoust. Soc. Am. 35:1773–1781.

Lindblom, B., B. Lyberg, and K. Holmgren. 1977. Durational Patterns of Swedish Phonology: Do They Reflect Short-Term Memory Processes? Department of Phonetics, Institute of Linguistics, Stockholm University, Stockholm.

Lindblom, B. E. F., and J. E. F. Sundberg. 1971. Acoustical consequences of lip, tongue, jaw and larynx movement. J. Acoust. Soc. Am. 50:1166.

Lisker, L. 1978. Rapid vs rabid: A catalogue of acoustic features that may cue the distinction. Status Report on Speech Research, SR-54, pp. 127–132. Haskins Laboratories, Yale University, New Haven, Conn.

Lisker, L., and A. Abramson. 1967. Some effects of context on voice onset time in English stops. Lang. Speech 10:1–28.

Lublinskaya, V. V. 1966. The recognition of the articulatory attributes of closed consonants in a shift from a vowel to a consonant. Akustich. zhurn. 12:213–221. (Soviet Physics-Acoustics translation.)

MacNeilage, P. F. 1970. Motor control of serial ordering of speech. Psychol. Rev. 77:182–196.

Malécot, A. 1956. Acoustic cues for nasal consonants, an experimental study involving a tape-splicing technique. Language 32:274–284.

Malécot, A. 1970. The lenis-fortis opposition: Its physiological parameters. J. Acoust. Soc. Am. 47:1588–1592.

Mártony, J. 1965. Studies of the voice source. Speech Transmission Laboratory Quarterly Progress Report 1:4.

Mattingly, I. 1977. Syllable synthesis. In Status Report on Speech Research, SR-49, pp. 111–119. Haskins Laboratories, Yale University, New Haven, Conn.

Miller, R. L. 1953. Auditory tests with synthetic vowels. J. Acoust. Soc. Am. 25:114–121.

O'Connor, J. D., L. J. Gerstman, A. M. Liberman, P. C. Delattre, and F. S. Cooper. 1957. Acoustic cues for the perception of initial /w j r l/ in English. Word 13:24–43.

Ohala, J. 1974. A mathematical model of speech aerodynamics. In G. Fant (ed.), Proceedings of Speech Communication Seminar, Stockholm, 1–3 August 1974. Vol. II, pp. 65–72. Almquist & Wiksell, Stockholm.

Ohala, J. 1977. The physiology of stress. In L. M. Hyman (ed.), Studies in Stress and Accent, pp. 145–168. Southern California Occasional Papers in Linguistics No. 4, Los Angeles.

Paget, R. A. S. 1924. The nature and artificial production of consonant sounds. Proc. Royal Society, Series A, 106:150–174.

Perkell, J. S. 1965. Cineradiographic studies of speech: Implications of certain articulation movements. Proceedings of the 5th International Congress of Acoustics, Liege, Paper A32.

Perkell, J. S. 1969. Physiology of Speech Production: Results and Implications of a Quantitative Cineradiographic Study. Research Monograph No. 53. The MIT Press, Cambridge, Mass.

Peterson, G., and H. Barney. 1952. Control methods used in a study of vowels. J. Acoust. Soc. Am. 24:175–184.

Peterson, G. E., and I. Lehiste. 1960. Duration of syllable nuclei in English. J. Acoust. Soc. Am. 32:693–703.

Pickett, J. M. 1957. Perception of vowels heard in noises of various spectra. J. Acoust. Soc. Am. 29:613–620.

Pickett, J. M. 1965. Some acoustic cues for synthesis of the /n-d/ distinction. J. Acoust. Soc. Am. 38:474–477.

Pisoni, D. B. 1975. Auditory short-term memory and vowel perception. Mem. Cogn. 3:7–18.

Pisoni, D. B. 1977. Identification and discrimination of the relative onset of two-component tones: Implications for the perception of voicing in stops. J. Acoust. Soc. Am. 61:1352–1361.

Potter, R., G. Kopp, and H. Green. 1947. Visible Speech. Van Nostrand Reinhold Co., New York. (Reprinted in 1966 by Dover Press, New York.)

Rothenberg, M. 1968. The breath-stream dynamics of simple released-plosive production. Bibliot. Phonet. 6:1–117.

Rothenberg, M. 1973. A new inverse-filtering technique for deriving the glottal air waveform during voicing. J. Acoust. Soc. Am. 53:1632–1645.

Sawashima, M. 1968. Movements of the larynx in the articulation of Japanese consonants. Ann. Bull. Res. Inst. Logoped. Phoniatr. (U. Tokyo) 2:11–20.

Sawashima, M., and S. Miyazaki. 1973. Glottal opening for Japanese voiceless consonants. Ann. Bull. Res. Inst. Logoped. Phoniatr. (U. Tokyo) 7:1–10.

Scripture, E. W. 1902. Experimental Phonetics, p. 450. Charles Scribner's Sons, New York.

Shafer, R. W., and L. R. Rabiner. 1970. System for automatic formant analysis of voiced speech. J. Acoust. Soc. Am. 47:634–648.

Shepard, R. N. 1972. Psychological representation of speech sounds. In E. E. David and P. Denes (eds.), Human Communication: A Unified View, Chapter 4. McGraw-Hill Book Co., New York.

Slis, I. H. 1970. Articulatory measurements on voiced, voiceless and nasal consonants. Phonetica 21:193–210.

Slis, I. H. 1975. Consequences of articulatory effort on articulatory timing. In G. Fant and M. Tatham (eds.), Auditory Analysis and the Perception of Speech, pp. 397–411. Academic Press, New York.

Slis, I. H., and A. Cohen. 1969. On the complex regulating the voiced-voiceless distinction (Parts I and II). Lang. Speech 12:80–102; 137–155.

Stålhammar, U., I. Karlsson, and G. Fant. 1974. Contextual effects on vowel nuclei. Quarterly Progress and Status Report 4/1973, Speech Transmission Laboratory, Royal Institute of Technology, Stockholm.

Stetson, R. H. 1928. Motor phonetics. Arch. Néerl. Phon. Expér. 3:1–216.

Stetson, R. H. 1951. Motor Phonetics. 2nd Ed. North-Holland, Amsterdam. (For motor theory of speech acquisition and perception, see pp. 135–154.)

Stevens, K. N. 1972. The quantal nature of speech: Evidence from articulatory-acoustic data. In P. B. Denes and E. E. David, Jr. (eds.), Human Communication: A Unified View, Chapter 3. McGraw-Hill Book Co., New York.

Stevens, K. N. 1975. The potential role of property detectors in the perception of consonants. In G. Fant and M. Tatham (eds.), Auditory Analysis and Perception of Speech, pp. 304–327. Academic Press, New York.

Stevens, K., and M. Halle. 1967. Remarks on analysis by synthesis and distinctive features. In W. Wathen-Dunn (ed.), Models for the Perception of Speech and Visual Form, pp. 88–102. The MIT Press, Cambridge, Mass.

Stevens, K. N., and A. S. House. 1955. Development of a quantitative description of vowel articulation. J. Acoust. Soc. Am. 27:484.

Stevens, K. N., and A. S. House. 1961. An acoustical theory of vowel production and some of its implications. J. Speech Hear. Res. 4:303.

Strange, W., D. Verbrugge, D. Shankweiler, and T. Erdman. 1976. Consonantal environment specifies vowel identity. J. Acoust. Soc. Am. 60:213–224.

Studdert-Kennedy, M. 1974. The perception of speech. In T. A. Sebeok (ed.), Current Trends in Linguistics, Vol. 12. Mouton, The Hague.

Studdert-Kennedy, M. 1976. Speech perception. In N. J. Lass (ed.), Contemporary Issues in Experimental Phonetics, pp. 243–293. Academic Press, New York.

Studdert-Kennedy, M., A. Liberman, K. Harris, and F. S. Cooper. 1970. The motor theory of speech perception: A reply to Lane's critical review. Psychol. Rev. 77:234–249.

Summerfield, A. Q., and M. P. Haggard. 1975. Vocal tract normalization as demonstrated by reaction times. In G. Fant and M. Tatham (eds.), Auditory Analysis and Perception of Speech, pp. 115–141. Academic Press, New York.

Sundberg, J. 1973. The source spectrum in professional singing. Folia Phoniatr. 25:71–90.

Tiffany, W. R. 1959. Nonrandom sources of variation in vowel quality. J. Speech Hear. Res. 2:305–317.

Titze, I. R. 1973. The human vocal cords: A mathematical model. I. Phonetica 28: 129–170.

Titze, I. R. 1974. The human vocal cords: A mathematical model. II. Phonetica 29:1–21.

Titze, I., and D. Talkin. 1979. A theoretical study of the effects of the various laryngeal configurations on the acoustics of phonation. J. Acoust. Soc. Am. 66(1):60–74.

Truby, H. 1959. Acoustico-cineradiographic analysis considerations with special reference to certain consonantal complexes. Acta Radiol. (suppl. 182).

Uldall, E. 1960. Attitudinal meanings conveyed by intonation contours. Lang. Speech 3:223–234.

Umeda, N. 1975. Vowel duration in American English. J. Acoust. Soc. Am. 58: 434–445.

Umeda, N. 1977. Consonant duration in American English. J. Acoust. Soc. Am. 61:846–858.

Vanderslice, R. 1967. Larynx vs lungs: Cricothyrometer data refuting some recent claims concerning intonation and archetypality. Work. Pap. Phonet. 7:67–79. Phonetics Laboratory, University of California at Los Angeles.

Williams, C. E., and K. N. Stevens. 1972. Emotions and speech: Some acoustical correlates. J. Acoust. Soc. Am. 52:1238–1250.

Willis, R. 1829. On vowel sounds and on reed organ pipes. Trans. Cambridge Philosoph. Soc. 3:231–268. (See also Boring, 1942, pp. 369–371, 395.)

Author Index

Subject Index

List of Spectrographic Examples

List of Summary Sections